# AMERICAN ECONOMIC HISTORY

# 2014 EDITION

**"I Saw a Startling Sight Today, a Politician with His Hands in His Own Pockets" - Mark Twain**

**"A Government Big Enough to Give you Everything you Want is Strong Enough to Take Everything you Have."**
Thomas Jefferson

*Richard E. Carmichael, Ph.D.*

**Printed in the United States of America**

**Library of Congress Cataloging - in Publication Data**

American Economic History: 2014 Edition
Richard E. Carmichael
Includes biographical references and index.
Library of Congress Control Number: TXU 1-127-033


Published by: R. Carmichael Company
Conover, NC 28613
April 19, 2014
ISBN: 9-78143821245-6


American Economic History 2014 Edition is also published in Electronic Format and is Available for the Kindle and E-nook Readers. The book is also available in electronic PDF format from Novelnook.com.

# ACKNOWLEDGMENT

I would like to thank my wife Kay and my son Greg for the numerous hours that they spent proofreading and making suggestions for improving the readability of this book. Kay has a degree in International Languages and Greg has masters in Education with a concentration in English. They were instrumental in editing this book.

The Internet was used extensively to obtain the latest government data on domestic and international trade. Two of the major sources that were used in developing this book were the Bureau of Economic Analysis database at (www.bea.gov) and the McMaster University Economic History database in Hamilton, Ontario Canada. Also, the tables in this book will be continuously updated when new information is available. In addition, an instructor's manual is available for this book. A free copy of the instructor's manual is available to all interested college professors upon request. All requests for a copy of the Instructor's Manual should be E-mailed to: rcarmichaelco@hotmail.com.

## INTRODUCTION

American Economic History: 2014 Edition contains an analysis of the historical contribution to economic theory provided by many of the great economists of the past. The book also contains the latest economic data available from The Bureau of Economic Analysis (Year end and quarterly GDP for 2013), the Department of Labor (December 2013 employment), the Federal Reserve Money Supply (December 2013), the Federal Government Debt and Deficit from the Department of the Treasury (Fiscal Year 2013) and The President's 2015 Budget.

The outlook in the twenty-first century for the world's industrial countries cannot be forecasted by use of mechanical extrapolation. This is because each of these countries, be it Western Europe, or Japan and the "Asian Tigers," or the United States, has its own separate history, its own culture.

In the twenty-first century, market niche competition will give way to head-to head competition among the industrial giants of the world. The key to competing in this environment will be the ability to create and sustain a competitive advantage over a company or country's economic rivals. Each country has a unique culture that determines how it approaches the marketplace. This will require that industrialized countries look to its history to determine its strengths and weaknesses, its opportunities and threats, relative to the competition. Also, many companies look to their national government for different levels of assistance in accomplishing their business goals. Some companies form a partnership with their government in order to enhance their competitive positions, while others emphasize a hands-off policy in trade and commerce. Therefore, this book examines the historical and continuing role of government in business.

The purpose of this book is to examine the evolution of economic thought and the historical events that affected the economic growth of the world's industrialized countries, with particular emphasis of the United States. During specific times in its history, the United States was the envy of the entire world. In the nineteenth century, the Europeans recognized that the America approach was different. It was the Europeans, who originally coined the term the "American System."

After World War II, the United States dominated the world in almost every aspect of global business, as they were clearly the world leader in manufacturing in both new product and new process development.

However, starting in the 1980's the rest of the industrialized world began to catch up and even surpass America in some sectors of manufacturing. During the 1990's there were many economists that were predicting that the European Union or Japan would overtake America and become the economic leader of the free world in the twenty-first century. However, these predictions neglected to estimate the importance of an invention by Intel, Inc. in the early 1970's. The invention was called the microprocessor and it was a catalyst for the strong comeback of American industry in the twenty-first century.

This is not a book about government, or industry, it is about the people, past and present that contributed to the current understanding of economic and political theory in an historical context. The major theories of micro and macroeconomics are discussed but the major emphasis is how these theories were developed and taught by those economists and political thinkers who invented them in the first place.

# CONTENTS

| CHP NO | CHAPTER TITLES AND SUBTITLES | PG NO |
|--------|------------------------------|-------|

# LIST OF TABLES AND FIGURES

## LIST OF PHOTOGRAPHS

The following photographs were provided by the McMaster University (Hamilton, Ontario Canada), Economic History Database. Additional Photographs and Biographies are Available at the Universities Web Site.

## <u>Description</u>

1.   Aristotle
2.   Jeremy Bentham
3.   Henry George
4.   Thomas Hobbes
5.   David Hume
6.   John Maynard Keynes
7.   Thomas Malthus
8.   Alfred Marshall
9.   Francis Quesnay
10.  David Ricardo
11.  Jacques Rousseau
12.  Joseph Schumpeter
13.  John Baptiste Say
14.  Adam Smith
15   Herbert Spencer
16.  William G. Sumner
17.  Anne-Jacques Turgot
18.  Thorstein Veblen

## LIST OF PHOTOGRAPHS

The following photographs are from the Biographical File at the U.S. Library of Congress.

## <u>Description</u>

1.      Edmund Burke
2.      Andrew Carnegie
3.      Henry Ford
4.      Henry George
5.      John Locke
6.      John Pierpont Morgan
7.      Karl Marx
8.      John Stuart Mill
9.      Ronald Reagan
10      John D. Rockefeller
11.     Franklin D. Roosevelt
12.     Frederick Taylor
13.     Mark Twain

# RICHARD E. CARMICHAEL, Ph.D.

## ABOUT THE AUTHOR

Richard E. Carmichael, Ph.D. is a professor in the College of Distance Learning and Continuing Education at Gardner-Webb University. He previously served as the Alex Lee Professor of Business at Lenoir-Rhyne College. He also served as a Visiting Professor of Finance at Washington College in Chestertown, MD and a Faculty Associate with the Johns Hopkins University Division of Business in Baltimore, MD. He has had teaching assignments in American Economic History, Macro and Microeconomics, Strategic Management, Business Economics, International Business, Small Business Management and Financial Markets and Institutions.

In addition, Dr. Carmichael has over fifteen years of business experience in the fields of Financial Management, Economic Forecasting and Marketing. He has held executive positions with First Interstate Bank of California as Vice President of Strategic Planning and Marketing, BankAmerica Corp., as Vice President of Market Planning and Research, Manufacturers Hanover Corp. as Financial Economists for the Bank's National Division. Also, he has over ten years experience with the U.S. Government as Budget Manager for the U.S. Bankruptcy Court in Maryland and as Branch Chief for Credit Programs for the U.S. Small Business Administration in Washington, DC. He holds a BS in Economics, an MBA in Financial Management and a Ph.D. in Business Administration.

# CHAPTER 1

---

# THE ECONOMIC WAY OF THINKING

*"Political Economy or Economics is a study of mankind in the ordinary business of life." --Alfred Marshall*

## WHAT IS ECONOMIC HISTORY

After World War II, the United States dominated the world in almost every aspect of global business. Mass marketing was effectively an American monopoly. American companies were superior in technology, their workers were better educated and more skilled, and American managers were the best educated and trained in the world. The United States was clearly the world leader in manufacturing in both new product and new process development. In the twentieth century almost everything that plugged into an electrical outlet was invented in America and this country was the clear leader in determining what new products would be manufactured and how they would be made. However, America no longer dominates the world in the field of new process engineering. Japan's consumer electronics industry is now the most productive in the world and the three largest chemical companies in the world are located in Germany. American Scholars invented one of today's most prevalent management theories "Total Quality Management," but its application was perfected in Japan.

America has lost its position of total world dominance in manufacturing. There is now a three-way race between the European Union, Japan, and the United States. The race is to determine who will be the leader of the industrial world in the twenty-first century. The question in the twenty-first century will not be who is perfect, but who is doing the best job, and who is creating the most value for its customers. In the nineteenth century, the American manufacturing strength was not as the original inventor of new products but as the innovator of new manufacturing processes. American businessmen acquired technological processes from abroad and then experimented with them, often greatly improving on the original invention. The Europeans themselves were the first to recognize that the American approach was different. It was the Europeans, who coined the term the "American System." America is still in the best position to remain the industrial leader of the twenty-first century; however, there will be increased competition for world dominance from the European Union and Japan. America needs to look at the past, and to understand what made it the greatest county in the world. For it is only with an understanding of past events that a country effectively plans for the future.

The purpose of this book is to examine the evolution of economic thought and how historical events have affected the economic growth of the world's industrialized countries. The first step in this analysis is to examine the field of economics itself. First, the basic theory of modern day economics will be explored in order to give the reader some understanding of what economics is and what economic theory attempts to accomplish. The theories of many famous European and American economists are then described and placed in a historical context.

Economics has always been a reflection of historical events and has evolved as a field of study that proposes to explain current events. Therefore, the focus of this book is to trace the evolution of economics, referred to as Political Economics until 1776, and to examine how the evolution of economic belief served to explain the growth of the economies of the leading industrialized countries of the world. Our exploration of economic history will begin with ancient history, which traces political economics all the way back to the writings of Aristotle. However, the emphasis of the book is the United States, and it's continuing debate as to the proper role of government in controlling economic activity. Still, this analysis will not arbitrarily end in the 1990's. In addition to attempting to explain the past, this book analyzes the strengths and weaknesses of the Industrial World's leading economies and provides a picture of what these countries might look like in the twenty-first century.

## BASIC ECONOMIC TERMS AND THEORY

Economics can be defined as the social science that seeks to examine and understand the choices people make in using scarce resources to meet their demands. Economic history is the subject that deals with the ways in which man has used his limited resources to satisfy his wants and with the institutions he has developed to organize economic activity.

"Political Economy or Economics," according to Alfred Marshall, "is a study of mankind in the ordinary business of life".[1] However, for practical purposes, the scope of this book is limited to the analysis of the questions that are most commonly asked by economists and other interested persons. Central to the study of economics is the question of what determines prices, how proceeds of economic activity are distributed and what determines the share of income that goes to wages, profits, interest and rents.

In every economy, certain basic choices have to be made. Among these choices, the most important are what goods will be produced, how they will be produced, who will do which jobs and for whom the results of economic activity will be made available. Each of these choices is made necessary because of scarcity, and each can be used to introduce key elements of the historical as well as the current economic way of analyzing a situation. To define the economic way of thinking, exploring the key elements of economic analysis, is useful.

### Deciding What to Produce

In any economy the number of goods and services that could be provided is immense. The impossibility of producing as much of everything as people want reflects a scarcity of the productive resources that are used to make all goods. Many scarce productive resources must be combined to make even the simplest product or to produce a simple service. These productive resources are referred to by economists as the factors of production and are usually grouped by labor, capital and natural resources. Labor can be defined as the contribution to production made by people working with their minds and muscles. Labor can further be divided into those persons who organize the factors of production, i.e., the business owners, and those who actually perform the physical tasks required to produce a product, the workers.

Capital is the means of production that are created by people, including structures, machines, tools and systems. In economics, capital is defined as goods that are produced and used for the purpose of increasing the quantity of future goods. Natural Resources is anything that can be used as a productive input in its natural state, such as farmland, residential and commercial building sites, forests, fossil fuel and mineral deposits.

## Deciding How to Produce

There is more than one way to produce almost any product. As a nation's economy advances, new methods of production are continually being developed. Business owners operate to make a profit. In order to make a profit, they have to find a way to allocate the factors of production efficiently. The owners of a business usually organize their company in an attempt to operate efficiently. Efficiency means producing a product with a minimum expense, effort and waste. However, over time, production potential can only be expanded by accumulating more of the factors of production and finding new technology to make the factors more productive. The act of increasing the economy's supply of production inputs made by people is known as capital investment. Investment is the act of increasing the economy's stock of capital. To accumulate capital, individuals have to save some of their income.[2]

## Deciding Who Will Do the Work

The question of who will do the work, who will organize the tasks, who will develop the systems and who will do the physical work is a matter of organizing the social division of labor. Will everyone do everything independently, or will people cooperate? Economists answer these questions by pointing out that it is more efficient to cooperate. Three things make cooperation effective; they are, teamwork, learning by doing and comparative advantage. Teamwork requires that people work together to accomplish a task more efficiently than if they work independently. Learning by doing implies that people get better at some jobs by doing the work repeatedly. Comparative advantage is the ability to produce goods or services at a relatively lower opportunity cost than someone else.[3]

## Deciding for Whom Goods and Services Will be Produced

In any economy, a decision has to be made about who will receive the benefits of production. Are goods and services to be distributed equally to everyone? Or are they to be sold to those willing and able to pay. If the goods produced are distributed only to those persons that are willing to pay, people with higher incomes will enjoy more and better products than people with lower incomes.

Distribution of purchasing power is never perfectly equal because some people have the financial resources to enjoy great quantities of goods and services. Other people, even in a nation as wealthy as the United States, live in poverty. No society has yet discovered how to provide equally for the demands of everyone, and at the same time, to provide the incentives that encourages high quality production and continued technological innovation.[4]

The question of distribution of output, among members of society, has implications in terms of both efficiency and fairness. Efficiency is the part of economics that is concerned with facts and the relationships among them. This is referred to as positive economics. However, a great portion of economic analysis is based on the fairness of distribution. This part of the analysis is called normative economics which is the area of economics that is devoted to judgments about which conditions and policies are good or bad.[5]

## Additional Questions that Concern Economists

Another question that concerns many economists is what variables depress or stimulate total economic growth and what are the causes of the uneven levels of severity of business cycles? Also, emerging as a ponderable question is why it is so difficult in the modern economy to find useful employment for people that are willing and able to work.

In addition to these questions, the role of institutions such as business enterprises, banks and central banks, and government policies must be considered. All these questions, the solutions past, present, and the courses of action that are taken are the subject of economic history.

## SCOPE OF THE BOOK

The study of American economic history is a study of change, from the merchant capitalism that preceded the American revolution, to the industrial revolution and the productivity revolution, through the Great Depression of the 1930's, two world wars, and culminating with the head to head competition of the modern day global economy.

Economics does not consist of one theory; it consists of many theories that have evolved throughout the history of the modern world. While examining every economic theory in the context of one book, is not possible, the objective of this work is to analyze historical events through the use of the most prevalent economic theory and the most noted economist of the time under evaluation.

Modern history has often presented a stage for the debate of the role of government in the economy. In 1576, Jean Bodin defined the role of the leaders of the new "Nation-State," as maintaining the climate for economic growth, keeping taxes low, and defending the realm. In the mid-eighteenth century, a group of French Philosophers called the Physiocrats created the idea of an economic system as an interconnected and interdependent structure. Their system contained a controlling natural law of economic behavior and a guiding rule of laissez faire, or a hand off policy by government in the affairs of trade. In 1776, Adam Smith wrote "The Wealth of Nations," where he defined the role of government as a source of calculable law, a defender of the nation and a promoter of the freedom of internal and international trade.

In the nineteenth century, economists such as David Ricardo, John Stuart Mill, and Karl Marx, continued the debate which by that time was centered on the fairness of the distribution of profit between the workers and the capitalists. Alfred Marshall took the theories of the classical economists and developed economics as a separate field apart from politics, history and moral issues. Classical economics or Neoclassical economics, as it was now called, supported the basic theory that there was a self-adjusting mechanism that prevented an economy from entering into a long and severe depression. Since, by theory, depression could not be sustained, it was not necessary for government to take an active role in controlling the economy.

During the Great Depression that started in 1929, the leading economists of the day urged their governments to do nothing to improve their economic situation. However, by 1933, the newly elected American president Franklin D. Roosevelt found an economy with 25 percent of its employable workers not able to find jobs. Roosevelt's solution was to put people to work in jobs provided by the federal government and the Federal Emergency Relief Administration was created for this purpose. By 1937, eight million Americans were employed by their government.

In 1936, a new economic theory was created by John Maynard Keynes in his book, "The General Theory of Employment, Interest, and Money." According to Keynes, it is not necessary to wait for the economy to self adjust to a depression. The government should take steps to overcome a shortage of total demand. In a depression, the desire of the federal government to balance their budget must give way to the need to stimulate economic growth. The great depression and the theories of Keynes started the transition of the United States and most of Europe, from the national state to the fiscal state. The depression gave rise to the belief that the national government should control its country's economic environment.

Joseph Schumpeter, a contemporary of Keynes, pointed out that as long as revenues were considered as a constraint, it was difficult for the government to act as either a social or economic agent. Following

World War II, most developed countries adopted the theories of Keynesian economics. Keynes assumed that a wise and efficient government would apply sound fiscal policy. However, in the hands of modern day politicians, government has become the master of the individual in society.

In 1964 President Johnson passed the tax reduction plan that was proposed by John F. Kennedy. The result of the tax reductions was a decrease in the unemployment rate to 4 percent. In addition in 1965 with the economy already running at nearly full capacity, Johnson instituted his "Great Society" social welfare program. At the same time America had begun a military involvement in South Vietnam which greatly increased defense spending. The combination of reduced taxes and increased spending led to the inflation of the 1970s.

In 1975, President Ford called into conference some of the country's better-known economists to prescribe a remedy for inflation, as there was a 13.5 percent increase in the consumer price index that year. The entire group agreed on only one remedy: government should remove any impediments to market competition. For practical effect this was no better than Ford's own prescription, which was wearing of buttons with the insignia (WIN – Whip Inflation Now). The Keynes system of using fiscal policy was proven in practice to be of limited value in fighting inflation. Keynes had assumed a benevolent government, however; Congress was not going to vote to increase taxes or to reduce expenditures to decrease inflation especially during elections. Consequently there remained only one viable course of action to use monetary policy to control inflation.

In 1981 President Reagan's advisors urged him implement a program of supply-side economics. The basic premise of supply-side economics is that it places supply over demand in the hierarchy of economics and therefore deals with enhancing economic production, efficiency, and growth within the context of the marketplace. This change in economic policy became known as Reaganomics and consisted of four key elements designed to reverse the high-inflation, slow growth economy of the 1970s. The key elements were as follows: (1) A restrictive monetary policy engineered through the Federal Reserve; (2) the economic recovery Tax Act of 1981 including a 25 percent across the board tax cut; (3) A promise to balance the budget through domestic spending restraint; (4) A program to roll back many restrictive government regulations. During the 1980s the American economy produced 17 million new jobs. When Reagan left office in 1989, the unemployment rate had fallen to 5.5 percent, the inflation rate had fallen to 4.1 percent, the Dow Jones Industrial Index had doubled in value and America had reaffirmed its position as the world's preeminent economy. However, the economic progress came at a cost as the federal government accumulated over $2 trillion in debt during the Reagan administration.

Schumpeter warned in 1918, that the fiscal state would in the end undermine government's ability to govern. Eighteen years later, Keynes hailed the fiscal state as the great liberator of a depressed economy. Keynes argued that government, no longer limited by restraints on expenditures, could effectively control economic growth by manipulating government spending and taxation. However, in the 1990's many economists and politicians believe that Schumpeter might have been right. By 1996, most of the governments of the industrialized world had run up such large federal deficits that fiscal policy became almost useless in fighting either recession or inflation. In 1997 and 1998 the U.S. economy continued to grow at historically high rates, which resulted in higher tax revenue for the federal government. In 1998 federal government tax revenues exceeded expenses resulting in a budget surplus for the first time in almost 50 years. A saying attributed to both John F. Kennedy and Ronald Reagan can be used to explain the government surplus: "A Rising Tide Lifts All Boats."

The debate continued into the 2000 American presidential campaign where both the Republican and Democratic parties have attempted to define their positions based on the perceived role of government. The Republicans led by Texas Governor George W. Bush defined their position as one of a reduced tax burden on its citizens, along with a smaller and less intrusive role of the federal government. Their position is similar to the theories of Alfred Marshall and Neoclassical economics. The Democrats under, Vice President Al Gore, defined their position more along the lines of Keynesian economic theory, calling for a larger role of government in controlling the economy.

The election of 2000 was one of the closest votes in American history. The election came down to who would be awarded the 25 electoral college votes from Florida. It took more than a month and a Supreme Court decision to decide the issue. On December 12th 2000 George W. Bush was officially declared to be the new president of the United States.  George W. Bush won the election with an electoral college vote of 271 to Al Gore's 266 but lost the popular vote by 541 thousand. However, Bush was not the only president to lose the popular vote and win the election; two other presidents were elected by receiving a majority of the electoral votes and losing the popular vote. The other two presidents were Rutherford Hayes in 1876 and Benjamin Harrison in 1888.

The 2008 presidential elections were held on November 4th. After a long primary campaign, Republican's choose John McCain a long time Senator from Arizona and a Viet Nam War Hero and Democrats choose Barack Obama a young senator from Illinois. Young and charismatic but with little experience on the national level, Obama smashed through racial barriers and easily defeated John McCain to become the first African-American destined to sit in the Oval Office as America's 44th president. As president, Obama faces daunting problems. How to fix a financial system no one seems to fully understand. How to defeat terrorist enemies sheltered in the territory of our putative ally Pakistan. How to live up to the high expectations so visible in the cheering faces of his followers.

The Business Cycle Dating Committee of the National Bureau of Economic Research met by conference call on Friday, November 28, 2008. The committee maintains a chronology of the beginning and ending dates (months and quarters) of U.S. recessions. The committee determined that the economy was in a recession that started in December 2007. Getting the economy growing again is one of President Obama's priorities in 2009 and beyond. The American Recovery and Reinvestment Act of 2009 passed Congress with no Republican votes in the House and only 3 in the Senate. The plan called for a fiscal stimulus package in the amount of $797 billion. Many Republicans criticized the bill for not providing enough tax relief. Only 36 percent of the stimulus was for tax reductions. Some Democrats argued that the amount of stimulus was not large enough to end the recession.

In March of 2013, President Obama released his budget proposal for fiscal year 2014. The budget called for large increases in expenditures and budget deficits in every year through 2019 and beyond. The total gross national debt is projected to increase by $5.6 trillion from fiscal year 2012 actual through 2018 planned data. This amount is greater than the total increase in the national debt for the entire eight years of the George W. Bush administration. The president's 2014 budget was turned down by the U.S. Senate by a vote of 98 to 0. Both the House and the Senate presented a budget for fiscal year 2014. However, the Senate and House bills vary widely on Income, expenditures and the federal deficit. In March of 2014 The President released his 2015 budget. The budget called for deficit spending through 2019 and beyond. The 2015 budget was not well received by the House which presented it's on version of the Budget in April of 2014.

As for the current generation of Americans and Western Europeans, we may never completely settle the question of the proper role of government in the economy. However, the actions of the Obama administration including the 2015 budget and the 2009 stimulus package will most likely lead to an increased roll of government in business over the next four years.

Business by its nature requires change, however, in life there is only one certainty, for as John Maynard Keynes once wrote: "In the long run we are all dead." Therefore, the main purpose of this book may, be summarized as follows

- To see economics as a reflection of the world in which specific economic ideas have developed over time.
- To isolate and emphasize the most lasting concepts of the leading economists of their time.
- To examine the contributions of the economic scholars and political leaders to events that shaped the history of economics, its evolving institutions, and it's continuing debate over the role of government in controlling the economy.
- To use the lessons from the past so that we can avoid repeating our mistakes in the future.

NOTES:

## Chapter 1
## The Economic Way of Thinking

1.   Marshall, Alfred, <u>Principles of Economics, 9th</u> Edition,
     London, England, Macmillan, 1920, p. 1.
2.   Dolan, Edward S. & Lindsey, David E., <u>Economics, Seventh
     Edition</u>, The Dryden Press, Orlando, FL, 1994,  p. 9.
3.   Dolan and Lindsey, p. 10.
4.   Hyman, David N., <u>Economics, Third Edition</u>, Boston, MA, Irwin,
     994, p.10.
5.   Dolan and Lindsey, p. 14

# CHAPTER 2

---

# THE ROOTS OF POLITICAL ECONOMICS

*"The lower sort are by nature slaves, and it is better for them as for all inferiors that they should be under the rule of a master. Indeed the use made of slaves and of tame animals is not very different."* —Aristotle

## THE GREEK INFLUENCE

Central to all economic analysis was the question of what determines the prices that are paid for goods and services and how the proceeds from this economic activity are distributed. Also, there was a continuing debate over what determines the share of income going to wages, interest, profit, rent and other fixed items that are used in production. Over most of the modern life of economics, the following two subjects have been of great concern:

• The Theory of Value and what determines prices.

• The Theory of Distribution and who has benefited.

In earliest times, neither the factors determining prices nor those setting levels of wages and interest, were of much relevance. With production and consumption centered on the household, there was no necessity for a theory of prices; with slaves there was no compelling need for a theory of wages. In nearly all of economic history, most people have been poor and a comparative few have been very rich. Accordingly, there has been a compelling need to explain why this is so.

## Aristotle 384 - 322 B.C.

Aristotle

The basic industry of both Greece and Rome was agriculture; the producing unit was the household, and the labor force was the slave. Discussion of the economic questions of this era is principally to be found in the writings of Aristotle. The most important reason that ethical questions were addressed to the exclusion of economic ones in the ancient world was the existence of slavery. According to Aristotle, at all times and in all places, the Greek world relied on some form of dependent labor to meet its needs. Since wages were not paid for labor, it followed that there could be no view of how wages were determined. Because slaves did the work, labor had a derogatory aspect that helped to exclude it from scholarly consideration.

The ethical justification of slavery became the most interesting economic question of the period. In defense of the institution Aristotle wrote, "The lower sort are by nature slaves, and it is better for them as for all inferiors that they should be under the rule of a master. Indeed the use made of slaves and of tame animals is not very different."

In Politics, Book I Aristotle adds, "It is clear then, that some men are by nature free, and others slaves, and that for these latter slavery is both expedient and right." Aristotle was equally certain as regards to women, "The male is by nature superior, and the female inferior; and the one rules, and the other is ruled; this principle, of necessity, extends to all mankind."[1]

Aristotle also strongly condemned the taking of money in the form of interest. Aristotle held that money was intended to be used in exchange, not as means to obtain a profit. Interest continued to be condemned throughout the middle ages. Without wages and interest in the ancient world, there could not be a theory of prices in any modern sense. Prices derive, in one way or another, from production costs, and production costs were not a visible function in the slave owner household.

Aristotle wrote about another problem that was to be a continuing one for economists. This is the question of value in use and value in exchange. Aristotle wondered why some of the most useful things have a low value, e.g., water, while some of the least useful items command a much higher price, e.g., gold or diamonds. Well into the nineteenth century, economic writers would still be struggling with the difference between value in use and value in exchange.

By Aristotle's time, they had established coinage of metal in Greece. After defining the nature of money and coinage, Aristotle goes on to an analysis of how money is made. According to Aristotle, the making of money, in its pure form, is not permissible. "Some men turn every quality or art into a means of making money; this they conceive to be the end, and to the promotion of the end all things must contribute."[2]

## THE CONTRIBUTIONS OF ROME

There was one major contribution to economic thought by the Romans. This was Roman Law that defined the rights of private property. It was Roman Law that gave formal identity to property and to its possessor the dominion or rights, which are now commonly agreed upon. These rights were comprehensive; they included the right not only of enjoyment and use of property, but also to misuse and abuse it. The intrusion on these rights in the future would from that time on require justification by the intruder.

No institution can compare in its importance to private property and no institution has been so productive of social, economic or political discord. If Roman economic comment was slight, it was, nonetheless, the Roman genius to distinguish and give form to the institution that would be central to personal satisfaction, economic development and political conflict in the centuries to come.

## THE MIDDLE AGES

Historians have looked, with little success, for any formal expression of economic ideas in the scholarly and priestly thought of the one thousand years that followed the dissolution of the Roman Empire. The basic economic life of the middle ages bore little resemblance to modern economic society. Specifically, the market though growing in importance was still a minor aspect of life in the middle ages. The great rural masses of men and women grew, made or killed what they ate or wore and surrendered a part of it to a hierarchy of Lords or Masters.

However, towns, though small by modern standards, began to appear. Some purchases and sales did take place and they attracted the mind and pen of the greatest of the religious philosophers of his time, the prolific Saint Thomas Aquinas (1225 - 1274). Saint Thomas was the first of the group of religious philosophers and scholars known to history as the Schoolmen.

The craft guilds were strongly characteristic of medieval economic life. They existed for several purposes, for example: assurance as to quality of workmanship, social observances, political influence and regulation of prices and journeymen's wages. This being the case, the question of fairness or justice of the price of a product arose, just as it had with Aristotle. It was to the fairness of prices that Saint Thomas Aquinas addressed his work. "I answer that it is wholly sinful to practice fraud for the express purpose of selling a thing for more than its just price. To sell dearer or to buy cheaper than a thing is worth is in itself unjust and unlawful." Saint Thomas thus enjoined a fair price as a religious responsibility; default from that obligation made the perpetrator subject not only to the moral condemnation of the community but to appropriate religious sanction.[3]

Saint Thomas also accepted and strongly affirmed the ban on the taking of interest. He also combined this belief with the consideration of the righteousness of trade overall. Trade, according to Saint Thomas, is praiseworthy, because it serves natural needs.

Money, one of the most magically alluring subjects of economics, drew the attention of another articulate religious scholar, Nicole Oresme (1320 - 1382). The term "Merchant Capitalism" is central to Nicole Oresme. The policy of the prince (the leader) should be to encourage trade and arrange the conditions that do so. For Oresme this meant the proper management of money.

Oresme showed how the coinage of such metals as gold, silver and copper, coins of fixed weight and reliable purity, could replace the awkward use of scales, in the weighing of metals. The responsibility for coinage he then placed squarely on the Prince or the government. According to Oresme, it is the sovereign's function to condemn and punish those who practice any fraud upon money.[4]

Oresme was particularly severe with the Prince of an adjacent province who slipped debased coins (less than claimed amounts of metal) into the monetary circulation of his neighbor, and he was convinced that merchants would avoid doing business in a land where the coinage was unreliable.

The rigid hierarchical structure of feudal society commanded and distributed goods and services not in response to price but in response to law, custom and the fear of punishment. The marketplace was an esoteric exception to the way trade was conducted, and most scholars did not spend time trying to explain it. Oresme, who did, was responding to a new and expanding world in which markets and moneys were strongly emerging as necessary factors of economic life.

## MERCHANT CAPITALISM (1450-1776)

Merchant Capitalism extended for three hundred years, from roughly the middle of the fifteenth to the middle of the eighteenth century. The end of merchant capitalism was sealed by the beginning of the industrial revolution, the American Revolution and the publication in 1776 of "The Wealth of Nations" by Adam Smith.

Mercantilism was the product of the minds of statesmen, civil servants, and the financial and business leaders of the day. The merchant emerged from the feudal shadows to become an affluent, distinctive, socially acceptable and a prestigious figure.

By the fifteenth century the merchant towns of Venice, Florence, Antwerp, and London had merchant communities of distinction. In the merchant towns the great merchants were not merely influential in the government; they controlled the power of government. Throughout all of Europe they were influential in the new national states.

The national state arose as a response to transnational drives. The Spanish Empire in the new world produced so much gold and silver that Spain, under Philip II, could finance the first standing army in the sixteenth century, since the Roman legions. Thus equipped, Spain launched the first campaign for the attempt to unify Europe under Spanish rule. Fighting Spain's threat became the motivation and the aim of the inventor of the national state, the French lawyer-politician Jean Bodin, (1530 - 1596). In 1576, Jean Bodin published, "Six Livres de la Republique," that defined the new national state.

What Bodin prescribed was a controlled civil service (answerable only to the sovereign), central control of the military, and a standing army managed by professional soldiers appointed by and accountable to central government. Bodin also recommended central control of coinage, taxes, customs and a centrally appointed professional judiciary, rather than courts staffed by local magnates.

These recommendations were the opposites of what had existed for a thousand years. All of them threatened powerfully entrenched "special interest," for example:

- An autonomous church and exempt bishops and abbeys.

- Local lords of all sizes, each with his own armed mercenaries, and each with his own jurisdiction and his own taxing powers.

- Free cities, self-governing trade guilds and scores of others.

However, the Spanish bid for mastery of Europe left no alternative. The choice was subjection to the national sovereign or conquest by a foreign sovereign. From then on, attempts similar to those of Spain to gain the mastery of Europe triggered practically every change in the political structure of the national states. Along with the proliferation of markets and the rise of the merchant class, three major developments reflected the economic attitudes and policies of this period.

The first were the voyages to America and the Far East. In 1492, Christopher Columbus, who was trained in Portugal and sponsored by Spain, found America. In 1497 the Portuguese navigator

Vasco da Gama sailed to India; and in ensuing decades, others from Spain and Portugal and then from England, France and Holland.

The result of these voyages was a flow of new and exotic products into Europe from the East, and more important, a flood of silver and gold from the mines of the new world. From 1531 to 1570, near the peak of the flood, silver represented an amount between 85 to 97 percent of the total treasury coming into Europe.

The effect of the great inflow of metal was a general rise in prices, an early example of the quantity theory of money. This is the historic theory which argues that if the volume of trade (the velocity of money) is held constant, prices will vary in direct proportion to the supply of money. The relationship between the supply of money and general commodity prices, was a key topic of the economic analysis of the time. Writing in 1576, Jean Bodin said; "I find that the high prices we see today are due to some four or five causes. The principle one is the abundance of gold and silver."[5]

The second development was the continuing effect that the great inflow of silver and gold had on the volume of trade. There was a view in this period that the role of money was essentially neutral. Money is a convenience in the buying and selling of goods, a bridge over the gap in time between the sale and purchases of goods, and a convenient way of holding wealth. It was believed that more fundamental factors govern the state of trade than the changes in the supply of money. Therefore, increases in the supply of money could not be used to stimulate merchant trade.

The third and most important development of the merchant capitalist period was the appearance and consolidation of the authority of the national state, as previously discussed. The earlier centuries had seen the decline of the feudal and compulsively feuding baronage and the emergence of princely and city authority. The national state was but the final step in a long chain of events. The rise of the national state caused the close association between the state authority and the interest of the merchants.

Mercantilism involved a market break with the ethical attitudes and instructions of Aristotle and of Saint Thomas Aquinas and the middle ages overall. The Merchants were patently in pursuit of wealth, in a society where they were influential. However, society no longer considered the pursuit of wealth by the merchants, to be evil or dubious. Merchants were easy in their conscience. Protestantism and Puritanism may have helped, but the church leaders accommodated religious faith to economic circumstances.

As wealth and the pursuit of wealth, by the merchants, become respectable, the right to charge interest on loans became acceptable. When the borrower invested and in turn made money from his loan, then, as a matter of simple equity, he should share the gain with the lender who made the investment possible and compensate the lender for their risk of loss of the principle. Both Catholic and Protestant Church doctrine made the necessary concession to economic circumstances. The financing of merchant operations with borrowed money became legitimate. They did not deny merchants access to heaven if they charged interest on their loans. After all, they were among the largest contributors to the Church.[6]

Wages had little or no part in mercantilist discussion and practice. They accomplished domestic manufacturing extensively in the household. In their home, husband, wife and children worked the raw material supplied to them by the merchant into finished textile products. Again no wages were paid as such; the merchant simply paid the workers whatever amount was necessary to obtain the finished product.

In summary, the major beliefs of the merchant capitalist were:

- Merchants had a very negative attitude toward competition. Because they didn't relish competition, monopoly or monopolistic control of prices and product offerings were approved.

- The Merchants were extremely influential in the state, and held a strong belief that the government should not interfere in trade or the economy.

- There was agreement that the accumulation of gold and silver should be a primary goal of personal and public policy, and this was the end to which all personal effort and public regulation should always be directed.

Of the total changes that took place during the years of merchant capitalism, none was more important than the arrival of the modern corporation. Initially this was merely a temporary association of individuals joining their efforts and capital for a common task or voyage and to ensure a non-competitive price for the products that they purchased and sold. The roots of such associations extended back to the guilds of the middle ages. In the fifteenth century, merchants selling cloth from England to the continent often formed a loose federation. The following were the most important of these federations to economic history:

- Muscovy Company of 1555

- The Dutch East India Company of 1601

- The British East India Company (1600-1874)

In the late seventeenth and early eighteenth centuries the chartering of joint-stock companies, as they came to be called, continued. Actually, most trade with the American Colonies was conducted with charted companies. Also, in the early 1700's, there was a further and even more spectacular forerunner of modern corporate business. This was the market for the sale of stocks and bonds that appeared in Paris and London.

Although we can understand mercantilist doctrine primarily through the policies of the time, there were men in all the new states of Europe that articulated its general principles. Thomas Mun, who was one of the most distinguished of these writers, published in 1664, "England's Treasure by Foreign Trade." Thomas Mun offers a dozen rules for maximizing England's wealth and well-being, for example:

- Always sell dear to foreigners what they do not have and sell cheap what they can otherwise obtain.

- Use ones own ships for exports.

- Buy cheaply from far away countries.

- Do not give business to nearby competitors.

## THE QUANTITY THEORY OF MONEY

Between the years of 1530 and 1650, price levels approximately tripled in Europe. This occurrence sometimes referred to as the "Great Elizabethan Inflation." As the peoples purchasing power was being eroded, many peasant revolts ensued, most often directed toward the grain merchants. It was only in 1568 that French mercantilist, Jean Bodin, discussed earlier in this chapter, drew attention to the most important economic development in this period; namely, the great influx of gold and silver from the Americas into Spain and the rest of Europe. Bodin speculated that there was a direct relationship between the quantity of gold and silver and the price level. Thus was born the first theory of money, the "Quantity Theory." John Locke the English political philosopher, in 1692 took this idea and stated the Quantity Theory of Money as a general rule. According to Locke, if the supply of money is increased, the prices of all goods will rise. Locke argued the Mercantilist line of maintaining a favorable balance of trade to ensure an inflow of money and thus that the price level of English goods remained higher than that of foreign goods.

### David Hume (1711-1776)

David Hume

David Hume was an early member of the classical school of economics, as well as a noted historian and philosopher. He was a colleague of Adam Smith at Edinburgh University in Scotland. Eighteenth century economists widely agreed that an increase in the money stock, chiefly gold and silver coins at the time, would raise the price level. Price increases had been observed, for example, when the Spanish began bringing gold back to Europe from the New World. A less settled question was whether an increase in the money stock would also cause real economic output to increase. Today economists refer to this issue as whether or not money is "neutral." On the subject of the neutrality of money, Hume said that "although an increase in the price of goods is a necessary consequence of an increase in the stock of gold and silver, it follows not immediately." The change in the money stock does not affect all markets at once. Hume continues by stating that, "At first, no alteration is perceived; by degrees the price rises, first on one commodity, then of another; till the whole at last reaches a just proportion with the new quantity of money." Agreeing with the modern theory, which states that the initial stimulus to real output is only temporary, Hume continues: "In my opinion, it is only in this interval or intermediate situation, between the acquisition of money and the rise of prices, that the increasing quantity of gold and silver is favorable to industry." In Hume's view, there is no long-run effect on real output. In the long run, unlike the short run, money is neutral. A one-time change in the quantity of money has a lasting proportional effect on the price level but on nothing else.[7]

Hume initiated a quote to describe his theory on the neutrality of money. Money was "Oil-in-the machine." He also outlined the famous Quantity Theory relationship between the supply of money and the general level of prices. According to Hume, "All augmentation of gold and silver has no other effect than to heighten the price of labor."

Though Hume's ideas had older roots, the direct relationship between money and prices was introduced by Jean Bodin and the theory itself was developed by John Locke. However, the bulk of the Mercantilists equated money with wealth. Thus, Hume's argument of money as a veil is often regarded as an attempt to assail the Mercantilist position on the creation of wealth.

**NOTES:**

**Chapter 2**
**The Roots of Political Economics**

1.    Aristotle, <u>Politics, Book I, In Early Economic Thought,</u>
      <u>Edited by A.E. Monroe</u>, Cambridge, MA, Harvard University
      Press, 1924, p. 10.

2.	Aristotle, Politics, Book I, p. 19.
3.	Saint Thomas Aquinas, <u>Summa Theological, in Early Economic Thought</u>, pp. 54-55.
4.	Oresme, <u>Traictie de la Premiere Invention des Monnoies,</u> in <u>Early Economic Thought,</u> p. 95.
5.	Bodin, Jean, <u>Les Six Livres de la Republic, In Early Economic Thought</u>, p 127.
6.	Galbraith, John Kenneth, <u>Economics in Perspective</u>, Boston, MA, Houghton Mifflin Company, 1987, p. 38
7.	Hume, David, <u>On Money, " In his Writings on Economics,"</u> Edited by Eugene Rotwein, Madison, WA, University of Wisconsin Press, 1955.

# CHAPTER 3

---

# AMERICA: THE EARLY YEARS

*"America was never in higher prosperity, her produce abundant and bearing a good price, her working people all employed and well paid." -- Benjamin Franklin*

## COLONIAL BUSINESS ENTERPRISE

During the colonial period, extremely small business dominated American industry. Most American businessmen were peddlers, blacksmiths, and small shopkeepers. These small business owners did not have the capital or ability necessary to cope with the needs of the widening market. Eventually the petty capitalists' position of dominance in America was taken over by a group of merchants who were better able to take care of the international and domestic economy that the colonies had become as a member of the British Empire.

The merchants came into existence in America, in the middle of the eighteenth century, in the major colonial cities. The original merchants were owners of general stores, shipping companies, brokerage and wholesale operations. The era of the merchant capitalists in the colonies spanned the period from 1750 to about 1850. Thomas Hancock, Stephan Girard and John Jacob Astor were all merchant capitalists. Before the American Revolution there were over 100 merchants in each of the three largest cities, Philadelphia, Boston and New York.

## THE INFLUENCE OF BRITISH MERCANTILISM

By the middle of the seventeenth century, Great Britain had not yet achieved her position of world economic domination. Attempts to build an empire were often frustrated by the power and activities of the Dutch and the French. In order to overcome the advantages enjoyed, especially by the Dutch, Britain adopted a set of policies that came to be known as merchant capitalism. Designed principally to build a strong state, mercantilist policies were intended to help the entire empire to compete in the world economy. However, merchant capitalism favored the interests of the "mother country" over those of the rest of the empire.

The American colonies were to be given assistance, but they were also regarded as producers of raw materials for Britain and consumers of British manufactured goods. The intention of the British government was to use force, if necessary, to maintain this arrangement. Beginning in 1649, Britain adopted the first Navigation Acts affecting the colonies, and for the next 200 years these acts were modified for the purpose of preserving the power of the British Empire.

After the French and Indian War in 1763, the regulations imposed by the Navigation Acts began to be applied with an emphasis toward raising revenue to help Britain offset some of the expenses of defending the colonies. In general, mercantilist legislation, as it pertained to international trade, provided for the following:

- All trade to England from the American colonies was to be carried in ships owned and manned by citizens of the British Empire.

- All goods imported into the colonies, except wine and salt from Southern Europe, had to be shipped via England.

- A major portion of colonial exports, such as tobacco, cotton, indigo, rice and naval stores (pitch, tar, resin, turpentine, hemp, masts, yards, and bowsprit), could be shipped only to England.

- Extensive tariff regulation was established.

- An elaborate system of rebates, drawbacks, export bounties on designated goods, and export taxes was developed.

The restrictions on imports and exports were economically disadvantageous to the colonists. An example of British legislation that particularly frustrated American traders was the Molasses Act of 1733, which imposed prohibitive duties on imports of sugar, molasses, and rum from the non-English West Indies. Designed to protect the English West Indies' sugar producers at the expense of the mainland, this Act proved to be a colossal economic and political blunder on the part of the British government.

However, the British system of mercantilism did present the colonies with some advantages. England protected colonial shipping on the high seas. Also, generous bounties were paid to the colonists on such goods as tar, pitch, hemp, silk, indigo and lumber. Being members of the British Empire, the colonists also had the advantage of exporting some goods to Britain at lower duties than were required of foreign shippers. In some cases, British restrictions gave the colonists an almost monopolistic position in trade, relative to other countries in Europe. For example, tobacco raising was prohibited in England and a prohibitive duty was imposed on non-colonial tobacco imports.

## GREAT BRITAIN'S VIEW OF COLONIAL TRADE

From the British point of view, the colonies never seemed to understand that their function in life was to devote their efforts to the interest of England, the center of the Empire. They were supposed to be producers of raw materials and consumers of English manufactured goods, i.e., the basic goal of English mercantilism.

New England was the worst offender of the system. Because of its geographical disadvantages, New England could not compete in agricultural production with the other colonies. New England did have a large seacoast, and abundant natural resources. This situation resulted in a comparative advantage that gave New England the ability to produce ships at a lower cost than English shipbuilders. Consequently, New England competed with, rather than complemented, England's international trade. This tendency toward competing directly with England with a manufactured product, i.e., sailing ships, was in direct contradiction with England's mercantilist policy.

The middle colonies, New York, New Jersey, Pennsylvania and Delaware, were also not living up to mercantilist expectations. The middle colonies carried on a large trade with Southern Europe and the West Indies. By 1770, the middle colonies had greatly increased their volume of foreign trade by selling wheat flour and provisions to Southern Europe, the West Indies and England.

The Southern Colonies came the closest to fulfilling the requirements of the mercantilist system. They raised raw materials, mostly tobacco, for export to England and imported manufactured goods from England. In 1700, Virginia and Maryland shipped enough tobacco and imported enough manufactured goods to account for two-thirds of all colonial trade with Britain.

Great Britain was prospering very well during this era, and manufacturing with a built in market for the goods produced, was the key. By far the world's leading manufacturing nation, England was building up an overseas financial empire by exporting more than that country was importing. When a country exports more than they import, they have a balance of payments surplus. However, when one country has a balance of payments surplus, at least one of its trading partners must have a balance of trade deficit. In this case, the colonies had a balance of payments deficit with Britain. In the short run, the colonies were able to cover their balance of payments deficit by borrowing, but eventually the debts became so large that they could not be paid. These debts by the colonies were one of the aggravations that fanned the anti-British feeling that eventually erupted in the revolutionary war.[1]

## COLONIAL BANKING

The history of American money and banking has been a story of conflict between different philosophies and disparate beliefs over what money should do and how it should be controlled. The two points of view about the role of money were between those who desired "easy money" versus those who desired "sound money" policies. Those who believed that easy money offered an open door to prosperity argued for a rapidly expanding money supply that was free from strict control by a central authority. For the colonies this meant Great Britain. Their views were opposed by those who believed in sustainable economic growth or a steady progress under a central authority whose primary objectives were safety, solvency, and stability. The debate began before the revolution and has continued ever since.

In early America, capital did not accumulate fast enough to raise the level of living very much. Therefore, many of the colonists, acting on the assumption that money was the same as capital, thought that each addition to the money supply would automatically increase the stock of capital by the same amount. It was commonly believed that a money system should have two functions: it should provide a medium of exchange, and it should augment the supply of capital. However, as David Hume pointed out, there is no direct relationship between the money stock and the amount of capital available for investment. The colonists, in a desperate attempt to expand their business, developed a series of monetary experiments. All of these experiments were resisted and sometimes thwarted by the British, who upheld the conservative view in the monetary debates of that period.

By the middle of the seventeenth century, in order to increase their stock of metallic money, i.e., gold and silver, the colonies resorted to devaluation; that is they cut the amount of metal in their silver coins. However, this attempt to inflate the money supply was also prohibited by British edict. Refusing to accept Britain's distaste for monetary inflation, the colonies, which were desperately in debt to England, began to print paper money. In 1690, Massachusetts issued one-year notes to pay retiring soldiers. The experiment worked out so well that more paper money was quickly printed. Meanwhile, the other colonies, encouraged by Massachusetts' action, also began to issue paper money. Some of these notes were issued by state banks, but there were no banks as we know them today. Colonial banks issued money against mortgages, but they did not accept deposits.

At first, paper money did not depreciate in value. However, in many colonies it was used unproductively and far too much money was printed. As a result of this over expansion of the state's money supply, prices increased on a broad scale. Extreme inflation can disrupt the economy and cause widespread suffering to certain groups of people. However, paper-money depreciation did act to the advantage of colonial debtors and to the disadvantage of British creditors, who eventually prevailed upon the British Crown to prohibit the practice.[2] According to Benjamin Franklin, the British anti-inflation policy was one of the five causes of the America Revolution.

## ECONOMIC SEEDS OF REVOLUTION

The major problem that confronted the British in North America after the French and Indian War was that of financing the protection of the colonies and liquidating the debts acquired during the war. The Seven Years War (the French and Indian War was the colonial phase) diverted capital away from British commerce and depleted the royal treasury. The English government believed that it was politically impossible to increase property taxes at home, and argued that the colonists should bear a larger share of the costs of their own defense.

The British response to their money problems created by the North American War was to introduce new revenue measures, tighten up the administration of the colonies, and force the mainland colonies to conform more closely to mercantile expectations. Fiscal reform began in 1762 with the passage of a wartime measure that ordered absentee customs officials to their colonial posts, increased the portion of revenues that they could keep for themselves, and gave the Navy authority to seize cargoes suspected of customs violations. Parliament changed the wartime measures into permanent law in 1763 and in 1764 added the Revenue Act. The Revenue Act included a revision of the Molasses Act of 1733, lowering the duty on molasses from the French West Indies, but also providing the means for strict enforcement of the Act. Also, the British altered the judicial aspects of the Navigation Acts in this 1764 program. The vice-admiralty courts received larger jurisdiction, customs officers were guaranteed freedom from retaliatory suits, and defendants in custom cases were generally denied the due process of law by having to prove their innocence in these cases.

In addition, in 1764 Parliament passed The Currency Act that caused the colonists to be seriously constrained for the first time in the management of their money supply. The Currency Act prohibited the creation of all new land banks throughout the colonies. Also this Act demanded the phased withdrawal of previous land-bank notes, banned additional issues of bills of credit as legal tender, and required a scheduled retirement of all past issues of bills of credit.

The 1764 Currency Act was designed to reduce the exchange rate of the colonial currency in terms of British Pound Sterling. This would increase the cost of colonial products to English buyers and reduce the cost of English products to colonial buyers. The Act resulted in strong protest from the conservative mercantile communities in Philadelphia, New York and Baltimore. In adopting the Currency Act, the English desired the following results:

- To increase the value of colonial currency in which the colonists paid taxes to England.

- To increase the value of debts owed by the colonist to English merchants. This would effectively lower the profit for the colonist on trade with England.

- To increase the colonial demand for English imports, as a result of the increased value of colonial currency, in terms of Sterling.

- To create a decline in English demand for exports as a result of the falling value of Sterling in terms of colonial currency.[3]

Given the negative balance of trade that was already being experienced by the colonial merchants, this Act effectively devalued the British Pound relative to colonial currency. As many American merchants were already in serious debt to their British counterparts, this Act served to worsen an already bad situation.

Further revenue measures followed. The Stamp Act of 1765 placed a levy on commercial papers, newspapers and other printed material. The Chancellor of the Exchequer, Charles Townshend, sponsored a set of duties, which were enacted in the Townshend Acts. These Acts taxed the colonists on their consumption of paper, glass, lead, paints and tea that was imported from England.

Soon after their introduction, these enactments were repealed: the Stamp Act in 1766 and the Townshend duties (except for the tax on tea) in 1770. However, the capriciousness of all these regulations was an important contributor to the development of a revolutionary atmosphere that was probably more significant than the direct economic burden the regulations themselves imposed. The unpredictability of British regulations, and the potential for substantial damage to colonial interest, fueled a growing lack of respect for British authority. For an example of the potential impact that the Currency Act could have caused, consider the modern monetary policy of the United States being conducted by the Bank of England. Thus, while other irritations and desires fueled the American Revolution, there was probably no single issue more important and more divisive, than the perceived role of government (in this case the British Parliament), in commerce and trade.

## AMERICAN COMMERCE AFTER THE REVOLUTION

In 1774 and 1775, the First Continental Congress prohibited trade with Britain. The British followed with the Prohibitory Act of 1775, banning almost all trade with the colonies. Accordingly, the British attempted to blockade the coast of the mainland colonies. This resulted in a decline in trade with Britain. However, American merchants got around the British blockade by developing new trading opportunities. The First Continental Congress opened American ports to all traders, except England, and promoted an expanded trade policy with the friendly European nations. In 1779, the French formed an alliance with America. The result of this alliance was that trade with the French West Indies and Europe expanded. Americans were able to purchase a large amount of European imports through the sale of tobacco and from the procurement of loans from France, Spain and The Netherlands.

When the War ended in 1783, Americans resumed trade with Britain. American consumers had become accustomed to British manufactured goods. Responding to this large market, British merchants again extended credit to American importers, although at levels that were smaller than before the War. However, Americans were able to engage in international trade with the rest of Europe, on a more favorable basis. Part of this improved trading position was a result of freedom from the mercantile system. Relieved of the restrictions of the Molasses and Sugar Acts Americans could trade with greater freedom and at a lower cost with the French West Indies.

American commerce profited in other ways from the demise of mercantilism. Americans gained the ability to export a much greater amount of goods (not just tobacco), directly to the continent, and trade with Northern and Southern Europe increased substantially. Americans were now free to export grain, flour, rice, potash and naval stores directly to France and the Netherlands. Americans also took advantage of their new freedom by developing a direct trade with Asia. As early as 1786, Americans began shipping beef, flour and naval stores to the French Island in the Indian Ocean and at the same time, they opened trade with China In summary, the end of British rule in the colonies brought about the end of merchant capitalism and the beginning of the industrial revolution in America

## THE CREATION OF THE U.S. CONSTITUTION

To fight the War of Independence, the colonies were loosely tied together by the Articles of Confederation and Perpetual Union that was ratified in 1781. However, after the war, the confederation was too weak to be effective as a framework of national government. In particular, taxing power to pay for the operation of government was left to the individual states. This delegation of responsibility left the new nation in debt and consumed by inflation when the war ended.

In January 1786, Virginia and Maryland appointed commissioners to analyze the potential development of a better form of government. The delegates from these two states met with representatives from the middle states at Annapolis and issued a call for a constitutional convention. The first meeting was held at Philadelphia on May 14, 1787. Four months later, on September 28, 1787, George Washington, who was president of the convention, sent the completed constitution to the thirteen states for ratification. The constitution required ratification by two-thirds of the states to become law. On June 21, 1788, New Hampshire became the ninth state to ratify the constitution. Congress declared the constitution to be the new law of the land on March 4, 1789. The first ten amendments to the constitution, the Bill of Rights, were passed by the First Congress and became law on December 15, 1791.

The representatives of the individual states were reluctant to give up any power and relinquished to the central authority only those rights they believed were necessary to create a strong central government. To strengthen the reserved rights, the Tenth Amendment was added to the constitution that said:

• The powers not delegated to the United States by the Constitution, nor prohibited by it to the states are reserved to the states respectively, or to the people.

The Constitution as written is remarkably simple. The 18 powers given explicitly to Congress are in Article I Section 8. These powers say, in summary, that Congress shall have the power to tax, borrow on the credit of the new government, regulate commerce, establish post offices, create patent and copyright laws, raise and support armies and declare war.

In addition to the powers given to Congress, the Constitution, in Article II, sets up the Executive Branch, and in Article III, sets up the Judiciary. Article IV contains the "Full Faith and Credit" provisions of the Constitution, ordering each state to recognize the laws and judicial practices of the other states.

Also, the Constitution secured the rights of individuals to own property, settled and reserved the rights of the states and its citizens, and provided a consistent body of knowledge based on English common law. Consistent and calculable law is a requisite for the economic growth and  development of an industrial nation and this body of law was provided in the United States Constitution.

**NOTES:**

**Chapter 3**
**American: The Early Years**

1. Krooss, Herman, <u>American Economic Development</u>, Englewood   Cliffs, N.J., Prentice-Hall, Inc., 1966,   p. 150
2. Lester, Richard A., <u>Monetary Experiments</u>, Princeton,      N.J., Princeton University Press, 1939.
3. Brownlee, Elliot, W., <u>Dynamics of Ascent</u>, Belmont, CA, Wadsworth Publishing Company, 1988, p. 104.

# CHAPTER 4

---

# THE FRENCH CONNECTION

*"Man is born free and is everywhere in chains. The natural state could only be achieved via wholesale social reform, which would result in a collective state with extra-personal dedication to a General Will."–Jean-Jacques Rousseau.*

## THE PHYSIOCRATS

Merchant capitalism and the craftsmen that it required to produce its products had also appeared in France. Paris had become a city of merchants along with their suppliers and workers. However, to a larger extent than any other country in Europe, France had retained a powerful agricultural interest and mystique.

In the latter half of the eighteenth century, a highly innovative French contribution to economic thought evolved. This was in the spirit of enlightenment, based on the writings of Cantillon, Quesnay, Marquis de Mirabeau, DuPont de Nemours, and Turgot. Central to this theory was the role of agriculture as the source of all wealth. The French philosophers combined an assertion of the traditional values of the land and its associated political power with the advocacy of reform.

Historians of economic thought have given these writers the title of "Physiocrats," those who assert the rules of nature. The Physiocrats were a closely-knit community and many of their ideas are associated with a common position. An important figure among the Physiocrats was Pierre Samuel DuPont de Nemours (1739-1817). In 1800, DuPont immigrated to the United States, and in 1802 with his two sons, he began construction of a powder mill on Brandywine Creek near Wilmington, Delaware. From these beginnings came one of the largest

American industrial corporations. In fact General DuPont became one of the most powerful industrial leaders of the last part of the nineteenth century.[1]

The major contributions of the Physiocrats to economic thought were as follows:

- Ledriot Natural (Natural Law): The first and central commitment of the Physiocrats was to the idea of natural law, for it was this, they held, which ultimately ruled economic and social behavior. The law of kings and legislators is tolerable only as it is consistent with natural law, the existence and protection of property according to natural law. A society is better off, it was reasoned, if things were worked out in accordance with natural motivations and restraints.

- Laissez Faire: A term coined by Vincent de Gourney, proposed that the guiding rule in legislation and in government should be laissez faire. The term laissez faire was the greatest legacy of the Physiocrats. However, this phrase has been defined in two different ways. In later times, economists would identify laissez faire with the achievements of the competitive market. The results of a market economy would be preferred to any intervention by the state. However, laissez faire would also be the rallying cry against government intervention in any form for any social purpose. Leave things alone in the widest conceivable area except national defense, and they will work themselves out.

- Product Net: There was another theory that was clearly in opposition to merchant capitalism. This was the idea of product net. It simply held that all wealth originated in agriculture, none in any other industry, trade, or occupation. Closely associated with the notion of product net was the physiocratic class structure. In this, there were the following categories:

  1.  The landlords or proprietors: The people who guided the production of agriculture. To them the product net ultimately accrued and they were accountable for the

social and political responsibilities of the community and the state.

2.	The productive class: The people who worked the soil. It was after their reward (wages) was paid that the product net went to the proprietors.

3.	The lower status: The merchants, manufacturers, and craftsmen, i.e., the unproductive class.

As with laissez faire, this was an idea that did not die. The notion that production somehow creates a surplus of revenue accruing to particular classes was to re-emerge in a different form in the next century. Then it would be the capitalists, not the landowners, whom they would accuse of receiving a surplus value, another and different product net.[2]

## Richard Cantillon (1680-1734)

Richard Cantillon was an Irishman with a Spanish name who lived in France. His treatise, "Essai Sur la Nature du Commerce en General" was written in French and published anonymously in England some twenty years after his death. His work was well known and used as a building block by the Physiocrats. However, Cantillon fell into obscurity until resurrected and popularized by William Stanley Jevons in the 1880s. Cantillon was one of the first to recognize the circular flow of income and set the foundation for the much of the Physiocrats work. Cantillon's system was clear and simple. He developed a two-sector general equilibrium from which he obtained a theory of price (determined by the costs of production) and a theory of output (determined by factor inputs and technology). He was also among the first political economists to reduce labor to the amount of necessities needed to sustain it, and thus, made employment a function of the land absorption necessary to produce the necessities to feed labor and the luxuries to feed landlords. In summary, Cantillon developed an early version of the "land theory of value". This theory was a critical part of the Physiocratic doctrine.

## Francois Quesnay (1694-1774)

Francois Quesnay

The cornerstone of the Physiocratic doctrine, which built upon the work of Richard Cantillon, was the Tableau Economique. The Tableau Economique was developed by Francois Quesnay. This system alleged to show how products flowed out from the worker to the landlords and onto the merchants, manufacturers and other non-productive classes, and how money flowed back to the cultivator. Thus Quesnay showed how each part of the economy served and was compensated by each of the others. He displayed the mechanism of purchase and sale of goods as a complete interlocking system. In 1973, Wassily Leontief was awarded the Nobel Prize for Economic Science. This award was for his work called input-output analysis. This system became the principle building block for the modern popular models for predicting the economic prospect and the effect of changes in prices, wages, interest rates, taxes and demand as these are reflected through individual industries. This was a concept developed by Francois Quesnay.

## Anne-Robert-Jacques Turgot (1727-1781)

Originally, the term Physiocrats was reserved for Quesnay and the inner circle of his disciples. However, Jacques Turgot should be included in this group. Turgot advanced a distinctly different and more advanced version of the Physiocratic doctrine. He developed his theory on Laissez-Faire in his "Elegy to Gournay" written in 1759 as a tribute to the Marques de Gournay. Turgot argued that the network of detailed mercantilist regulation of industry was but a veritable system or coerced cartelization and special privilege conferred by the State. For Turgot, freedom of domestic and foreign trade followed equally

Anne-Jacques Turgot

from the enormous mutual benefits of free exchange. According to Turgot, self-interest is the prime mover in the process, and the individual interest in the free market must always coincide with the general interest. The buyer will select the seller who will give him the lowest price for the most suitable product, and the seller will sell his best merchandise at the highest competitive price. Turgot concluded that the general freedom of buying and selling, is therefore, the only means of assuring, on the one hand, the seller of a price sufficient to encourage production and, on the other hand, the consumer of the best merchandise at the lowest price.

Turgot's economic writings, most notably his "Reflections on the Formation and Distribution of Riches" (1769), were particularly influential on Adam Smith and many of the insights in the "Wealth of Nations" can be traced back to Turgot. Among his most notable contributions was the introduction of the concept of "Capital" into the Physiocratic system. Turgot pointed out that wealth is accumulated by means of consumed and saved annual produce. Savings are accumulated in the form of money and then invested in various kinds of capital goods. The capitalists must first accumulate saved capital in order to advance their payment to laborers while the product is being worked on. In agriculture, the capitalist must save funds to pay workers, buy capital, pay for buildings and equipment until the harvest is reaped and sold and he can recoup his advances. And so it is in every field of production.[3]

Turgot, in his "Paper on Lending at Interest" (1770) focused on the problem of interest and why borrowers are willing to pay interest for the use of money. Turgot wrote that, since a sum of money actually owned now is preferable to the assurance of receiving similar sum years later, the same sum of money paid and returned is scarcely an equivalent value, for the lender gives up the use of money and receives nothing in return. Therefore, the interest that the lender receives is to compensate him for the use of his money. Turgot in his "Reflections" was the first person to point out the concept of capitalization, that is, the present value of land or other capital good on the market tends to equal the sum of its expected annual future rents, or returns, discounted by the market rate of time preference or rate of interest.[4]

## THE PHILOSOPHES

The European Enlightenment developed in part due to an energetic group of French thinkers who thrived in the middle of the eighteenth century: the philosophes. This group was a heterogeneous mix of people who pursued a variety of intellectual interests: scientific, mechanical, literary, philosophical and sociological. They were united by a few common themes: an unwavering doubt in the perfectibility of human beings, a fierce desire to dispel erroneous systems of thought (such as religion) and a dedication to systematizing the various intellectual disciplines.

The rallying cry for the philosophes was the concept of progress. By mastering both natural sciences and human sciences, humanity could harness the natural world for its own benefit and learn to live peacefully with one another. This was the ultimate goal, for the philosophes, of rational and intentional progress. Of the French philosophes, the most influential in regard to political economics were Jean-Jacques Rousseau, Francis Marie Arouet (Voltaire), Denis Diderot, and the baron de Montesquieu.

### Voltaire, Diderot, and Montesquieu

Voltaire concentrated on two specific philosophical projects. First, he untiringly worked to introduce empiricism into French intellectual life. Second, he persisted in proselytizing for religious tolerance; in fact, most of his works that are still read today had as their theme religious tolerance. Voltaire's argument was very simple; the most inhuman crimes perpetrated by humanity throughout its entire history have been perpetrated in the name of religion. Voltaire believed that individual governments should not impose religious systems on an entire state. The ultimate argument of his book "A

Treatise on Tolerance," published in 1763, was that secular values should take precedence over religious values; until that happens, human history will be marked by viciousness and inhumanity.

The great manifesto of the philosophes movement was Diderot's Encyclopedia. The Encyclopedia was the collective effort of over one hundred French thinkers. The central purpose of the work was to secularize learning and to refute what the authors felt were dangerous carry-overs from the Middle Ages. For the philosophes', human improvement was not a religious issue, but simply a matter of mastering the natural world though science and technology and mastering human passions through an understanding of how individuals and societies work.

The baron de Montesquieu concerned himself entirely with political theory. His "Spirit of the Laws," published in 1748, sought to explain how different groups of people end up with different and varying forms of government. He argued that climate, terrain, and agricultural conditions largely predetermined both human behavior and various forms of authority. However, Montesquieu also believed that there was a single, best form of government and human beings could overcome any and all geographical and climatic conditions. For Montesquieu, the best form of human government was embodied in the English constitution after the Great Revolution. In particular, the English constitution divided state powers into three independent branches of government: the executive, legislative, and the judicial. Since no one person or group was in charge, the maximum amount of political and economic freedom was made available to the general population. He called this equal distribution of power "checks and balances," and his theories of government would be the single most powerful influence upon the formation of the American government at the end of the eighteenth century.

## Jean-Jacques Rousseau (1712-1788)

While others contributed, the center of gravity for social reform in the eighteenth century was a single writer: Jean Jacques Rousseau. Rousseau's most important contribution to economic history was his "Discourse on Political Economy" published in 1775. In his Discourse,

Jean-Jacques Rousseau

Rousseau shared with his fellow philosophers the faith in the existence of a "natural state" of society. This faith could in turn be extended to social equilibrium and the natural value concepts that were ingrained in the thinking of the Physiocrats. However, Rousseau was a pessimist about existing human society. He recognized that this natural state was perverted by civilization and that the appetites and motivations of civilized man had been consequently corrupted and constructed by his interaction with society. "Man is born free and is everywhere in chains" as he wrote in the opening to his "Social Contract" published in 1762. According to Rousseau, what marks a state as legitimate is its guarantee to all its members of the freedom to enact their own laws. The institutional device, which Rousseau relies on to allow this freedom, is direct democracy. If those who are subject to a states jurisdiction assemble together to make laws, the state is legitimate, since all of its members then have a direct and equal legislative voice. Rousseau's main test of legitimacy is to justify the tight connection between direct democracy and legislative freedom by identifying the contextual requirements and institutional conditions which a direct democracy must meet."[5]

In his "Discourse on Political Economy," Rousseau begins to answer the question of how a legitimate state might be established and what administrators must do in order to follow the political will of those to be governed. Rousseau presents three maxims designed to answer these questions. The first maxim of legitimate government, according to the essay, is to follow the "General Will" of the people in all things. The mechanism that has been developed to guide government into dealing fairly with its people is a system of laws. "It is to the law alone that men owe justice and liberty. It is this statutory tool of the will of all which reestablishes natural equity on a legal basis among men." The leader's essential duty is to oversee the observance of the laws of which he is the minister and upon which all his authority is founded. Rousseau concludes that the first rule of public economy is that the administration should conform to the laws.[6]

In the second maxim of public economy, Rousseau details how to create the civic virtue that is a precondition to the successful operation of a legitimate state. Rousseau suggests three means for creating civic virtue: state protection for personal safety, economic equality, and public education. On economic equality, Rousseau states that "It is therefore, one of the most important concerns of government to prevent extreme inequality of fortunes, not by taking away wealth from those who possess it but by depriving everyone of the means of accumulating it, and not by building poorhouses but by protecting citizens from being impoverished." On the subject of public education, Rousseau writes: "The homeland cannot subsist without liberty, nor liberty without virtue, nor virtue without citizens; you will have everything if you train citizens; without that, you will only have malicious slaves."[7]

The third maxim is about the need for economic equality. Rousseau's concern over political corruption leads him to set aside economic efficiency and growth in favor of equality, simplicity, and self-sufficiency as the values that the economy should serve. He writes in the essay: "It is not enough to have citizens and to protect them; it is also necessary to consider their subsistence, and providing for the public needs is an obvious consequence of the general will." Once public resources are established, the leaders of the state are rightfully the administrators of them. From this rule, Rousseau derives the most important maxim in financial administration, which is to take far greater pains to prevent needs than to raise revenues. "The distribution of commodities, money, and merchandise in just proportions, as indicated by times and places, is the true secret of finances and the source of wealth." Rousseau emphasized the use of the tax laws to provide economic equality. He states that taxes levied on the people are of two kinds, property taxes that are collected on things and personal taxes that are paid by a head count. Rousseau argues for a taxation system that is proportionate to income and wealth. "But if the need tax is exactly proportionate to the means of private individuals, as the tax in France known as the Capitation, could be and which is, thus, both real and personal, it is the most equitable and, consequently, the best suited to free men." Rousseau backs a tax system proportionate to income and wealth. He also argues that those who can afford only the necessities of life pay no tax at all. "Anyone who has only the bare necessaries should not pay anything at all; the taxation of anyone who has more than he needs can, when the occasion demands, be extended to the amount that exceeds the necessities."

Rousseau summarizes the social pact between the rich and the poor with a facetious quotation. "You need me, for I am rich and you are poor; let us make an agreement between us; I shall permit you to have the honor of serving me on the condition that you give me what little you have left in return for the trouble I shall be taking to command you."[8]

## The American and French Revolutions

The French Revolution swept away the world that the Physiocrats had sought to defend and save. Left, however, for generations to come were the ideas of an economic system as an interconnected and interdependent structure of concepts; a controlling natural law of economic behavior, the prominence of agriculture, laissez faire, the product net, and the Tableau Economique.

Since the philosophes believed that human beings and human society was perfectible, the philosophes were energetic activists and agitators, sometimes incurring great personal risk for their beliefs. However, the most effective agitators, using the ideas of the philosophes movement, were the American revolutionaries in the latter quarter of the century. The foundation and formation of the American Republic was, by and large, the product of putting many philosophes ideas into practice at great personal risk to those who declared their independence from England.

**NOTES:**

**Chapter 4**
**The French Connection**

1.  Galbraith, John Kenneth, <u>Economics in Perspective</u>, Boston, MA, Houghton Mifflin Company, 1987, p. 50.
2.  Galbraith, p. 52.
3.  Turgot, Anne-Jacques, <u>Reflections on the Formation and Distributions of Wealth</u>, Printed by E. Spragg, J. Good, Bookseller, No. 159, London, EN, 1793, p. 18.
4.  Turgot, p. 20
5.  Rousseau, Jean-Jacques, <u>Rousseau's Political Writings</u>, Edited <u>by Alan Ritter and Julia Bondanetta</u>, NY, W.W Norton & Company Inc., 1987, p. 107.
6.  Rousseau, p. 63.
7.  Rousseau, p. 72
8.  Rousseau, p. 80
9.  Rousseau, p. 82
10. Turgot, Anne-Jacques, <u>Reflections on the Formation and Distributions of Wealth</u>, Printed by E. Spragg, J. Good, Bookseller, No. 159, London, EN, 1793, p. 6.
11. Rousseau, Jean-Jacques, <u>Rousseau's Political Writings,</u> <u>Edited by Alan Ritter and Julia Bondanetta</u>, NY, W.W Norton & Company Inc., 1987, p. 107.
12. Rousseau, p. 63.
13. Rousseau, p. 72
14. Rousseau, p. 80
15. Rousseau, p. 82

# CHAPTER 5

---

# THE FOUNDATIONS OF CLASSICAL ECONOMICS

*"It is not its silver or gold that measures a nation's wealth. It is the annual labour of every nation that is the fund which originally supplies it with all the necessaries and conveniences of life." —Adam Smith*

## ADAM SMITH (1723-1790)

Adam Smith

The industrial revolution, which came to England and Southern Europe in the last third of the eighteenth century, brought workers to the factories and the factory towns. These workers previously produced goods in their cottages or food and wool on their farms. The capital that merchants had invested in raw materials and sent to the villages to be made into cloth was now being invested in factories. However, to operate these new factories a much larger investment was needed in the factors of production, i.e., land, labor, and natural resources.

The dominant figure in this change was the industrialist whose purpose was the increased production of goods. The industrial revolution profoundly shaped the development of economics and from it emerged one of the most celebrated figures in the history of the subject. Adam Smith was the prophet of the industrial revolutions achievements and the original source of its explanation.

Adam Smith is considered to have been the founder of economics as a distinct field of study, although he wrote only one book on the subject "An Inquiry into the Nature and Causes of the Wealth of Nations," published in 1776. Smith was 53 years old at the time. His friend David Hume found the book such hard reading that he doubted that many people would read it. However, Hume's prophecy was wrong. People have been reading The Wealth of Nations, for more than 200 years.

Adam Smith wrote that the wealth of a nation was not a result of accumulating gold and silver, as the mercantilists believed. The wealth of a nation is measured by the outcome of the activities of ordinary people working and trading in free markets. To Smith, the remarkable thing about the wealth produced by a market economy, is that it is not a result of any organized plan but the unintended outcome of the actions of many people, each of whom is independently pursuing the incentives the market offers with his or her own interests in mind. Smith writes that: "It is not from the benevolence of the butcher, the brewer, or the baker that we expect our dinner, but from their regard to their own interest. Every individual is continually exerting himself to find out the most advantageous employment for whatever capital he can command. By directing that industry in such a manner as its produce may be of the greatest value, he intends only his own gain, and he is in this, as in many other cases, led by an invisible hand to promote an end which was no part of his intention."[1]

Much of the discipline of economics as it has developed over the past two centuries consists of elaborations on ideas found in Smith's work. The idea of the "invisible hand" of market incentives that channels people's efforts in directions that are beneficial to their neighbors remains the most durable of Smith's contributions to economics.

In his book, Smith describes the work of a pin factory, but one that was far from characteristic of the industrial plants of later decades. What captured Adam Smith's attention was not the machinery that characterized the industrial revolution but the way the job was divided so that each worker became an expert on his minuscule part of the task. The great efficiencies of contemporary enterprise, combined with man's natural propensity to truck, barter, and exchange one thing for another came from this specialization, this division of labor.

## Smith's Lasting Contributions to Economics

Adam Smith's contributions to economics were many. There are, however, four critical areas that provide a  starting point. These are his views on economic motivation, the distribution of revenue that was earned from the sale of goods, how prices are determined and the role of government in business and international trade. These issues still survive in today's college textbooks as the study of microeconomics.

**Economic Motivation:** This for Smith centers on the role of self-interest. The private and competitive pursuit of things that are in ones best interest is the source of the greatest benefit to the public. Smith adds, an invisible hand leads the individual to promote and end which was not part of his original intention. The person concerned with self-enrichment had previously been and object of doubt, suspicion and mistrust, feelings that went back through the middle ages to biblical times. Now, because of his self-interest, he had become the driving force behind the industrial revolution's propensity to produce a whole spectrum of new products.

**The Distribution of Revenue:** Prices and who gets the proceeds were the second of the basic issues of economics that Smith addressed. In this regard, Smith analyzed the reasons for the distribution of revenue among the workers, the landlords and the owners.  As workers were assembled in the factories, what determined their pay became highly relevant. As the capitalists assumed control of production, the question arose concerning a fair distribution of income to the workers and to the owner of the business.

The wage's that were paid to workers,  Smith regarded generally as the price of attracting labor and the cost of sustaining them on the job.  Profit, according to Smith is the appropriation of a surplus value that the worker creates over and above what the capitalist pays them. The capitalist, according to Smith, has a seemingly rightful claim. The question here was not if the capitalist deserved a return on the capital that they invested, but how much that return should be. In many circumstances, the amount of return that went to the capitalist was a result of the power that they held over the workers and not their contribution to the value of the goods sold.

The compensation paid to landlords as rent, entered into the composition of the price of commodities, in a different way from wages and profit. High or low wages and profit are the causes of high or low price; high or low rent is the effect of it. "The rent increases in proportion to the goodness of the pasture."[2]

**How Prices are Determined:** The interesting and disturbing circumstance that many of the best or most nearly essential things in life are virtually free, puzzled Smith. For example, water which was highly useful was very cheap while diamonds which were then, as now, expensive, were not really very useful. From this analysis came the troubling difference between value in use and value in exchange.

Smith resolved the problem in his time by simply setting value in use aside and asserting a value in exchange. This was a version of what came to be known as the "labor theory of value." According to Smith, the value of labor measures the worth of any possession and ultimately the amount for which it can be exchanged.[3]

**Government's Role in Business and International Trade:** Adam Smith's strongest recommendation as to public policy urges the freedom of internal and international trade. Many of Smith's recommendations come from his observation of the pin factory. According to Smith, only if there is freedom to barter and trade, can some workers specialize on pins. Also, others can devote their efforts to additional tasks, so that all of these efforts will come together for the exchange that satisfies several individual needs. If freedom of trade does not exist, each worker must concentrate incompetently on making his own pins; the economies from specialization are gone. From this analysis, Smith concludes that the wider the trading area, the greater the opportunity for specialization; for the division of labor, and the greater the productivity of labor.

Smith's case for free trade extends to a direct assault on the mercantilist view of gold and silver as the foundation of national wealth and to the belief that trade restrictions can enhance the stock of precious metals. In the opening words of The Wealth of Nations, Smith proclaims that it is not its silver or gold that measures a nation's wealth. It is "the annual labour of every nation that is the fund which originally supplies it with all the necessaries and conveniences of life." Wealth, Smith held, is enhanced by "the skill, dexterity, and judgment with which its labour is generally applied, and, secondly, by the proportion between the numbers of those who are employed in useful labour, and that of those who are not so employed."[4]

According to Smith the matters of labor and production are the most important ones to address. If they are managed successfully, prices will be low, and supplies of marketable products will be plentiful. Gold and silver will come in from abroad to purchase the products, and the supply of specie will take care of itself. Other countries cannot prevent their people from exchanging their gold and silver for useful products. Smith observes that, "All sanguinary laws of Spain and Portugal are not able to keep their gold and silver at home." Smith adds, "It is not by the importation of gold and silver, that the discovery of America has enriched Europe. By the abundance of the American mines, those metals have become cheaper."[5]

Smith was not totally rigid on the matter of free trade. He would allow tariffs for industries essential for defense and possibly in retaliation for tariff abuse abroad. Also he would be tolerant of protecting new enterprises from competition abroad and recommend a gradual withdrawal of tariffs as these enterprises became capable of competing on an international level. Alexander Hamilton who recommended tariff protection for new and developing enterprises in America after the revolution, took this argument up later.

## Smith's Laws of Accumulation and Population

Smith attempted to answer the question of what pushes a society toward the pursuit of wealth. Smith thought that part of the answer is the workings of the market system itself. The competitive force of the marketplace encourages businessmen to invent, innovate, to take risks, and to expand. Smith identified two basic laws of behavior that propel the market system toward increasing levels of productivity.

The first is the Law of Accumulation. The industrial revolution in its early stages provided many opportunities to obtain wealth for those who were industrious enough and smart enough to take advantage of the situation. The basic objective of most of the early industrialists was to accumulate their savings. Prior to the Civil War in America, bank loans were usually made for purchasing land and investment banking had not yet been developed in this country. Therefore, the money to build manufacturing facilities essentially came from the profit of the enterprise or the accumulated savings of the capitalist.

Smith believed that the accumulation of capital was a great benefit to society. For it was the capital that society invested in new facilities and machinery that provided the division of labor necessary to increase the workers' productivity. However, Smith identified a potential problem as he feared that accumulation could lead to market saturation. This was because accumulation would mean more machinery, and this would increase the demand for workers. The increased demand for workers would lead to higher and higher wages until profits would disappear.[6]

They would surmount this hurdle to economic growth, according to Smith, by the second great behavioral law, "The Law of Population." Smith believed that if wages were high, then the population would increase because families with higher incomes could afford more children and the infant mortality rate would decrease. Therefore, if the first effect of accumulation was to raise the wages of the working class, the second effect would be to encourage the increase in the number of workers. This meant that accumulation might continue for long periods. The increase in population controls the supply of workers and their ability to command higher wages. The growth in population limits the cost of labor which is the major obstacle to increased profits.

Through the laws of accumulation and population, Smith constructed for society an endless chain of increased productivity. The mechanism of the market and the price system first serves to equalize the distribution of income to labor and capital, sees to it that the products demanded are produced in the proper quantities, and further encourages competition that drives prices down to where they are equal to the cost of production. Smith believed that the new industrial society was dynamic, that accumulation of wealth would continue, and that accumulation would result in increased facilities for production and in a greater division of labor.[7]

Smith was the economist of preindustrial capitalism. He saw an evolution for society, but he did not see a revolution. His system presupposes that eighteenth-century England will remain unchanged forever. The system would grow only in quantity, more people, more products and more wealth, but its quality would stay the same. Smith's system is a static one that grows but one that never matures.

Adam Smith emphasized the commitment to competition as a prerequisite to all capitalists' societies. Smith assumed that competition in a capitalist system, would ensure optimal industrial performance. Adam Smith addressed an audience that was ready to receive his message and with his message the remnants of the out-of-date regime of merchant capitalism ended.

For one hundred years after Smith's death, economists would attempt to amend and sharpen his conclusions, and struggle to resolve his ambiguities. In the years following Adam Smith's death, three great figures one French and two British emerged. The main emphasis of their writing was to refine and extend Adam Smith's economic theories. All three witnessed the industrial revolution in full flower, and, improving on Smith, they sought to bring economics abreast of this enormous change. In addition, there was the beginning of economic commentary from America.

## JEAN BAPTISTE SAY (1767-1832)

Jean Baptiste Say's business background led him to observe the distinctive role of the entrepreneur; the man who conceives or takes charge of an enterprise; sees and exploits opportunity, and is the motivating force for economic change and improvement. Say later in life was a professor ending his career at the College de France.

However, Say's major, and for a full 130 years, his lasting and most influential contribution to economic theory was his Law of Markets. To this day, economic textbooks continue to refer to Say's

Jean Baptiste Say

law. Say's Law held that out of the production of goods came an effective aggregate of demand sufficient to purchase the total supply of goods.[8]

Put in more modern terms, from the price of every product sold comes a return in wages, interest, profit or rent, sufficient to purchase that product. There can never be a shortage of demand. It is, indeed, possible that some people will save from the proceeds of the sale. However, the amount saved by consumers will be invested by companies in new production facilities. In other words, businesses would spend the saved income of consumers. Even if they hoard the receipts, this does not change the situation; prices adjust themselves downward and adjust to the lesser flow of income. There can still be no general excess of goods, no general shortage of purchasing power.

## THOMAS ROBERT MALTHUS (1776-1834)

Thomas Malthus

Thomas Malthus was a British clergyman whom the British East Indian Company employed. Malthus wrote two books on classical economics and the industrial revolution, "An Essay on the Principle of Population" and "Principles of Political Economy." These works cover a wide range of subjects, but to the history of economics he contributed two theories.

Malthus' most noted contribution was the law he saw controlling the growth of population, and on how increased population affected the allocation of wages to the workers. From Thomas Malthus' observations came his basic conclusion:

- The mean of subsistence will limit population growth.

- Population increases when the mean of subsistence allows, and does so geometrically, while the best hope for increase in the food supply is arithmetic.

- This asymmetry will persist, so that the food supply will hold the population in check unless prior checks on its increase are operative. The possible prior checks are moral restraint, vice and misery.[9]

Using data from the United States, supplied by Benjamin Franklin, Malthus asserted that population tends to double every twenty-five years. Franklin also reported that some villages in the new country doubled in only fifteen years. Although Franklin did not provide any information on the food supply, Malthus concluded that output could never keep pace with population. Unchecked population grows at a geometric ratio, Malthus held, whereas food increases at merely an arithmetic ratio.

A geometric ratio means that a number continually multiplies itself by a constant, for example, a perpetual doubling. An arithmetic ratio simply adds a constant. Malthus provided a good example of his theory: where humans would increase by 1,2,4,8,16,32,64,128,256, while food would grow by 1,2,3,4,5,6,7,8,9. In this case if each person had one basket of food at the beginning of a period, two hundred years later, and 256 people would have to share just nine baskets of food.

Malthus did not present a pleasant prospect for humanity. He did provide a powerful case against public or private charity and a greatly serviceable support to those who found it convenient to forgo help to the unfortunate.

Malthus' other claim to fame was his doubt about Say's Law. Malthus held that supply would not create its own demand, given the poverty of the workers. The workers have reduced themselves to the lowest levels of sustainable wages by their propensity to reproduce. There would be a tendency for more goods to be produced than could be bought and consumed by these workers. Also, at this time, banks did not make loans to business firms. Therefore, the only way that business owners could obtain capital, was by deferring consumption. This would result in increased savings at the expense of current consumption demand.

## DAVID RICARDO (1772-1823)

David Ricardo

David Ricardo rescued Say's law from Malthus' attack. According to Ricardo, the flow of income from the production of goods did indeed create its own sufficient demand. Ricardo's writing was not similar to the method used by Adam Smith. Ricardo's work is grim and difficult. Ricardo offered an influential change of method. Ricardo was theoretical and inductive; proceeding from some empirical evidence, he continued by abstract reasoning to the plausible, or perhaps inevitable conclusion.

Ricardo's writing used a method that, in the future, would greatly appeal to economists. His method of writing reduced the research that is necessary to analyze a theory. It served Ricardo well. His method and his conclusions would lead the later defenders of capitalism, and its most passionate opponents, equally to firm conclusions.

One of Ricardo's most lasting contributions to economic theory was his Law of Comparative Advantage. During Ricardo's time wealthy English landowners attempted to persuade Parliament to impose tariffs on the import of grain. The price of grain had soared during the Napoleonic Wars, partly because of Napoleon's embargo, and the landowners feared that a drop of prices would take place. On the other side of the argument were the new businessmen of the Industrial Revolution who preferred to see lower prices for food. The reason that businessmen preferred low prices is that the price of food affects their major cost, the wages paid to the workers. The landowners won the battle of influence, and in 1815 Parliament passed an act that prohibited imports of grain below a certain price, virtually granting

English farmers a monopoly. British dictionaries define "corn" as grain such as oats, rye, wheat and barley. Thus they called the acts "Corn Laws."

Ricardo thought that Britain had two choices as to their position in international trade: as a projectionist island or as an extroverted trader. Ricardo recommended a free trade policy for Britain. Ricardo developed his theory to show that countries should specialize in whatever leads them to give up the least opportunity. This is their "comparative advantage." In addition, the sacrifice they make by not producing a product, is their "opportunity cost." Thus according to Ricardo, specialization is determined by whoever has the lower opportunity cost.

For Ricardo, free trade makes it possible for households to consume more goods regardless of whether trading partners are more or less economically advanced. Ricardo's position on the "Corn Laws" was that if the French farmers are willing to feed English consumers for less than it would cost to feed themselves, Englishmen would be better off by eating French food and spending their time doing something else. In spite of his constant argument on this topic, Ricardo could not persuade Parliament to repeal these laws and they remained in effect until 1846. Ricardo did, however, provide a powerful argument for subsequent generations of economists. Ricardo's argument is that protection is usually bad for an economy as a whole, though sometimes good for a particular group of people. This debate continues today though in another form, between those who support managed trade and those who still believe that totally free trade is possible.

Ricardo follows Smith in identifying the main concerns of economics. Of the factors determining the value of price (value in exchange) of a product, Ricardo believed that the first must be utility. "If a commodity were in no way useful, in other words, if it could in no way contribute to our gratification, it would be destitute of exchangeable value."[8] Here emerges, in early form, the other side of the modern view of price making, the interaction of supply and demand. After establishing the need for "exchangeable products," Ricardo then saw the value of exchangeable products resulting from scarcity or from the quantity of labor required to obtain them. It is

Ricardo's commitment to a firm labor theory of value in exchange that is central to the influence he exercised in the years to come.

Next Ricardo addressed the return to landlords of rent, which he defined as, "That portion of the produce of the earth, which is paid to the landlord for the use of the original and indestructible powers of the soil." From the possession of the better land the landlord would receive a surplus over the cost or rent. The owner of good land was thus the beneficiary not only of his own good fortune but also of the increasing misery or poor fortune of all others. Rent did not force up prices; it was a residual accruing passively from the increase in population and the general progress of the society. The rise of rent is always the effect of the increasing wealth of the country, and of the difficulty of providing for its augmented population.[10]

Returning to wages, Ricardo said, "That wages are the price that is necessary to enable the laborers to subsist and to perpetuate their race, without either increase or reduction." This theory, "The Iron Law of Wages," was to enter history extending far beyond formal economics. The law established that those who worked were meant to be poor and were not to be rescued from their poverty by a compassionate state or employer or through trade unions or by other actions of their own. This, as we shall see was a very fortunate conclusion for the capitalist who received a seemingly excess value for their investment.

The Iron Law was the natural or equilibrium price of labor, the level to which, all else equal, wages tend to settle. However, Ricardo concluded that not only workers' necessities but also conveniences that were essential to them based on previous habit, should be considered. Taken together, these are what economists would now call the workers' accustomed standard of living. Also, the market price of labor in an improving society could be above the market rate in the short run. This could result when the demand for labor was greater than the current supply of labor. However, since higher wages encourage increases in population and as the number of laborers is increased, wages again fall to their natural price and sometimes fall below it. In modern terms, if the demand for labor is greater than the supply of labor, wages will increase. However, when living standards increase, families tend to have more children. This increases the supply of labor and reduces wages to a natural or equilibrium level.

It was for his controlling law of wages that Ricardo was to be remembered. From this controlling law came his commitment to the inevitable misery of those who live under capitalism and to the uselessness of any corrective action by government or by the workers themselves. This action Ricardo specifically condemned as he wrote; "Like all other contracts, wages should be left to the fair and free competition of the marketplace, and should never be controlled by the interference of the legislature." [11]

In the years to come there would be an increasingly angry division between those who spoke for the system and those who spoke for the masses who were perceived as the victims of the industrial revolution. From Malthus and especially from Ricardo came ideas that would serve both sides of the debate.

## HENRY CHARLES CAREY (1793-1879)

Until the civil war and even after, what distinguished the American scene was a spacious abundance, a prospect of income and opportunity for farmer and worker, as well as businessman and capitalist, unimaginable in England. The leading American economic scholar of this time was Henry Charles Carey.

In his early work, Carey was a follower of the British classical theory. However, as he sought to apply classical theory to his American surroundings, he came to have his doubts. David Ricardo had seen increasing population and limited land resources pressing labor to an even lower marginal return. Carey saw the same processes leading labor to an ever higher return as it became more productive.

In the new world settlement had begun on the hilltops, where forests were less dense and resistant. Since property on a hilltop usually represented the most prestige to those of noble European heritage, settlers tended to assign the most value to these locations. In America, when the pioneers moved, it was often to more fertile, more productive valleys, thus achieving not a diminishing but an expanding return. The same was true when attention turned to the frontier and the great unexplored resources there.

This tendency rejected the views of Ricardo, and it destroyed those of Malthus. An increasing population was not dividing a stagnant or decreasing food supply, but one that was rapidly increasing. Henry Carey was not averse to the thought that on some distant day there might be too many people. However, he was content to believe that this evil was sufficient unto its own time. God had said "Be fruitful and multiply."[12]

**NOTES:**

**Chapter 5**
**The Foundations of Classical Economics**

1.    Smith, Adam, <u>An Inquiry into the Nature and Causes of  The Wealth of Nations</u>, R.H. Campbell, A.S. Skinner and       W. B. Todd, Editors., Oxford, En, Clarendon Press, 1977  [1776], Introduction.
2.    Smith, Book I, Chapter 2.
3.    Smith, Book I, Chapter 5.
4.    Smith, Introduction.
5.    Smith, Book 4, Chapter 1.
6.    Gailbraith, John Kenneth, <u>Economics in Perspective</u>, Boston, MA, Houghton Mifflin Company, 1987, p. 75.
7.    Heilbroner, Robert L., <u>The Worldly Philosophers</u>, New York, Simon & Schuster, Inc., 1986, p. 65.
8.    Heilbroner, p. 66.
9.    Malthus, Thomas A., <u>An Essay on the Principle of  Population, 6th Addition</u>, London, England, Ward  Lock, 1890, p. 15.
10.    Sraffa, Piero, <u>The Works and Correspondents of David Ricardo</u>, Cambridge, England, Cambridge  University Press, 1951, p. 11.
11.    Ricardo, p. 77.
12.    Gailbraith, pp. 100-101.

# CHAPTER 6

---

# THE RISE OF POLITICAL PARTIES

*"The true natural rights of men, then, are equal justice, security of labor and property, the amenities of civilized institutions and the benefits of orderly society." — Edmund Burke*

## THE EVOLUTION OF POLITICAL THEORY

All societies have conservative elements within them, acting to preserve the institutions that those societies developed. Concurrently, the same societies have liberal elements within them, working to change or even eliminate those institutions. The terms liberal and conservative has become central to political debate in the western world ever since the monarchies of Europe began to be overthrown in the late eighteenth century.

### The Age of The Enlightenment

Modern political liberalism began in the Age of Enlightenment, which provided the philosophical basis for both the French and American revolutions. Modern conservatism began as a response to liberal philosophy. For almost a thousand years, prior to the eighteenth century, Western Europe was divided into many kingdoms; each ruled by a monarch. The entire feudal system was hereditary; kings, nobles, and peasants were all born into a clearly defined class system.

This class system operated with the sanctions of the Church which was the glue that held the political structure of feudal Europe together. This alliance between the monarchs and the Church was the catalyst to a concept known as the "Divine Right of Kings." The European feudal system was essentially conservative with resistance to change built into it. The changes that did take place were the result of the gradual evolution of the institutions in the society. The most important of these changes was the rise of the new merchants who were positioned between the nobles and the peasants.

By the seventeenth century, the Age of Enlightenment had begun in Europe. The Enlightenment consisted of the individual efforts of many philosophers and scientists who changed the way people thought about reality and about mankind. The philosophers of the time effectively replaced the reliance on the faith in God and the Church as the ultimate authority on questions of reality with the reliance on human reason. This concentration on the study of finding ways to promote human well-being is the major link between the Enlightenment and modern liberal political thinking.

## THE SOCIAL CONTRACT

The Enlightenment's questioning of faith as the supreme authority on social order was a clear threat to the monarchs of Western Europe. Since, in theory they ruled by divine right established by faith. If faith was replaced by human reasoning, by what right could monarchs continue to rule? One answer to this question was provided by English philosopher Thomas Hobbes.

Thomas Hobbs

**Thomas Hobbes (1588-1679)**

According to Hobbes, a strong form of central government was necessary because human beings tended to be selfish and even predatory. Some sovereign power had to be given the authority to make decisions and to enforce social order. For Hobbes, the best form that a government could take was a monarchy. This was an implied contract between the people and the monarch.

Hobbes theory was essentially a conservative one because it was to justify the existing social order and to place security above human rights in preserving that order. These two elements, a preference for maintaining the existing institutions and the overriding concern for the security of the nation, are basic to conservative political theory.

## John Locke (1632-1704)

John Locke

Another form of the theory of a social contract was developed by English philosopher, John Locke. He believed that men were essentially good and meant to be happy. Locke argued that a social contract was needed only because individuals couldn't judge for themselves the boundaries between their legitimate rights and the rights of others. Locke believed that what people thought, and consequently how they behaved, was strongly influenced by their environment. If man was unhappy or immoral, the fault must be in their environment which was perverting their basic nature.

The theories of John Locke and to a lesser extent Thomas Hobbes contained the basic elements of modern democracy. If all people were essentially equal, if they all had the same natural rights as stated by Locke, to Life, Liberty, and the Right to Property, then shouldn't they all have an equal vote in how they are governed? The masses would have to surrender some of their rights by agreeing to a social contract, but if they became unhappy with that contract, did they have the right to break it? Hobbes would say "no." Locke would say "yes" to this question.

# SOCIAL-CONSERVATISM VERSUS TO SOCIAL- LIBERALISM

The nineteenth century developed many theories of social conservative and liberal philosophy. These two philosophies can be generalized into several categories.

## Social Conservatism

Russell Kirk in his "The Conservative Mind" developed six canons of social conservative thought:

(1) Belief in a transcendent order, or body of natural law, which rules society as well as conscience. True politics is the art of apprehending and applying the justice which ought to prevail in a community of souls.
(2) Affection for the proliferating variety and mystery of human existence, as opposed to the narrowing uniformity, egalitarianism, and utilitarian aims of some opposing liberal systems.
(3) Conviction that civilized society requires orders and classes. Ultimate equality in the judgment of god and equality before courts of law are recognized by conservatives.
(4) The persuasion that freedom and property are closely linked. Economic leveling, they maintain, is not economic progress.
(5) Faith in prescription and distrust of "Sophisters, calculators, and economists" who would reconstruct society upon abstract designs. Custom, convention, and old prescriptions are checks both upon man's anarchic impulse and upon the innovator's lust for power.
(6) Recognition that changes may not be salutary reform. Society must change, but a statesman must take providence into his calculations, and a statesman's chief virtue is prudence.[1]

## Social Liberalism

To catalogue the principles of social liberalism is equally difficult. At least five schools of liberal thought have competed for public attention during the nineteenth century: The Philosophes lead in France by Rousseau, Voltaire, Diderot and Montesquieu and in England by Hume and Smith, the Utilitarianism of the Benthamites, the Materialism of John Stuart Mill and Positivism of Comte's school, the Collectivism of the Socialist and Communists, and the theories of Social Darwinism. In general, nineteenth century social liberalism tended to attack the conservative arrangement of society on the following basis:

(1) The perfectibility of man: Education, positive legislation, and the alteration of the environment can produce godlike men; they deny that humanity has a natural tendency toward violence and sin.
(2) Contempt for tradition: Where reason, impulse, and materialistic determinism are preferred as guides to social welfare. Formal religion is questioned and various ideologies are presented as substitutes.
(3) Political leveling: Order and privilege are condemned; total democracy, as directed by practicable, is preferred. Allied with this spirit is a dislike of old parliamentary arrangements and a desire for centralization and consolidation.
(4) Economic leveling: The ancient rights of property, especially land, are usually suspect, and collectivist reformers attack the institution of private property.

In general social liberals were united in their dislike of Edmund Burke's description of the state as "ordained by god," and his concept of society as "joined in perpetuity by a moral bond among the dead, the living, and those yet to be born-the community of souls."

## EDMUND BURKE (1729-1797)

Edmund Burke was a British statesman and orator, who championed many human rights causes and brought attention to them through his eloquent speeches. Burke was born in Dublin and educated at Trinity College. He studied law briefly in London before embarking on a literary career.

Edmund Burke

His first important work was "Vindication of Natural Society" (1756), a satire ridiculing the reasoning of the British statesman Henry Bolingbroke. This work, published anonymously, attracted considerable attention. Soon afterward he published an essay, "The Philosophical Inquiry into the Origin of Our Ideas on the Sublime and Beautiful" (1756). The following year, he began a 30-year association with The Annual Register, a British yearbook.

After 1761, when he became private secretary to the British chief secretary for Ireland, William Hamilton, he demonstrated his aptitude for political service. Four years later he became private secretary to the new British prime minister Charles Watson-Wentworth, 2nd marquis of Rockingham, and in 1766, Burke was elected as a "Whig" to Parliament. The Whig political party originated in 1679 in England, and the name was applied to the English opponents of the secession of the Roman Catholic Duke of York (later James II). The Revolution of 1688 assured a Protestant succession and the constitution supremacy of Parliament over the king. Almost immediately, Burke sought repeal of the Stamp Act. In a pamphlet, "Thoughts on the Cause of the Present Discontents" (1770), and in two speeches, "On American Taxation" (1774) and "Conciliation with America" (1775), he urged for justice and conciliation toward the American colonies.

Burke later appeared as the champion of the feudal order in Europe with the publication of "Reflections on the Revolution in France" (1790). The text, which was read throughout Europe, encouraged European rulers in their hostility to the French Revolution.

Burke was a major contributor to Conservative Political thought in the nineteenth century. Burke developed the conception of the individual as himself the product of society, born to an inheritance of rights (which are all the advantage for which civil society is made) and the reciprocal duties, and in the last resort, owing these concrete rights to convention and prescription. Society originates not in a free contract but in necessity, and the shaping factor in its institutions has not been the consideration of any code of abstract (the inherent rights of the people such as the theories of the philosophies) but convenience. And, of these conveniences or rights, two are supreme: government and prescription, the existence of a power out of themselves by which the will of individuals may be controlled and the recognition of the sacred character of prescription. In whatever way a particular society may have originated in the process of time, its institutions and rights come to rest upon prescription. The privileges of every order, the rights of every individual, rest upon prescription embodied in law or established by precedent. This is, according to Burke, the compact or agreement which gives its corporate form and capacity to a state.

For Burke, the essential condition of every right is the state itself. There can be no right, which is incompatible with the very existence of the state. Justice is not to be sought in or by the destruction of that, which has given us the idea of justice, has made us the moral beings we are. The state is no mere prudential contract for material ends, security of property and life; it is according to Burke "The partnership between men from which has sprung science and art and virtue-all human perfection; a partnership which links one generation to another, the living to the dead and the unborn. It is more; each contract of each particular state is but a clause in the great primeval contract of eternal society, which is the law of God and holds all physical and all moral natures, each in their appointed place."[2]

According to Burke, The true natural rights of men, then, are equal justice, security of labor and property, the amenities of civilized institutions, and the benefits of orderly society. Social and political equality, he declared do not fall within the category of the real rights of man; on the contrary "Hierarchy and aristocracy are the natural, the original, framework of human life; if we modify their influence, it is from prudence and convention, not in obedience to natural right." Burkes reverence for the wisdom or our ancestors, through which works the design of Providence, is the first principle of all consistent conservative thought.[3]

As time went on, Burke became more and more vehement in his denunciation of the French Revolution. To Burke, countering the philosophy and fanaticism of the French Revolution with a deeper philosophy and an equal zeal, was a crusade; and he pressed for it passionately before Prime Minister Pitt until Pitt's hand was forced by France's invasion of Holland.

Burke retired from Parliament in 1794, after a career remarkable for its laborious, earnest, and brilliant discharge of duties.

## THE EMERGENCE OF POLITICAL PARTIES

The American Revolution was the logical culmination of much of the political and social theory of the Enlightenment. The revolution like the theory of a social contract was liberal in its ideals but essentially conservative in spirit. The new social contract drawn up after the American Revolution was the Constitution of the United States. The Constitution reflected two basic social concerns: the desire to assure that the new American government would never degenerate into tyranny, primarily a liberal concern, and the need to maintain order, which was essentially a conservative idea.

The issue of protecting the rights of individuals from the tyranny of the majority clearly defines the differences between the liberal and conservative beliefs of the framers of the Constitution. Those like Alexander Hamilton and John Adams distrusted the unguided desire of the majority. Those of a more liberal belief, such as Thomas Jefferson, felt that the people had the right to exercise power over their government.

The founders initially believed that each political conflict that comes up could be resolved on its own merits. Eventually, however, ideology and self-interest replaced good intentions and political parties developed. When political parties did evolve they developed along either conservative or liberal lines. The first to emerge in the United States was the Federalist Party, a conservative faction, led by Alexander Hamilton. The opponents of the Federalists called themselves simply the Anti-Federalist Party. The Federalist Party lost the election of 1804 to Thomas Jefferson and his renamed Democratic-Republican Party. The Democratic-Republican Party won the presidential elections of 1808, 1812, and 1818, and by 1820, the Federalists did not run a candidate for president. This, for the time being, ended the two-party system in the United States. In 1828, the two-party system was re-established with the emergence of the National-Republican party. This party, led by John Q. Adams, was created to face incumbent Andrew Jackson in the presidential election. The Jackson campaign catered to popular prejudices, portraying the contest between democracy (represented by his Democratic-Republican Party) and the more conservative aristocracy as represented by John Q. Adams. Jackson won the election and was re-elected in 1832. The Democratic-Republican Party, the party of both Jefferson and Jackson, is the forerunner of the modern Democratic Party in the United States.

In the election of 1836, a new party the Whigs evolved in response to Jackson's perceived heavy-handed tactics, especially his battle to defeat the Second U.S. Bank. The American Whig Party was named after the eighteenth century British party whose most distinguished member was Edmund Burke. The Whigs were successful in only two presidential campaigns. Whig senate leaders Henry Clay and Daniel Webster, however, fearing disunion over slavery, played key roles in securing the Compromise of 1850, which included a strong Fugitive Slave Law that offended many northern Whigs. In 1852, many southern Whigs defected in reaction to the party's nomination of General Winfield Scott for president. Furious sectional controversy over the Kansas-Nebraska Act dealt the final blow. The bulk of the party's remaining members dispersed in 1856. During the election of 1856, a new party of northern Whigs and Democrats combined to become the Republican Party. The Republicans were a pro-tariff, conservative, nationalistic party that was founded to oppose the spread of slavery into the United State's territories. The first Republican president was Abraham Lincoln who was elected in 1860.

## Politics, Government, and Business

In one major area, the question of government interference in the business economy, liberals and conservatives have, in effect, changed places. While Jefferson and the Democratic-Republicans favored a hands-off policy, Hamilton and the Federalists felt that government should be directly involved in the nation's economy. The Federalists originally favored a strong national bank, a strong national currency, and government policies that promoted trade and commerce.

However, after the Civil War, businesses got bigger and were better able to promote and protect their own interests. During the last two decades of the nineteenth century, the federal government became concerned with the tendency of large businesses to create monopolies and eliminate competition. During this time, the federal government under the leadership of Republican president Theodore Roosevelt began to exert more control over business by signing anti-trust legislation. However, the Democratic candidate for president in 1912, Woodrow Wilson, made the regulation of business an issue through an aggressive campaign calling for vigorous application of anti-trust laws against big business. This, conservatives felt, was hurting both business and the economy in general. Consequently, as the Democrats became more and more concerned with using government to control and regulate big business, Republicans became more and more concerned with keeping government out of business affairs. This perception, of the role of government in the affairs of business, continues to be a distinction between the modern day Democratic and Republican parties.

**NOTES:**

**Chapter 6**
**The Rise of Political Parties**

1.  Locke, John, <u>The Second Treatise of Government</u>, Edited by Peter Laslett, Cambridge, EN, Cambridge University Press, 1988, p. 268.
2.  Kirt, Russell. <u>The Conservative Mind,</u> Washington, DC, Regnery Publishing Company, 1995, p. 9.
3.  The Cambridge History of English and American Literature, <u>Volume XI. The Period of the French Revolution</u>, p. 36.
4.  Kirt, p. 65

# CHAPTER 7

---

# FINANCE AND BANKING
## (1800-1913)

*"The whole community derives benefit from a bank. It facilitates the commerce of the country. It quickens the means of purchasing and paying for country produce and hastens on the exportation of it." --*
*Thomas Paine*

## THE ROLE OF COMMERCIAL BANKS

Financial intermediaries play an important role in industrialized countries. The major function of a commercial bank is to gather the savings of many individuals and convert these funds into mortgage and business loans. Companies invest dollars in new plant and equipment and additions to inventory in order to increase the output of goods or services or to reduce the unit cost of producing these products. In modern times many of these investment dollars come from the savings of individuals. Banks collect these dollars in demand and time deposits and in turn make loans to corporations. In addition, individuals may choose to invest their dollars directly in corporations by buying their stocks and bonds through a stockbroker. The key to a bank's profitability is making loans to individuals and firms at a rate of interest that is higher than the interest that they give savers on their deposits. Also, the interest rate charged must be sufficient to cover Administrative costs and provide a margin of profit. This in banking is called the interest rate spread. Also, prudent banks try to match the maturities of their deposit liabilities with lending assets. For example, if the bulk of a bank's savings and demand deposits mature on an average of six months, the bank should limit the maturities of their lending portfolio to between six months and one year.

When a bank mismatches its maturities, that is has the bulk of its liabilities maturing in six months or less and the bulk of its assets maturing at one year or greater, it runs the risk of becoming illiquid. If depositors become worried that they may not be able to convert their deposits into currency, a run on the bank may occur. This would cause the bank to become insolvent and probably would force the bank to stop doing business. Therefore, a bank must practice prudent and sound lending practices if it wishes to increase the probability that it will stay in business in the long-run.

## BIMETALLIC MONEY

In 1792 Congress chose the dollar as the official United States currency. Congress defined the dollar as containing either 371.25 grains of silver or 24.75 grains of gold or a relationship between the two metals of fifteen silver to one gold. The government offered to buy and sell unlimited amounts of gold and silver at the fifteen to one ratio. These purchases could be in either coin of bullion. As long as this relationship held in the bullion markets, the system worked well. However, if the relative values of gold and silver as bullion differed from the fifteen to one ratio, people would exchange the overvalued metal for that which the U.S. mint undervalued.

Early in the nineteenth century, gold could be exchanged for sixteen times its weight in silver in the bullion markets. The result of this difference in the valuation of gold and silver as bullion versus the valuation of these metals as a medium of exchange was that U.S. gold coins disappeared from circulation. In 1834 Congress changed the mint relationship to sixteen silvers to one gold, but by this time the ratio overvalued gold. As a result of the changed relationship, silver coins became extremely scarce. The discovery of gold in California in 1848 only made the situation worse.[1]

When the United States defined the dollar as containing a specific amount of gold or silver, it determined the exchange rate between the dollar and foreign currencies, whose metallic content was also fixed. Dollars would exchange for British pound sterling in proportion to the rate that each currency could be exchanged for gold. Since gold could move freely between nations, there was only a limited extent to which the United States could both control its own monetary affairs and maintain fixed exchange rates.

## BANKING BEFORE THE CIVIL WAR

Gold and silver coins were only part of the United States money supply. Most of the money that circulated was created by commercial banks. Prior to the Civil War, the use of bank checking accounts had become widespread, particularly in the Northeast and Mid- Atlantic states. In addition to checking deposits, banks could print notes that they could lend to customers. Today, in comparison, only federal reserve notes can circulate as U.S. currency. During the fifty years after 1800, the number of banks grew much faster than the rate of population, and bank assets, notes in circulation, and deposits grew even faster.

Since money's value depends on its scarcity, there are limits to a bank's ability to increase the money supply. Bank money has limited value if it is not convertible into legal tender. In the nineteenth century, legal tender meant gold or silver. Banks had to be able to exchange their notes and checking deposits for legal tender on demand from their customers. Under normal circumstances, only a small fraction of an individual bank's outstanding liabilities, would be presented for conversion to specie, on any given day. Thus, banks only had to retain about 10 to 30 percent of their notes or deposits in the form of gold or silver. The remaining deposits could be used to fund loans or to purchase securities.

If a bank's ability to convert its own money into specie was in doubt their notes would be accepted in trade at less than face value or at a discount. The discount would vary with the degree of uncertainty about the issuing bank's ability to redeem its obligations in full on demand. Information about the stability of banks generally became more difficult to obtain, when the issuing bank was located a great distance from the bank receiving the note. Therefore, most banks' notes were discounted at rates increasing with the distance from their point of origin.

## ATTEMPTS TO REGULATE BANKS

Various attempts were made prior to the Civil War to regulate the state banking system. States often contributed to a bank's capital and did gain some control as stockholders. In general, banking laws specified the amount of capital that had to be subscribed by the bank's owners, limited the amount of notes that it could issue, and made some provision for inspections to insure compliance with these regulations. The extent of regulations and its enforcement was inconsistent, stricter where merchant communities were well established, and very lax in the rural areas. Often the regulation of banks was left up to the institutions themselves. Some self- regulation did occur in the eastern states but very little in the western states. An example of self-regulation was the Suffolk Banking system that attempted to regulate banks in the New England region of the country.

In 1820, the newly established Suffolk Bank in Boston offered to accept the notes of any rural bank in New England that would keep a permanent deposit of $5,000 over the funds required by the state clearinghouse. The Suffolk Bank also allowed rural banks to redeem their notes at the same rate of discount for which Suffolk had accepted them. Rural banks, that did not cooperate, found that the Suffolk bank would accumulate large quantities of their notes and present them, without notice, to the rural bank for redemption for specie. The Suffolk system caused the notes of all New England banks to circulate within the region at their face value, therefore eliminating the need to discount bank notes within the region. This made bank money a better medium of exchange and made trade run smoother within the system.[2]

New York State attempted to alleviate the propensity of small local banks to fail and therefore cause large losses to their depositors, through an institution similar to the modern Federal Deposit Insurance Corporation. In 1828, the state required that all banks in New York contribute 1.5 percent of their capital annually, up to a maximum of 3 percent, to a fund that would be able to make good the notes of failed banks whose assets were not sufficient to cover their outstanding notes. Banks were required to join the system as a condition for renewal of their corporate charters. Although the safety fund created by this legislature apparently was capable of protecting investors against the occasional failures of individual banks, it proved insufficient to deal with the bank collapses of the latter part of the 1830's.

Left to regulate themselves, most state banking systems had serious weaknesses. Regulation varied greatly between states. This resulted in the instability of the entire United States banking system because there was no source of additional reserves available for the entire system. If enough people began to fear that their bank notes or demand deposits could not be converted into gold or silver, a run on the bank took place.[3]

## ATTEMPTS TO ESTABLISH A CENTRAL BANK

The major function of a central bank in industrialized countries is to regulate the nation's money supply. Ideally, central banks attempt to prevent rapid changes in the money supply. Their major tool for this purpose is the control over private bank reserves. Also, central banks serve as government depositories and disbursing agencies performing clearinghouse functions for the settlement of inter-bank debts. In the first half of the nineteenth century, no country had fully developed the central bank, but the United States had two banks that exhibited some central bank characteristics.

### The First Bank of the United States

During the first half of the nineteenth century two United States banks were established by Congress. In 1791, Congress granted a federal charter to the First Bank of the United States. The Bank had branches and did business throughout the country and served as the government's depository. This structure enabled the Bank to return its deposits of the notes of other banks for prompt collection. This practice aggravated the smaller banks as it tended to restrict their lending or as we might say in modern times, it required the smaller banks to follow more prudent bank lending practices. The practice of restricting the lending of smaller banks was a continuous point of argument between Alexander Hamilton and Thomas Jefferson; Hamilton on the side of safe banking. The charter of the First Bank of the United States expired in 1811, and a bill to extend its charter for twenty more years was defeated in Congress by only one vote.[4]

## The Second Bank of the United States

In 1816, Congress granted a new charter, to the Second Bank of the United States. The Bank was headquartered in Philadelphia, then the country's financial center, and like the First Bank of the United States, had branches throughout the country. The Bank served as the federal government's depository, receiving all payments to the government. The Bank also accepted deposits and made loans in the same manner as the country's other commercial banks. The first two presidents of the Bank were not strong leaders and as a consequence the Bank was not very well run. In 1823, Nicholas Biddle became president of the Bank. Under Biddle's leadership, the Bank assumed some of the roles that are characteristic of a central bank. For example, the Bank began to use its position as a net creditor to the state banks to control the amount of their note issues. As a result of this policy, the state banks were forced to limit their note issues to the growth of their reserves. This practice while good for the safety of the banking system, served to reduce the potential profit available to the state banks.

In addition to its other operations, the Bank could function as a lender of last resort. On occasion, the Bank made some loans of specie to state banks that were experiencing short term financial difficulty. Still, the Bank was first and foremost a profit making institution. Because of its profit motive, the Bank made loans with the first priority given to its own reserve position and its own profit potential. In addition, it occasionally increased its own reserves to meet a crisis by selling bonds to the public. This action when implemented by a central bank serves to reduce the money supply and therefore reduces business expansion. However, neither the First nor Second Bank of the United States could expand the money supply since they could not control the amount of reserves held by state banks.[5]

In 1832, President Andrew Jackson vetoed a bill passed by Congress to extend the Bank's charter for twenty more years. The Bank did obtain a state charter from Pennsylvania, and continued in operation until 1841. However, after 1841, federal deposits were withdrawn from the Bank. These deposits were then placed in banks owned by Jackson's political allies. Finally, after the financial panic of 1837, in which the government lost large amounts of dollars that were deposited in these state banks, the government's deposits were kept in an independent treasury system. The era of a federal bank came to an end in 1832, and the country from then on, operated under a state chartered banking system until the Federal Reserve System was created in 1913.

## THE STATE BANKING SYSTEM

In 1838, Michigan and New York passed laws that greatly eased the previous banking restrictions. These banks were no longer required to obtain individual charters from the state legislature. Instead they could enter the banking business by depositing approved securities with the states' banking officials and by observing a few basic rules. Other states instituted their own rules, which became known as "Free Banking" laws. As a result of the reduction of bank regulations in many states, the number of state banks increased from 691 in 1843, to 1,520 in 1860.[6]

Although the history of banking is full of colorful tails about irresponsible practices, by 1860 it was commonly agreed between bankers and regulators that banks should keep reserves against all liabilities. The enforcement of state regulations began to improve, and some states even provided for periodic examinations. Therefore, it does not appear, based on modern studies, that free banking resulted in any serious damage and did not retard the economic growth in the new country from 1800 through 1860.[7]

## THE ERA OF DUAL BANKING

Prior to the Civil War, there were many controversies over money and banking. These controversies usually revolved around the quantity theory of money and the operation of the state banking system. Many people still held the conviction that capital could be created and prices could be increased by expanding the money supply. During the war, the union government could no longer make payments of money in the form of silver or gold. The Union government had to choose between increasing taxes to pay for the war or to begin printing money. Congress, unwilling to increase taxes to pay for the war, authorized the issue of $450 million in paper money. This authorization was in the form of United States Notes. These notes, commonly called "Greenbacks" were declared by Congress to be "Legal Tender" that could be used for payment of all debts.

In 1863, Congress passed the National Banking Act to provide a uniform currency to eliminate the oversupply of state bank notes, and to create a market for government bonds. One of the major provisions of the Act was to establish a bond-secured national currency. The Act created the national bank structure under the supervision of the Comptroller of the Currency. To obtain a national charter, groups of businessmen were required to deposit a specific amount of United States bonds with the Comptroller. These bonds could then be used as collateral that allowed the national chartered banks to issue national bank notes. National banks were also required to maintain reserves against their deposits, originally set at 25 percent for city banks and 15 percent for country banks.

After the Civil War, Congress amended the National Banking Act by imposing a 10 percent tax against state bank notes. The result of this tax was to drive state bank notes out of existence effectively creating a system of national currency. In addition, the National Banking System changed the philosophy of commercial banking by emphasizing the "Real Bills Doctrine." This doctrine confirmed that commercial banks should make only short term self-liquidating loans to businesses. Under the National Banking System, loans were made against commercial paper (short term unsecured liabilities of businesses) and were theoretically self-liquidating. This practice helped banks to better match the maturities of their assets and liabilities. This practice tends to increase the liquidity of the banking system by providing the ability to weather any crisis caused by a withdrawal of deposits. When the maturities of a bank's assets and liabilities are matched, it enables the institution to liquidate their loan and securities portfolios in order to accommodate any run on the bank's deposits.

While the National Banking System brought about many improvements in commercial banking, it also had some major weaknesses. The banking system allowed the practice of pyramiding bank reserves in New York City. Pyramiding of reserves occurred as out-of-town banks piled up deposits in New York. When additional funds were needed in rural areas, these country banks rapidly drew down their deposits forcing the New York banks to call in their short term loans to brokers. This practice set in motion a chain reaction as brokers called in their margin loans to customers. The result was the reduction of the money supply during business contractions and the aggravation of financial panics.

Another weakness of the National Banking System was that it relied heavily on the real-bills doctrine, with its emphasis on commercial loans. This reliance on the real-bills doctrine, intensified tendencies toward boom and bust economic conditions. To add to this weakness, there was no central bank that could assist individual banks when they got into financial difficulty. In addition, there was no institution that could step in to stabilize the economy by discouraging speculative expansion during prosperity and softening the impact of deflation during panic and depression. Also, there was no national clearinghouse which continued the inefficient way in which check payments were made between different regions of the country.

In summary, the National Banking System made banking safer for national bank note holders and depositors; however, it made the currency less elastic (the supply of money does not expand or contract with the rise and fall of business activity) and capital funds less mobile. These weaknesses continued until the establishment of the Federal Reserve System in 1913.

## JOHN PIERPONT MORGAN (1873-1913)

John Pierpont Morgan was born on April 17th 1837 in Hartford Connecticut. His grandfather Joseph was an extremely successful businessman who left his son Julius    (J.P. Morgan's father) more than $1 million when he died.

John Pierpont Morgan

In 1854 Julius Morgan formed a partnership with prominent American banker George Peabody and moved to London. At the time London was the center of the financial world. The partnership would eventually establish Julius as one of Europe's most prominent investment bankers. Pierpont, as he was often called, attended the University at Grottingen Germany, however; he spent much of his time in the German beer halls consuming large quantities of brew.

Alarmed by his son's behavior, Julius sent young Pierpont to work at Duncan, Sherman a merchant-banking firm in New York City. Morgan's apprenticeship at Duncan, Sherman lasted four years. He then persuaded his father for support in opening his own firm J.P. Morgan and Co. Julius supported Pierpont's request with the intention that the firm was to execute trades and represent Peabody and Co., at his father's direction. Pierpont had other ideas such as  expanding the scope of the company into an investment-banking firm.

Banking in the latter half of the nineteenth century had a different set of rules than today. Lending money to a company usually meant also taking a board seat so that the investor could protect their interests. This was necessary then, for Wall Street was full of unscrupulous manipulators who regularly fleeced investors. By 1870 Dabney, Morgan & Co. was thriving. In 1871, when Dabney retired, Julius arranged for Morgan to form a new partnership with a prestigious banking firm in Philadelphia called Drexel and Co. The new firm was named Drexel, Morgan and Co.

Morgan was optimistic about America in the 1870's and always alert for promising new industries. In a bold move, he agreed to finance a young inventor named Thomas Edison and his experiments with an electric light bulb. The success of this and other ventures eventually lead to the formation of the General Electric Company which remains today as one of America's largest and most respected companies.

America slipped into a steep industrial decline in 1893. More than 15,000 businesses and 600 banks failed and clashes were commonplace between owners and workers. Railroads were particularly hard hit, since they were burdened with heavy debt. English investors who owned a large portion of the railroad debt urged Morgan to help them. His solution was the voting trust. Morgan developed a reorganization plan, often referred to as "Morganization," that offered relief to shareholders of a bankrupt company if they would transfer their shares to the voting trust in exchange for non-voting trust certificates. Morgan then engineered a restructuring of the company's finances, becoming not only the trustee for the voting trust but also the banker for the entire company. By the end of his career, Morgan had reorganized approximately 33,000 miles of railroad track, about one-sixth of all the nation's tracks.

By 1895, Morgan was in total control of his firm. The Drexel's retired from the company and Morgan reorganized the bank renaming it J.P. Morgan and Co., the firm that survives today. Recognizing the benefits from increasing market share through mergers, other corporations followed Morganization techniques with business-friendly states such as New Jersey offering liberal rules for forming trusts. Such changes enabled Morgan to even further consolidate his control over America's finances.

However, with all his other ventures, J.P. Morgan is probably most famous for rescuing the stock market during the financial panic of 1907. On October 24, 1907, Ransom Thomas, president of the New York Stock Exchange, rushed from his office to 23 Wall Street across the street where J.P. Morgan, the most powerful banker in America was located. The United States was in the grip of a financial panic and numerous banks had failed. As a result, Thomas faced the probable failure of 50 brokerage firms and even the New York Stock Exchange itself.

At two that afternoon, Morgan held a meeting in his office with several of the city's most important bank presidents. He persuaded them to pledge $24 million at 10 percent interest. At 2:16 p.m., an announcement of the $24 million in available broker call money was made on the floor of the stock exchange. A cheer immediately erupted as the relieved traders were giving the mighty financier an ovation for rescuing them from near financial disaster. In 1987 a similar situation emerged which was referred to as a liquidity crisis, and the Federal Reserve provided the necessary funds for the market to recover. However; in 1907 the Federal Reserve System was still six years away.

Morgan's accomplishments were many, not only did he save the New York Stock Exchange in 1907, he also rescued the U.S. government from bankruptcy 12 years earlier. He created the General Electric Company and U.S. Steel, at that time the world's largest company. At one point he controlled more railroads than anyone in the United States did. His investment banking firm, J.P. Morgan & Co. remains today as one of the most influential firms of its kind in the world and with its recent merger with Chase Bank is now the second largest banking firm in America.[8]

**NOTES:**

**Chapter 7**
**Finance and Banking (1800-1913)**

1.  Puth, Robert, C. American Economic History, Orlando,   FL, The Dryden Press, 1993.
2.  Esterlin, L. Davis, American Economic Growth: An Economists History of the United States, New York, N.Y., Harper and Row, 1971.
3.  Calomiris, C., Is Deposit Insurance Necessary? A   Historical Perspective, Journal of Economic History,   June 1990.
4.  Lee, S. and Passell, P., A New Economic View of   American History, New York, N.Y., Norton, 1979, pp.   112 - 113.
5.  Puth, p. 240.
6.  Bureau of the Census, Historical Statistics, 1:1020.
7.  Fogel and Engerman, The Reinterpretation of American Economic History, New York, N.Y. Harper and Row, 1971.
8.  Gillen, Thomas F., Cigar Aficionado, New York, N.Y., p. 82-102 Note: The primary source of information for this article was taken from Ron Chernow's book, The House of Morgan.

# CHAPTER 8

---

# THE EVOLUTION OF CLASSICAL ECONOMICS

*"Those organizations which are best fitted to their environment, or which change to fit themselves to their environment, will survive. The least fit will die out, leaving the strongest and best." --Herbert Spencer*

## THE THEORY OF MARGINAL UTILTIY

The primary concern of economics, throughout the nineteenth century, was with how prices, wages, rent, interest and profits, are determined. Ricardo had anchored the value of price of any manufactured product firmly on cost; the cost, in turn, was that of the labor going into the output under the least satisfactory circumstances of production. The price of the labor was only the cost of sustaining the laborer. The wages paid to labor were in equilibrium at the level sufficient to maintain their life. The difference, between the price of labor and the cost of labor, then accrued as rent to the landlord or as profit to the owners of the business.

This analysis was proper when the distribution was viewed from the point of positive economics. However, far too often, it was observed that profit was handsomely in excess of the outlays for wages. The distribution of profit to the owner was approved of if it was a result of their entrepreneurial ability. However, it was argued, that the unequal distribution of profit was due to the monopoly power that was held by the capitalist, not the ability to manage the factors of production.

Another earlier flaw in the classical system was corrected as the century passed. During the second half of the nineteenth century economic analysis shifted from cost to supply as a determinant of price, and to demand as a determinant not only of price but also, of the factors of production. For example, there were attempts by economists to explain why some workers could command greater wages than others. The demand for workers was based on the supply of workers that had the particular skills that were necessary to operate the factories and machine tools available at the time. This development grew out of the efforts to solve the old and seemingly stubborn problem of why the most useful things like water, has a small price and why things with little practical use like diamonds commanded a far greater price.

During the last part of the nineteenth century, economists became preoccupied with solving the problem of value in use and value in exchange. In 1871 there was a breakthrough in explaining the question of value. In that year, William Stanley Jevons (1835-1882) in England and Karl Menger (1840-1921) in Austria, followed a few years later by John Bates Clark (1847-1938) in the United States (professors respectively at London, Vienna and Columbia Universities), recognized the role of marginal utility in determining price. Marginal utility was first explained as the proposition that the utility of any good or service diminishes, all else equal, with increasing availability. These economists held that it is the utility of the last and least wanted; the utility of the marginal unit, that sets the value of all goods and services.[1]

In fact, the marginal utility of a good was merely the first step to a further and final formulation of theory. The concept of marginality could be applied not only to demand but also for supply. Goods are produced at different levels of costs. Accordingly in industry as in agriculture, there is an omnipotent law of diminishing returns, or increasing cost at greater levels of production.

Because of the diminishing marginal utility to buyers, there is a collective reduction, on their part, to pay the listed price. In order for the producer to sell the remaining inventory of a product that had reached the level of diminishing marginal utility, the price of the product would have to be reduced. The result of this analysis was the downward sloping demand curve that stated that as marginal utility decreased, lowering prices in order to clear ever larger supplies from the market, would be necessary. Also, the cost of producing a product would increase as the productivity of the factors of production decreased. From the rising marginal costs of less efficient uses of the factors of production came the rising costs of additional supplies. The more of a good or service that is demanded, relative to the supply, the more that must be paid to producers to encourage them to produce that product. The determination that ever higher prices are needed to cover marginal costs and attract increased supplies to the market led to the discovery of the upward ascending supply curve. Thus the law of supply and demand was proposed with its supreme achievement at the intersection of the two curves; the price.

Also, there now appeared and was recognized as a major exception in the system, the monopoly. The monopolist extended production to where his more rapidly falling marginal return just covered the added costs. That was where profits were maximized. Production was at a theoretically smaller output than the competitive equilibrium. The monopolist could increase his profit by controlling supply and therefore keep prices artificially high. Accordingly, it was agreed that although the classical system generally was benign, monopoly was not. Monopoly established itself as the single great flaw in an otherwise thought to be perfect system.

## UTILITARIANISM AND JEREMY BENTHAM (1784-1832)

Jeremy Bentham

One of the early defenses of the classical system came from outside the central current of economics. This was the Utilitarianism defense, which identified happiness or utility with that characteristic in any object that tends to produce benefit, advantage, pleasure, good, happiness or similarly prevents mischief, pain, evil or unhappiness. In early nineteenth century England, nearly every intellectual wanted to follow the direction of the great physicist, Sir Isaac Newton, and attempt to discover precise answers to the basic economic, political and moral questions of the time. Smith, Ricardo, and Malthus wanted to be the Isaac Newton of economics, by discovering the laws of nature. Jeremy Bentham, the acknowledged leader of the Utilitarianism movement, sought to be the Isaac Newton of the moral universe.

According to Bentham's gospel, nature has two masters, pain and pleasure.[2] Since all human beings like pleasure and hate pain, they choose to do that which gives them pleasure. Bentham continues by stating that when choices affect others, people should choose the alternative that maximizes the total pleasure of all. "The greatest happiness for the greatest number," was the leading emphasis of the Utilitarian movement. Bentham even devised a method of quantifying the amount of pleasure and pain in a situation, called the "Felicific Calculus." In his system, any single experience could be measured by four basic factors: (1) intensity, (2) duration, (3) certainty, and (4) proximity.

Utilitarian theory as it applies to economics held that the maximization of pleasure or happiness could and indeed did come from the maximization of the production of goods, which was the unchallenged achievement of the industrial revolution. What encouraged production was useful or beneficial whether it resulted in incidental suffering for the lesser number or not; the basic rule was the provision of, "The greatest happiness for the greatest number." The unhappiness, even if acute, of the lesser number must be accepted as a matter of practical policy.

Bentham was also involved in politics. He and his followers carried on the battle for free speech and democracy. They fought the Stamp Act, which taxed periodicals, and opposed various restrictions on the right of assembly, and the Corn Laws. Bentham also denounced the barbaric English prison system, arguing that punishment should be used to deter crime, not to wreak vengeance on those convicted of a crime and sent to prison.

## JOHN STUART MILL (1806-1873)

Among the visible problems of the classical system there was first, the appalling difference between the wages and resulting living

John Stuart Mill

standard of the workers and those of the employers or capitalist. Next there was the unequal distribution of power inherent in the system. The worker, adult or child, was subject to the discipline that came from dependence on the job, and many times for the next meal. These necessities the employer could give or withhold at will, and he often did. The unequal distribution of power was an obvious flaw in the classical system, a flaw that required a defense.

John Stuart Mill's writing and political career reflect an enlightened and expanded version of Utilitarianism. Mill held that the greatest happiness depends upon more than just pleasure. His publications enhanced Utilitarianism by invoking Platonic virtues of honor, dignity and self-development. This is the reason that Mill became an ardent advocate of public education.

In one of his earliest books, "On Logic," Mill developed a distinction between positive and normative economics. Positive economics, according to Mill, describes and predicts what actually takes place in the world. Normative economics advocates what should take place based on one's moral philosophy. This distinction was carried onto many other of Mill's later works.

In 1848, John Stuart Mill published his most famous work in economics that was entitled "Principles of Political Economy." For decades this work dominated the economics textbook market and was the principle textbook used in the major universities in England until 1919. In "Principles of Political Economy," Mill developed a comprehensive review of accepted economic doctrine and he added numerous improvements to existing theory. He wrote about the management of a firm; supply and demand as an equation rather than a ratio, and demand as a major factor in Ricardo's law of comparative advantage.[3] Mill firmly attributed the poverty of the working man to the immutable physical law of diminishing returns to labor and the relentless desire of the masses to reproduce themselves. The law of diminishing returns to labor states that as more and more workers are added to a fixed amount of capital there will come a point where the productivity of labor declines. Mill continues by writing that, "Little improvement can be expected in morality until the producing families are regarded with the same feelings as drunkenness or any other physical excess."

Mill also examined the value of providing relief to the poor. Mill wondered how society could give relief to the poor without dissuading them from obtaining work. Mill distinguished the able-bodied from the disabled, elderly, and the very young. Mill did not believe that society should cut its relief efforts for the disabled. However, he was not as lenient with those who were physically fit. He proposed that recipients of aid from the state, exchange their labor for welfare payments. Mill feared that if welfare was too easily doled out, generations of poor people would be born into families weaned of the work ethnic. In addition, Mill thought that higher welfare payments would only promote higher birth rates. Thus, Mill rejected socialist proposals for increasing relief benefits or wages for the masses.[4]

Ricardo, Malthus, and John Stuart Mill, still have a large amount of influence in the attitudes towards the problems of our large inner cities. Also, the critics of the welfare state can find a lot of ammunition in their theories. Requiring physically fit persons to perform work in return for welfare payments is in 1994, still a critical topic of concern for the American Congress.

Thus, in summary, John Stuart Mill both advertised dramatically the hardship that the Utilitarian's accepted as necessary to progress and, as would many who followed him, appealed for patience and hope to withstand it. This remedy, like the knowledge that one was being sacrificed to the larger good, was never wholly satisfactory to those afflicted.

## KARL MARX (1818-1883) AND THE GRAND ASSAULT

It is widely believed that Communism was born in the mind of Karl Marx in the middle of the nineteenth century. Also it is believed that Communism received its first definitive expression in 1848, when Marx and Frederick Engles published, "The Communist Manifesto."

In 1848 there were no communist states in the world and no

Karl Marx

revolutionary governments of any sort. A few countries of Northeast Europe and the United States were industrializing rapidly, but there was no city in the world with a population greater than two million people, and no state; even Great Britain, in which a majority of the people did not live in the country and farmed for a living. While the skilled workers in the industrialized countries were beginning to form a middle class, over 90 percent of the World's population lived in poverty.

Into this world Karl Marx was born in 1818, in the Western German city of Treves. Treves was then a part of Prussia, the second most powerful of the independent German States. The Marx family was originally Jewish as both parents were descendants of rabbis. However, when Marx was six, his family was baptized as Lutherans, in order to save his father's career, in what was officially Lutheran Prussia.[5]

Marx's father wanted his son to become a lawyer like himself, and sent him through the best schools in Treves. In 1835, Marx was sent to the University of Bonn, and then in 1841 to the University of Berlin to study law.

In his years at the University of Berlin, some of Karl Marx's philosophy began to evolve. He came to believe that all of the various sciences and philosophies were part of one over-arching system, which when completed would give a true and total picture of the universe and man. The romantic philosophers of the time had transformed this faith, which they had inherited from their scientific predecessors. Marx believed that the core of such a science and philosophy was the growth, development, progress, and evolution of the world, human society, and the individual. He believed that nature and men evolve according to certain inexorable scientific laws, whose working can be embodied but not opposed by even the greatest of leaders.

Marx found the most thorough statement of these views in the works of the recently deceased philosopher, George Frederick Hegel.

However, unlike Hegel, Marx came to believe that there was no God.[6] Marx became convinced that Europe was on the edge of reaction and revolution and that most of mankind was unhappy, held down by society, and cut off from its own true nature. Such convictions were a variety of radical Romanticism that the Germans called "Left Hegelianism."[7]

Having become a radical, Marx decided to give up his pursuit of the law and became a journalist in 1842, when he joined the staff of the "Rheinische Zeitung," a liberal newspaper in Cologne. However, the paper was closed down in 1843 by the Prussian police due to its radical editorials, mostly written by Marx.

During 1843 and 1844, Marx was acquiring yet another set of convictions. He read the works of Malthus, Ricardo and other British economists of the time. Marx accepted much of the classical economic analysis, but disagreed with their pessimism and their political judgments of the workingmen. Instead, Marx picked the industrial workingmen (for whom he adopted a term out of ancient Roman history, the Proletarian) as the key to the future development of society.

By the end of 1844, Marx had established his lifelong friendship with Frederick Engels. Engels was born of a Calvinist father in 1820 in Barmen, Prussia, which was south of the Ruhr. Young Engels had become converted to radicalism, in 1841, at the University of Berlin. During the middle of the 1840's, Marx and Engels produced a number of works where they depicted the ghastly condition of the growing working class. Also, they began to set forth their own version of a new social theory that they called "Communism," in the 1840's. Thus, since 1850, Communism has been considered to be a revolutionary form of Socialism.

Marx and Engels were atheist Socialists, who being far different from those who wanted to reform society by peaceful means, urged violent revolution to be followed by a brief dictatorship of the proletariat. In 1847, Marx and Engels were commissioned by the Communist League in London. The commission was to develop a theoretical and practical platform for the new Communist party. The result of this commission was the writing of the Communist Manifesto, which was published in February of 1848 in London. To this day the

Communist Manifesto has survived as the first definitive statement of the Communist variety of Socialism and has become one of the most widely read and influential pamphlets in the history of the world.

The first chapter of the Communist Manifesto, pictured Europe as being in the middle of a tremendous struggle for control between the rising bourgeoisie and the developing proletariat. Marx defined the bourgeoisie as the people in the class of modern capitalists, owners of the means of social production and employers of wage labor.[8]

Chapter one begins by stating that "The history of all hither to existing society is the history of class struggles." Marx continues by stating that, "Society as a whole is more and more splitting up into two hostile camps; into two great classes directly facing each other, the bourgeoisie and proletariat. We see, therefore, how the modern bourgeoisie is itself the product of a long course of development, a series of revolutions in the modes of production and of exchange." According to Marx, "The bourgeoisie has at last, since the establishment of modern industry and of the world market, conquered for itself, in the modern representative state, exclusive political sway." Marx continues by saying, "The executive of the modern state is but a committee for managing the common affairs of the whole bourgeoisie."[9]

Marx did not question the productive achievements of the industrial system. What Marx did question was the vulnerable points in the capitalist system which he interpreted as the distribution of power, the highly unequal distribution of income, susceptibility to depression, and monopoly.

## The Distribution of Power

The power in capitalism, according to Marx, resides with the capitalist; it is the natural attribute of the productive property he owns. The payments proceeding there from command the obedience and submission of people, who have no property and thus no alternative income. Nor is the power of the capitalist confined to the enterprise. He extends this power to the society and the State.

## The Highly Unequal Distribution of Income.

The worker at the margin receives payment in wages reflecting his added contribution to the total revenue of the enterprise. That contribution diminishes as workers are added and the marginal wage sets the wage for all. However, those back from the margin, though paid the marginal wage, contribute more to earnings than their wage. They are in the infra-marginal, more fruitful stages of diminishing return. This is surplus value they create, and this surplus value accrues not to those who earn it but to the capitalist. It rightly belongs to the worker, but the Capitalist intervenes to appropriate it, i.e., steals the surplus value.

## The Susceptibility of an Economy to Depression

The productive power of capitalism would press its goods relentlessly on markets, and as the labor supply became fully employed, wages would inevitably rise. The result would be a falling rate of profits, a loss and retrenching by the producing firms, and imbalance in the productive process. Balance would be restored only as diminished production, unemployment and falling wages allowed production to be profitable again. It was an important point for Marx that the system is stable only when wages are held down by a reserve of unemployed workers.

## Monopoly

A flaw conceded by the Classical tradition. To the Classicists, monopoly was the exception to the competitive rule, and it presented no threat to the system as a whole. For Marx, monopoly was much more than a flaw; the increasing concentration of economic activity in the hands of ever fewer capitalists was an organic tendency of capitalism, one that proceeded with irresistible force.[10]

Thus, according to Marx, the economic system celebrated by the classical tradition would come to an end brought about by characteristics, some of the most important of which had already been identified by the Classical Economists themselves. However, capitalism is not dead yet for it has produced a middle class that indirectly owns some of the means of production through the stock markets. Some of Marx's defenders point to the growth of government in capitalist nations as the surprising savior of capitalism. Social welfare spending protects the capitalists from deeper depressions and revolution. Marx's defenders are probably right. However, we must remember, that Marx predicted that the political system would stay static, resistant to change and that inflexibility would destroy the entire system. In this respect as well as others, Marx will go down in history as a false prophet.

## HERBERT SPENCER AND INDIVIDUALISM (1820-1903)

Herbert Spencer

The rise of socialism and its cry for social justice required still another defense from the supporters of classical economics. Because Karl Marx's criticism of capitalism was based on Ricardo's labor theory of value, a theoretical defense of the system was needed.

One answer to Marx and capitalism was the nineteenth century philosophy of individualism, which developed as the ideology of the capitalist enterprise in the years after the Civil War, and endured until 1914. The basis for this new theory was a reinforced version of laissez faire, which defended the interest of the successful capitalist.

An English philosopher and economist Herbert Spencer, and an American sociologist, William Graham Sumner (1840-1910), were the leaders in the development of the philosophy of individualism. Spencer was an evolutionist even before Charles Darwin. In 1850, Spencer published "Social Statistics," where he argued that all social systems develop and change by a natural process those results in a maximization of individual welfare. This process of natural development stems from competition among individuals. Spencer held that any interference on the part of the government prevents full achievement of society's ideal goal.[11]

Spencer's early writings were followed by a ten-volume work entitled "Synthetic Philosophy," that sought to show that evolutionary progress occurred in all phenomena, in the biological world, in the human mind, in society, and in ethics. Where Darwin explained evolution in the terms of "Natural Selection," it was Herbert Spencer who coined the deathless phrase "Survival of the Fittest," as the source of economic and social progress. Spencer held that institutions conducted their business in such a way as to benefit the organization involved. "Those organizations which are best fitted to their environment, or which change to fit themselves to their environment, will survive. The least fit will die out, leaving the strongest and best."[12] According to Spencer the weakest individuals and the least useful social institutions gradually are eliminated. Since the individual member of society is the decision maker, the social organization that emerges from the process of change is more closely adapted to meeting the needs of the individual.

The ideas of Spencer led to a description of the ideal society, conceived as a static equilibrium between people and their surroundings, brought about by the full exercise of individual rights. The role of government was therefore limited to the protection of people and property and the enforcement of private contracts, nothing else.

One cannot avoid admiration for the comprehensive way in which Spencer and Social Darwinism served the defense of the system. Inequality and hardship were made socially benign and the mitigation of hardship was made socially acceptable. The fortunate and the affluent could have no sense of guilt, for they were the natural beneficiaries of their excellence, and nature had selected them as part of a relentless progress to an improved world.[13] Spencer's books sold hundreds of thousands of copies; his visit to New York in 1882 had some of the aspects of the coming of Saint Paul. A generation of American scholars echoed his thoughts.

## William Graham Sumner (1840-1910)

Spencer's greatest follower in America was William Graham Sumner, an Episcopalian minister and economist at Yale University. Sumner's major work in the field of sociology was "Folk Ways," published in 1907. In this book Sumner examined social mores, which

William G. Sumner

he defined as institutions and conventions that developed and continually change by process of adaptation to individual needs. If such institutions, according to Sumner, do not contribute to welfare and survival, they are gradually replaced by more effective methods, and the social system evolves into a higher and better form.

Sumner goes on to say that within the social system, individuals are also rising and falling. The person with ability, intelligence, and drive will rise to prominence by competing with all others. The lazy, ignorant, and weak will fall out of sight. The emergence of leading individuals brings progress, because these are the ones who innovate, who think, and who develop new ideas.

In a series of essays, most notably "The Concentration of Wealth: Its Economic Justification," Sumner applied his theory of society to questions of contemporary political and economic policy. Concentrated wealth, Sumner held, was justified because it was used to produce for others. The economic elite rose to the top only because they expanded activity and provided the goods and services that society demanded. In fact, Sumner proclaimed that "The millionaires are a product of natural selection. They get high wages and live in luxury, but the bargain is a good one for society."

Individualism was the evolutionary philosophy applied to the social system. It justified the wealth of the owners of production, on the ground that only social good could come from competition. It justified the unequal distribution of income on the ground that wealth existed only because it served others. It justified lack of social responsibility on the ground that anyone destroyed by competition could be considered "unfit," not capable of making a large enough contribution to the social order to survive.[12]

Rugged Individualism was a rigorous philosophy that associated success with right and failure with wrong, wealth with public service and poverty with uselessness. Thus the stage is now set for our understanding of the mind set of the industrial capitalist of the period and also, of the response of the workers and the less fortunate, who needless to say, never completely bought into this philosophy.

**NOTES:**

**Chapter 8**
**The Evolution of Classical Economics**

1.  Galbraith, John Kenneth, Economics in Perspective, Boston, MA, Houghton Mifflin Co.,     1987, p. 108.
2.  Bentham, Jeremy, Introduction to the Principles of Morals   and Legislation, New York, NY, Haffner,    1948, p. 1.
3.  Buchholz, Todd G., New Ideas From Dead Economists,     New York, NY, Penguin Books, 1989, p. 99.
4.  Buchholz, p. 102.
5.  Marx, Karl and Engels, Friedrich, The Communist Manifesto, Edited by Francis B. Randall, New York, N.Y., Simon & Schuster, 1964. p 11.
6.  Marx, p. 16.
7.  Marx, p. 16.
8.  Marx, p. 57.
9.  Marx, p. 61.
10. Galbraith, p. 133
11. Fusfeld, Daniel R., The Age of the Economists, Fifth Edition, Glenview, IL, Scott Foresman and Co., 1986, p. 72
12. Fusfeld, p. 72.

# CHAPTER 9

---

# THE INDUSTRIAL REVOLUTION
## (1800-1900)

*"Not only is labor not dishonorable among such a people, but it is held in honor. In the United States, a wealthy man would think himself in bad repute if he employed his life solely in living." —Alexis de Tocqueville*

## THE EVOLUTION OF AMERICAN CITIES

Between 1790 and 1860, the land area of the United States tripled. However, during the same period the size of the population on the land increased at an even swifter pace. Urbanization increased in a sustained fashion from 1820 and continued until the 1870's. Urbanization resulted in the creation of a form of economic organization that was conducive to innovation. This was due to the increased opportunities for the exchange of information among persons living close to each other and living close to their place of work. In the new cities that were created, owners of both capital and labor could more easily make decisions that worked to their best economic interest. In a period in which communication over long distances was very difficult, cities were the only logical areas in which the marketplace was fully functional.

Urbanization also served as a medium for the circulation of information throughout the economy. Urbanization included not just a concentration of population but also a developing system of cities that enhanced the exchange of existing and new information and innovations. Also, the larger commercial seaports, particularly New York, served as central areas of information collection. The large seaports collected news from Europe, from other large American cities, and from smaller sized cities and in turn disseminated information throughout the entire urban system. By 1840, the nation had made major advances in the exchange of information, through the development of urbanization.

Urbanization did not proceed uniformly across the nation. Regional variations occurred in productivity and manufacturing, with the Northeast leading the way in industrialism. The regions with the highest income levels in 1840, New England and the Middle Atlantic States, also were leaders in urbanization and industrialization. The Southern States decline in per capita income, during the period, indicates that the cotton producing slave economy was unable to compete with the long-term growth potential of the Northern states. This was due to the manufacturing base that had already been established in the North.[1]

## DISTRIBUTION OF INCOME AND WEALTH

A product of the first half of the nineteenth century was that the distribution of income and wealth was becoming less equal. The trend toward concentration of wealth was localized in the new urban areas, particularly in the largest northeastern cities. The growth of the urban population resulted in an increase in their numbers relative to the total population. The result of this relative growth was that the distribution of wealth, in the nation as a whole, was becoming more uneven. There were several factors behind the trend of concentration of income, in the northeast's large urban cities.[2]

### Technology, Skills, and Immigration

**Technology:** The rate of technology change proceeded unevenly, both within the economy as a whole and within the urban sector in particular. Key factory based manufacturing industries led the way in creating productivity gains, with commerce, banking and transportation following. The pattern of technological change favored the intensive use of investment capital, such as machinery, and employment of people with the skills necessary to operate the new machinery. As the price of machines fell due to the many advances in the machine tool industry, the demand for skills, including management skills that were required to operate the machines grew rapidly. Consequently, the distribution of wealth among individuals became more concentrated in the hands of relatively fewer skilled individuals.

**Unskilled Workers:** They received lower incomes and spent a larger share of their earnings on basic goods that were produced less efficiently, such as fuel and food. As a consequence, the cost of living for most unskilled workers increased more rapidly than for skilled workers.

**Immigration:** During the 1840's and the 1850's the expansive flow of immigrants, who tended to be less skilled and less well informed about the marketplace than the native population, reduced even further the wages of the unskilled workers. In more modern terms, the demand for skilled workers increased relative to the supply. This resulted in an increased cost for skilled labor. However, the supply of unskilled workers increased relative to their demand. This reduced the price that the owners of capital would be willing pay to obtain their services.

## GROWTH IN MANUFACTURING

Manufacturing led economic growth in nineteenth century America, even though early in the century manufacturing was mostly limited to a handful of states in the Northeast. The story of the development of industry rests on the success of American manufacturers in competing with the Western Europeans, particularly with the British. During the first half of the nineteenth century the British were riding on a more advanced wave of the industrial revolution, but American ingenuity would soon serve as a key ingredient gradually to close the gap.

Every young economy must devote most of its resources to agricultural production, for food is the basic necessity of life, and until a good supply is assured, manufactured goods must remain in the planning stage. However, the American people were determined to make their plans a reality. They were able and willing to use technology to supplement their labor and abundant raw materials. Nature had endowed America with ample supplies of most of the essential raw materials. There was plenty of iron and timber, and cotton could be cultivated on a large scale, but the entrepreneur found himself without the capital goods with which to process the raw materials. Gradually, the labor force, the land area, and capital were accumulated in amounts large enough to make a steady climb in the total manufacturing output possible. The mechanism that propelled the American factories toward increased output  was technology development and improvement.

Technological progress means the application of analytic methods of science to the industrial arts. Anything that speeded up the process of invention, encouraged business entrepreneurs to experiment with new devices, or improved the skills of labor, accelerated technological change and industrial development. As the American economy advanced, numerous influences contributed to make this change progressively more rapid. The accumulation of capital, the creation of a workable money system, and the enlargement of the market area all served to stimulate the growth of manufacturing in America. However, changes in technology occurred gradually and continuously rather than sporadically. Almost every era in American history was rich in invention and innovation. Yet each period was dominated by a particular type of technological development: the early years, by the accumulation of machines and tools; the late nineteenth century, by the intensive development of bigger machines and better metals; the early twentieth century, by scientific management and research and development.

The American forte was not as the original inventor but as the innovators. American businessmen acquired technological processes from abroad and then experimented with them, often greatly improving on the original invention. The Europeans themselves were the first to recognize that the American approach was different from theirs. It was the Europeans, who coined the term the "American System." To the Europeans this term meant a system of mass production, of standardized interchangeable parts with heavy emphasis on utility, and a great disregard for aesthetics.[3]

The thrust of American technological development was toward the use of labor saving, capital-using innovations. Manufacturers in the United States learned how to use more capital per unit of labor than their British counterparts. The result of this propensity to substitute capital for labor, in ever increasingly innovative ways, was the enhancement of their own competitive position. The competitive success of American manufacturers also depended on the rapid technical advance in the development of machine tools. British engineers invented most of the basic machine tools, but Americans devised the most important new machine tools of the nineteenth century, most notably milling machines, grinding machines and the turret lathes. By the 1850's Americans had more specialized machine tools than those available in England, especially those used in woodworking and small arms' manufacturing.

However, the American superiority in machine tools was only one of the key ingredients toward the long-term goal of manufacturing superiority. In 1850, the English were still far ahead in most manufacturing fields, but what was most impressive was that a nation that was just getting off the economic ground should excel versus the British in any field.

In summary, American industry was able to compete with the British because of the relative cheapness of its raw materials. The availability of fertile land helped Americans become competitive by allowing them to compensate for the high costs of scarce labor and capital with the savings achieved on raw materials. Consequently, industries specializing in the processing of agricultural products thrived, with the cotton textile, lumbering, boot and shoe, flour milling and men's clothing industries leading the way. In addition, Americans competed with the British in the iron fabrication and especially the machinery industry as a result of their unique ability to take existing technology and adapt it to their own particular use. This is demonstrated by the output of America's leading industries in the year 1859 as follows:

| | Gross Value Added | | Gross Value Added |
|---|---|---|---|
| Industry | ($ in Millions) | Industry | ($ in Millions) |
| 1. Cotton Goods | $54.7 | 6. Iron Fabrication | $35.7 |
| 2. Lumbering | $53.6 | 7. Machinery | $32.6 |
| 3. Boot and Shoe | $49.2 | 8. Woolen Goods | $25.0 |
| 4. Flour and Meal | $40.1 | 9. Wagons | $23.7 |
| 5. Men's Clothing | $36.7 | 10. Leather | $22.8 |

Source: Secretary of the Interior, The Eighth Census, Manufacturers of the United States in 1860 (Washington, D.C.: U.S. Government Printing Office, 1865), pp. 733-742.

## INTERNATIONAL TRADE

The international economy underwent a period of marked expansion during the nineteenth century and the American economy profited from participation in that growth. International expansion brought large amounts of foreign investment capital to the United States. Foreigners were willing to invest in America because of the possibility of the high returns that were available. The expansion of the world marketplace required the development of many institutions that are central to international economic growth. Nations had to develop capital markets that could provide the medium for increasing levels of international investment. Credit had been extended in international commerce for centuries, but only in the nineteenth century did firms appear whose primary function was judging the possible returns on a wide assortment of commercial activity. Following the rise of international bankers, such as the Rothschild's and the Baring Brothers, mobility of international funds increased. The American government also participated in the growth of international trade by sharply reducing tariffs in 1832.

America's development of its particular set of comparative advantages was reflected in the growth and structure of the nation's exports. The trend of exports was strongly upward throughout the period. After 1839, exports grew as rapidly as the national product.

The result of this growth was an export level that amounted to 6 percent to 7 percent of the gross national product, during the period. However, the composition of American exports remained essentially the same from previous decades as agriculture and fiber products constituted most of the country's exports before the Civil War.

Manufacturing exports during the period consisted mostly of low quality cotton textiles. Raw cotton dominated the American exports throughout the period. Cotton had replaced the traditional colonial exports of tobacco, rice, lumber and naval stores as the leading export product. Exports of wheat and flour gained importance in the 1840's and 1850's, when the Irish potato famine, the Crimean War, and the repeal of the Corn Laws in 1846, increased European demands. Great Britain was the major importer of American goods.[4]

Despite the increasing export trade, the United States had an unfavorable balance of trade, with Europe, from the 1820's until the 1870's. With its balance of payments account in a negative position, America made up for the trading imbalance primarily through exporting gold and silver and the returns from service charges such as immigrant remittances and earnings from shipping. During the 1850's the excess of imports over exports was supported by the California mining boom, which allowed an outflow of almost $400 million in gold and silver from the United States. Thus, the new discovery of gold and silver in the West was a major contributor to the ability of all Americans to increase their consumption of foreign manufactured goods beyond their ability to export goods to Europe.

Trade, both international and domestic, promoted economic growth during the period before the Civil War, as it permitted a greater division of labor. Those institutional changes that widened trade encouraged greater regional and national productivity. Growing trade with Europe permitted Americans to rely more heavily on foreign producers for articles of consumption, enabled southern farmers to specialize in profitable cotton production, and provided a small but growing foreign market for American manufactured goods.[5]

However, internal commerce absorbed the vast bulk of Western and Northeastern production, and the specialization that resulted from this trade was more significant to the development and strengthening of industrialization in the United States than was the flourishing international trade.

## THE GROWTH OF MASS PRODUCTION

Throughout most of American history, agriculture dominated the economy. After 1860 the economy continued to become industrialized and by the end of the nineteenth century production had shifted from the home to the factory and hand-crafted products were being replaced by factories with machines. One of the things that contributed to the overall growth of manufacturing was the natural increase in the factors of production. Gradually, the labor force, the land area, and capital expanded sufficiently enough to make a steady climb in total manufacturing output possible. At the same time, these factors of production were operating in a way that increased productivity in the entire economy, and especially in manufacturing. The tool that was used to increase production was the development of and the improvement in existing technology.

Technological progress includes the substitution of natural energy for human exertion. Improvements to technology can be used for the mechanization of industry, improvements in transportation and communications, and the development of mass production. The means of improving technology are through specialization and this is achieved through the division of labor. Technology improvement incorporates the application of human brain power and skill to improve physical property, factories, tools and equipment. As the American economy advanced, many things contributed to making this economic growth more rapid. The accumulation of capital, the creation of a workable state banking system, the growth of the mass market and the emergence of a more efficient transportation system were all large contributors to the growth of manufacturing during this period. However, of all the forces that were at work, three things were fundamental to the explanation of the economy's rapid growth during this period: the scarcity of labor, the expansion of education, and from the point of view of the business owner, the prospect of profit.

### Technology and the Scarcity of Labor

One of the main reasons for the growth in technology was the scarcity of labor. It was through application of tools, machines and capital goods that the small labor force was able to produce more. Starting with a small population, compared to the land mass, the Civil War made the problem even worse by either killing or wounding more than one million of the country's most productive workers. However, America's population was young and the American culture encouraged the accumulation of material things. Because the population was not divided by social status, there were no peculiar class tastes or needs, anyone could buy goods provided they had the price.

For the most part American workers did not oppose the increased use of technology. The revolts against technology changes that took place in England during the last half of the nineteenth century had no counterpart in America. For in America where labor was scarce, machinery increased production that resulted in increased wages paid to the workers rather than to their unemployment.

The American value system based upon individualism, frowned upon leisure. It made work a fetish and production almost a religion. An often quoted English writer de Tocqueville, once said of the American system, "the notion of labor is presented to the mind of every side as necessary, natural, and honest condition of human existence. Not only is labor not dishonorable among such a people, but it is held in honor. In the United States, a wealthy man would think himself in bad repute if he employed his life solely in living."[6]

## Education

Scientific information had been accumulated during the first half of the nineteenth century, but it was not yet a part of college instruction. As a result, scientific findings had not yet begun to filter down to industry. However, during the second half of the century engineering and mechanical education progressed at a rapid rate. In 1850 the Rensselaer Polytechnic Institute in New York became an engineering school. In 1862, the Federal Government through the Morrill act, started to subsidize state colleges. These colleges were created to teach agricultural and mechanical arts. In 1864, the

National Academy of Sciences was founded and in 1865 scientific instructions began at the Massachusetts Institute of Technology. By the end of the century, 147 institutions were offering technical education.[2]

Technological progress was accelerated not only by the expansion of scientific education, but also by changes that occurred in the inventive process. This process began to move from the individual home or storefront into the laboratories of business organizations. The process of invention became more systematized, more disciplined, more collective and less individual. It became a profession, with a good share of it organized on a group basis and financed by business enterprise. As the process of invention shifted more towards the corporation, it became more efficient and more productive and more able to give the business owner better tools and products for mass production.

## The Prospect of Profit

Technology and education are requisites of increased production, but the final ingredient was the business owner who assembled the factors of production. In America, the more enterprising businessmen recognized that there was profit to be made through mass production and they took ample advantage of these opportunities. Business enterprise accelerated the development of the new machinery by emphasizing both mass consumption and mass production. Without large-scale business the technological growth that occurred in America would not have taken place, because only large-scale business could afford to adopt the expensive machinery that technology produced. However, large-scale manufacturing brings with it large fixed costs. Therefore, mass consumption is necessary for mass production to exist. Early in American history businessmen realized that their opportunities relied on the expansion of mass consumption, and they set their goals accordingly. As early as the Jackson period, businessmen were suggesting that, a characteristic of American business, in the future, was to sell products to many customers at a low price, rather than at a high price, to just a few. Thus, it was a combination of labor scarcity, education, and entrepreneurial initiative that gave impetus to the growth and development of mass production in America.[7]

## THE RISE OF THE INDUSTRIAL CAPITALIST

By 1870, transportation of goods improved in America as there was, by this time, over 50,000 miles of railroad in operation. The improvement in railroad transportation made it possible to ship large amounts of goods from more distant locations. For example, cattle from the Southwest could be driven to Kansas City for processing and then shipped by rail to the east coast. Also, in addition to the improvements in transportation, almost one-quarter of America's population was by that time living in cities. Mass production, mass marketing, and mass consumption was now possible. However, to take advantage of this new market potential, business required a system of enterprise that would include new techniques for expanding fixed assets, new methods off distribution, and new ways to finance large-scale business, and improved methods of supervising a large labor force. To fill this need, the industrial capitalist appeared.

The industrialist was primarily concerned with driving down unit cost through mass production and therefore increasing the supply of consumer goods. Indeed, operating in a vastly untapped market, the industrialist often took demand for granted. Often starting on a smaller scale as a business merchant, the industrialist of the late nineteenth century raised a large portion of their own capital, by plowing back earnings into the business. He distrusted the financial institutions of the era. As an individualistic owner, the industrialist believed in centralized authority and preferred to run a so-called one-man style of business. He regarded all office work, with the exception of accounting, with contempt. He maintained a paternalistic attitude toward his employees and paid almost no attention to public relations. He believed in individualism and the philosophy of Social Darwinism and that economic life was governed by the principle of "Survival of the Fittest." He distrusted government and politicians and in the hierarchy of social values, he argued that the interest of his business came first and that he had no responsibility to sacrifice the profit potential of his organization for the attainment of social goals.[8]

## The Robber Barons

The Robber Barons was a term used by U.S. political and economic commentator Matthew Josephson to describe the industrial capitalists during the latter part of the 19th and the beginning of the 20th centuries. At the turn of the century there were twenty two industrialists whose fortunes amounted to nearly one billion dollars. Nine out of the twenty-two fortunes were railroad fortunes made, constructing and operating the 200,000 miles of railroad track that were built to cover the United States in the nineteenth century. Also, between 1870 and 1900, many of the large businesses of the new industrialists were created. Charles Pillsbury organized C.A. Pillsbury and General Henry DuPont formed the Gunpowder Association in 1872. Philip Armour opened his meat packing plant in Chicago in 1875. Wanamaker opened the Grand Depot in 1876 and the partnership between Gustavus and Edwin Swift was created in 1878. Two of the most powerful of non-railroad industrialists were Andrew Carnegie in steel and John D. Rockefeller in oil.[9]

## Andrew Carnegie (1835-1919)

Andrew Carnegie

In 1848 Carnegie's father lost his job in Dunfermline Scotland and the family moved to Pittsburgh, PA. At the age of 17 Andrew Carnegie was hired as an assistant to the Pennsylvania railroad superintendent. By age 24, Carnegie was hired as an assistant to the Pennsylvania railroad superintendent. By age 28, Carnegie was running the western branch of the railroad and investing his own money in oil, iron and other companies. By his mid 30's he built his own steel mill using the latest technology and hiring the best available employees. He secured every facet needed for steel making, from iron deposits and coal mines to railroads and ore ships.

Extremely competitive, Carnegie was soon out producing and underbidding and crushing rivals, and became the largest steel maker in the world. In 1892, Carnegie's partner, Henry Clay Frick, crushed Carnegie Steel's union in bloody clashes at its Homestead steel plant outside of Pittsburgh that resulted in a public outcry. In 1901 Carnegie sold his steel company to J.P. Morgan for $480 million. Carnegie received over $250 million in the deal making him one of the richest men in the world. After selling his steel interests Carnegie turned to philanthropic enterprise were by the time of his death in 1914 he had dispensed major portions of his fortune building more than 2,500 libraries and other institutions.

### John D. Rockefeller (1839-1937)

J. D. Rockefeller

Rockefeller and his partners built a business in Pennsylvania refining crude oil into kerosene. He brought to the venture a talent for watching the company books and scrupulously securing every economy in a boomtown business full of imprudent wildcatters.

During the latter part of the nineteenth century the oil industry had an assortment of problems, not the least of which was the cost of transporting oil to market. Rockefeller solved that by securing clandestine contracts with the railroads that afforded huge rebates. With the lower transportation cost, he was able to squeeze out the competition.

In 1870 the Rockefeller Brothers and Henry M. Flagler reorganized their oil refining business under the name of Standard Oil (Ohio). This was because prices and profit margins on petroleum products were falling. This was due to over expansion of production. Rockefeller and his associates responded to this problem by establishing an aggressive and ruthless policy of horizontal integration by purchasing rival refineries, and also developed a long range plan for vertical integration. During the 1880's and 1890's, Standard Oil continued to buy small marketing businesses. The company also acquired the remaining minority interest in its marketing affiliates, organized new units, and accumulated miles of pipelines and fleets of oil tankers. Meanwhile, Standard Oil also began to purchase companies in the oil and gas production industry. By 1893 Standard Oil had become fully integrated from the oil well to the gas station. They controlled the supply of oil and therefore the price.[10]

## The Industrialist's Efforts to Control Prices

One of the results of increased mass production in the United States during the last quarter of the nineteenth century, was that production capacity was increasing at a rate that was greater than demand. When supply increases at a greater rate than demand for the products produced, businessmen usually have to reduce the price of their products in order to sell the quantity produced. Thus the industrialists were confronted with a new problem, one of excess capacity and the possibility of ruthless price competition. The businessmen recognized that price wars would benefit consumers at the expense of the producers as they would result in losses in profit and the potential of a large amount of business failures. The strategy that was devised to avoid the potential of business losses was to control the price of the products produced.

The first attempt to control price competition was through trade associations. In the 1850's, the so called "Gentlemen's Agreements" began to appear regularly in manufacturing companies. For more than twenty years, businessmen tried to control price competition, through these associations. However, not all of the participants in an association could be trusted to control their output. Members found it easy to evade the self-imposed restrictions and sooner or later one party was sure to sell their goods below the agreed-upon price. Controlling the price of goods in an industry required the cooperation of all members of the association; however, when even one of the member cheats, the whole system usually collapses.

It soon became clear to the industrial capitalist that the best way to control prices was to eliminate the competition by buying a controlling interest in rival companies in the same industry. This method of consolidation is known as a horizontal merger. The

Gunpowder Association presents a good example of a horizontal merger. This association was controlled by General Henry DuPont, who owned a block of stock in each of the member companies, and the General used this power to control price competition within the association.

However, horizontal integration did not solve all of the business problems of the time for this provided little control over the supply of natural resources. The industrialist of this period solved this problem by integrating vertically. Vertical integration requires expanding forward to the customer through the purchase of wholesale or retail operations and backward to the producer of raw materials. The initial expansion was usually in the direction of the consumer as businessmen gradually took over the marketing of their products.

Two of the pioneers in building a marketing organization to integrate forward to the consumer were the McCormick Reaper Company and the Singer Sewing machine Company. McCormick began to sell agricultural products through commissioned agents and gradually this was built up to a franchise agent system. Edward Clark, the marketing brain in the Singer Company recognized that his company would have to demonstrate the sewing machine and provide instruction and service to customers. To provide these services, Singer established branch stores, 14 of them by 1859.[12]

## EXPANSION OF INCORPORATION AND THE TRUST

The corporate form of organization was used in a small number of companies as far back as the colonial period. In early years, corporate charters were granted by special acts of legislation and limited liability was not available. However, state law gradually changed and limited liability to stockholders was common by 1850.[7] However, what made the corporate form of business even more important was that it suited the needs of expanding companies. Through the sale of stocks and bonds, businessmen began raising capital in much larger amounts then would have been possible through the proprietor or partnership forms of business. As a result of these advantages, the industrial capitalist resorted more and more to the corporate charter in the late nineteenth century. The experience of two industrial states, New Jersey and Ohio, can be used to illustrate the trend toward the use of the corporate structure. In 1870 these states issued almost 150 corporate charters to manufacturing companies. In 1883, the same states issued about 450 new corporate charters to manufacturers.

These early corporate charters were granted mostly to "Closed Corporations," whose stock was not bought and sold in the open market. The Carnegie steelworks was a typical example of the closed corporation. In the Carnegie organization, there were 25 stockholders, whose ownership ranged from less than 1 percent to over 58 percent. Under the terms of the corporate charter, stockholders could sell their shares only to the company. Moreover, the shares of any holder's stock, could be bought at book value if 75 percent of the stockholders voted that way.

Because of the limitations to raising capital inherent in the closed corporation, corporate lawyers and business owners soon created a new form of organization called the "Trust." This form of organization gave the corporation much more flexibility to expand its capital raising powers and at the same time gave control of the company to a small group of insiders.

A trust (often referred to as a cartel) by definition is a group of producers that attempt to maximize their profits by joining together to control output and thereby fixing prices. In the United States there has historically been a populist sensitivity that tends to associate large size with the potential for monopoly power. A trust is a combination of firms in which the companies haven't actually merged, but they act as a single unit usually for the purpose of controlling output and fixing prices. Therefore, trusts often acted as if they were monopolies.

Standard Oil provides a good example of the trust activities of the late 1800's. Standard Oil under John D. Rockefeller, demanded that the railroads pay it kickbacks on freight rates. These payments allowed Standard Oil to set lower prices for its products than other companies which had to pay the railroads the full price on freight. This arrangement enabled Standard Oil to sell its products at lower prices than its competitors. By 1882, Standard Oil had driven many of its competitors out of business. The company then created a trust and invited its remaining competitors to join or be forced out of business.

The trust innovation was mainly the idea of Standard Oil's legal advisor, Samuel C.T. Dodd. Under the 1882 agreement, 41 stockholders, in 40 different companies, turned over their stock to 9 trustees in exchange for $70 million in "Trust Certificates," that represented all the shares in 14 companies and most of the shares of 26 other organizations. Stockholders continued to receive dividends. In theory they owned the companies, but in practice they did not participate in the management of the firm and effectively did not have control over the trust.[13]

Once they had gained control of the majority of their competitors, Standard Oil used the monopoly power that it had gained to close down refineries, raise prices and limit the production of oil. The price of oil rose from a competitive level to a monopolistic level, and the consumer ended up paying a higher price for oil.

The Trust idea caught on very quickly, and trusts were soon formed in cottonseed oil, whiskey, distilling, sugar refining and other businesses. The device enabled a group of business owners to control many different companies in many different states thus giving them the ability to control pricing. Separately this practice was not permitted under existing corporate law, but by operating through the trust structure the law could be circumvented. It also enabled the industrialist to raise capital to support the huge investment in the fixed assets required for mass production without relinquishing any of their control over the organization. These trust certificates could be issued to the public and were traded on the major stock exchanges of the era.

However, the word "Trust" soon became synonymous in many people's minds with the word "Monopoly," and states began to take legal actions to dissolve them by antitrust proceedings. The most noticeable of these actions was in Ohio in 1892, when that state delivered a serious blow to the Standard Oil Trust, by ordering Standard Oil to withdraw from the trust.[14]

## MONOPOLY AND THE GOVERNMENT

To understand the government's response to the large corporate combinations of this period, it is useful to first define monopoly in economic terms. Monopoly is a market structure in which there is a single supplier of a product. A monopolistic firm is the only supplier of a particular product. In addition, a monopoly firm must sell a product for which there are no close substitutes. For example, Standard Oil (Ohio) was able to form a monopoly position by eliminating competition through horizontal and vertical mergers, in a product (oil) where there was no close substitute.

## ANTITRUST POLICY

The problem often faced by government policy makers is to determine whether a firm is acting in a way that fosters competition and to decide what to do when a firm's behavior reflects its intention to control prices, supply or in other ways, restricts competition. Antitrust policy is the term used to describe government policies and programs designed to control the growth of monopoly and prevent firms from engaging in undesirable business practices. The federal government's right to regulate business in the United States is based on the commerce clause of the Constitution. As previously discussed, Article 1, Section 8, of the Constitution, states that "Congress shall have power to regulate commerce with foreign nations, and among the several states, and with the Indian tribes." Three laws currently define the United States Government's approach to antitrust policy:

- Sherman Antitrust Act (1890)
  Section 1: outlaws contracts and conspiracies in restraint of Trade.
  Section 2: forbids monopolization and attempts to monopolize.

- Clayton Antitrust Act (1914)
  Section 2: bans price discrimination that Substantially lessens competition or the ability to compete.
  Section 3: prohibits certain practices that might keep other firms from entering an industry or competing with an existing firm.
  Section 7: outlaws mergers that substantially lessen competition.

- Federal Trade Commission Act (1914)
  <u>Section 5</u>: prohibits unfair methods of competition   and    unfair
  deceptive acts.[11]

Economic theory presents sufficient evidence against monopoly to justify the presumption that impairments to competition are harmful. Even classical economic theory conceded that monopoly was the one flaw in their otherwise, thought to be, perfect system. Determining if the firm's actions are beneficial for society, and, in addition, if large size is harmful to society, is the aim of our government's antitrust policy.

The United States government tries to distinguish between beneficial and harmful actions, by companies, through focusing on unreasonable monopolistic restraints. The first phase of antitrust policy in this country began in 1890 with the passage of the Sherman Act. The courts used the "Rule of Reason" for judging the individual firm's acts. On the basis of the rule of reason, to be illegal an action must be unreasonable in a competitive sense and the anti-competitive effects of the actions must be demonstrated.

The second phase in antitrust policy began in 1914 with the passage of the Clayton Antitrust Act and the Federal Trade Commission Act. At this time the courts began to use the "Per Se Rule" to judge individual firm's actions. Actions that were potentially monopolizing tactics were determined to be illegal under the per se rule. Currently the courts have returned to the looser rule of reason standard. Since the 1980's, collusion or price fixing, has been the only tactic deemed intrinsically illegal under the Antitrust Acts.[15]

The results of antitrust legislation in the United States have been mixed at best. If antitrust legislation was intended to establish a more competitive market structure, historically it has failed to accomplish this goal. With the exception of the dissolution of the Standard Oil Company and the American Tobacco Company in 1911, the Sherman Act and subsequent laws, has not changed the existing market structure. However, the Sherman Act clearly established the principle that competition was to be favored over monopoly. The prohibition of price-fixing, did not end attempts by firms to reduce competition, but the antitrust laws did reduce these attempts and limited their impact. As a result of these laws it was more difficult for firms to collude and practically impossible for them to prevent or punish cheating. As a result, price-fixing combinations became more difficult to create and less effective in operation.[16]

**NOTES:**

**Chapter 9**
**The Industrial Revolution (1800-1900)**

1.      Brownlee, W. Elliot, <u>Dynamics of Ascent - A</u> <u>History of</u>    <u>the</u> <u>American   Economy,</u>   Wadsworth   Publishing   Company, Belmont, CA, 1988,  p. 129.
2.      Brownlee, p. 135.
3.      Krooss,   Herman,   E.,   <u>American   Economic   Development,</u> Englewood Cliffs, N.J. Prentice-Hall,   Inc., 1966. p. 349.
4.      Krooss, Herman, E., p. 351.
5.      U.S. Congress (1913), <u>The Concentration of Control of Money and Credit, Pujo Committee Report</u>, Washington, DC: GPO,
6.      Brownlee, p. 186.
7.      Krooss,   Herman   E.   <u>American   Economic   Development, Second</u> <u>Edition</u>, Englewood Cliffs, NJ, Prentice-Hall, Inc., 1966, p. 343.
8.      Krooss, p. 343.
9.      Krooss, p. 155.
10.     Krooss, p. 160.
11.     Krooss, p. 161.
12.     Krooss, p. 162.
13.     Krooss, p. 163.
14.     Krooss, p. 164.
15.     Boyes, William and Melvin, Michael, <u>Economics</u>, Boston,  MA, Houghton Mifflin Co., 1991, p. 715.
16.     Puth,   Robert   C.,   <u>American   Economic   History,   Third Addition</u>, Fort Worth Texas, The Dryden Press, 1993, p.   348.

# CHAPTER 10

---

## NEOCLASSICAL ECONOMICS

*"The institution of a leisure class is found in its best development at the higher stages of the barbarian culture. And the tribal rites of the latter have their counterpart in the dinners, dances and other entertainment's at the great houses in New York and Newport." --Thorstein Veblen.*

### ALFRED MARSHALL (1842-1924)

Alfred Marshall

William Stanley Jevons contributed many important ideas about marginal utility, but it was Alfred Marshall who developed the idea of Marginalism into a practical economic theory. Alfred Marshall was born in 1842 in Bermondsey England. Marshall's father wanted him to attend Oxford University, where he could study Latin and prepare for the ministry. However, to his father's disappointment, Marshall did not hear a voice from God. Instead of a voice from God, Marshall heard cries of the poor, urging him to study economics. Up until the nineteenth century three educational disciplines reigned in English Universities: Theology, aimed at spiritual perfection; Law aimed at justice; and Medicine, aimed at physical soundness. Marshall offered a fourth great vocation, the study of economics. Throughout his life Marshall fought for economics as a separate field apart from politics, history and moral issues. In 1885, Marshall was appointed as the Chair in Political Economy, but it wasn't until 1903 that Cambridge University decided to establish a separate economics course.

In 1890 Marshall published his most famous work, "Principles of Economics," where in the beginning of his book he describes his basic belief "Natura Non Facit Saltum," Nature makes no sudden leaps. Whereas classical economists followed a Newtonian Scientific approach searching for laws of nature, Marshall emphasized a more evolutionary approach. For Marshall, the theories of Charles Darwin and biology were more important than the physics of Isaac Newton. In this regard, Alfred Marshall's concepts about Marginalism, are similar to the theory of evolution, if this theory was applied to economics. According to Marshall, the businessman and the consumer make no great leaps, but gradually attempt to improve their situations. Individuals, companies, and governments all conform to changing situations and changing prices. In the long run only those firms that can adapt to change, only those firms that are the fittest, survive.[1]

Marshall realized that like biological time, economic time, was not a constant. Marshall's way of dealing with time constraints was to create an ingenious system of analysis. While he was looking at one factor, he set aside all other into a "pound." He called the pound "Ceteris Paribus," meaning "other things being equal." Prior economists had already devised a ceteris paribus assumption, but Marshall derived an explicit method and constructed rigorous theories according to it. Today, microeconomics textbooks are still based on Marshall's method of analysis.

According to Marshall, economic events must be analyzed in conjunction with the time that is necessary for both consumers and producers to make adjustments. Marshall's analysis broke time into three different areas. First there was the very short run. This is the time period of just one day where only demand can fluctuate. This is because producers generally cannot adjust supply in such a short period. Next there was the short run. In the short run according to Marshall, producers can supply more of a product by hiring more labor and purchasing additional amounts of raw material. However, the short run does not last long enough to increase the capacity of existing equipment or to build additional manufacturing capacity. The third period Marshall called the long run. This was a period when producers have enough time to build new machinery and new factories, as well as to vary labor and materials. Also, in the long run, new producers could enter the industry; old and less efficient companies would be forced to leave and the surviving firms would earn profit margins that were normal for the industry. This analysis has a key implication for the long run growth of any economy. Government intervention can serve to increase or reduce economic activity in the short run, but in the long run the output of any economy can only increase through increases in productivity, i.e., output per man hour of work.

## Marshall on Supply and Demand

Marshall did not agree with Ricardo's claim that the value of a product reflects the amount of labor it took to produce it. He thought that the supply and demand for a product were equally important. Based on the marginalist theory, economists had previously developed the downward-sloping demand curves, but Marshall developed the "Law of Demand," which stated that the greater the amount of products to be offered for sale, the smaller must be the price of those products. "The amount of a product demanded increases with a fall in the price, and diminishes with a rise in price."[2]

Marshall's analysis was based on the principle of "all other things being equal," but he knew that factors other than price entered into the analysis of demand. The most important of these factors were, consumer taste and preferences, customers' disposable income, and the price of substitute goods. In modern terms, a change in quantity due to a change in price is depicted as a movement along a demand curve, whereas a change in factors other than price would be represented as a shift in the demand curve.

Marshall developed a similar framework for suppliers. As producers supply more of a product, the total costs of production will rise. Therefore, supply will rise only if the price paid to the producer increases. The producer will compare the additional cost of producing one more unit to the price he can obtain when selling that output. This, according to Marshall, is the reason that the supply curve slopes upward, whereas the demand curve slopes downward.[3]

Marshall held that, in the same way that the consumer compares the marginal utility of spending on various products, producers constantly compare the potential returns from spending. In this case, the producer is comparing the potential returns from investing in capital equipment versus labor. The business owner in order to be successful must engage in a constant balancing act among capital, labor and natural resources, i.e., between new and used equipment and between skilled and unskilled labor. For this reason Marshall came out strongly against unions that supported make-work projects and featherbedding, as their lack of productivity would only serve to reduce profits and in the long run hurt their members.

## Marshall on Social Concerns

While Marshall's "Principle of Economics" tended to be theoretical, he insisted that economics must also be practical. Marshall frequently served on royal commissions and testified before parliament. He supported public education and a moderate redistribution of wealth, because it would heighten productivity and social welfare. However, he was not by any means a socialist and at one point called this philosophy the "greatest present danger." Just like philosophers and economists as far back as Aristotle, Marshall feared that collective ownership would "deaden the energies of mankind, and arrest economic progress; unless before its introduction the whole people had acquired an unselfish devotion to public good."

Marshall thought that the classical pessimists and the romantic Marxists were both wrong. The stationary state had not arrived. Population did not outstrip food as Malthus had predicted. Landlords did not reign. Although poverty still degraded a portion of the people, Marshall held that the "hope and poverty and ignorance may gradually be extinguished and this philosophy was supported by the steady progress of the working class during the nineteenth century. The steam-engine had relieved them of much of their exhausting and degrading toil; wages had increased; education had been improved and the railway and the printing press had enabled members of the same trade in different parts of the country to communicate easily with one another.[4]

Alfred Marshall remained a professor at Cambridge until he was over eighty years old. John Maynard Keynes, who was his pupil, once praised the "old professor of Cambridge" as he wrote, "The master economist must, like Marshall, be a mathematician, historian, statesman and philosopher to some degree. He must study the present in light of the past for purposes of the future."[5]

## AMERICAN CONTRIBUTIONS TO ECONOMIC THOUGHT

In the nineteenth century the United States was a world of improving land, life and well being. During that time the U.S. was a country of owner-operated farms. In the Southern states until the Civil War, wages were excluded from consideration because slavery, as in Aristotle's time, greatly focused attention on such ethical and moral issues as emancipation rather than on economic ones.

In the U.S. the discussion of economics was based on practical economic topics. These included the tariff, monopoly, the social behavior and defense of the very rich, and the diverse questions pertaining to banks and money. The American Economic Association, formed in 1885, was initially a protest against the highly conservative support accorded industrial capitalism by the accepted classical theory and the companion commitment to laissez faire. Only at the end of the nineteenth century did two distinctively American economic figures emerge: Henry George and Thorstein Veblen.

### Henry George (1839-1897)

In his time and into the 1920's Henry George was the most widely read of American economic writers. His major work, first published in 1879, was entitled "Progress and Poverty." Henry George's principle idea centered on the accidental and unjust enrichment that came from the ownership of land and the further meaning this had for the financing of the modern state. From his vantage point of San Francisco, Henry George saw the lush enrichment of landowners: as the frontier moved forward, the population increased, and economic development proceeded. David Ricardo had previously witnessed that the tendency of a growing society to enrich

Henry George

the holders of its land would have an adverse affect on the capitalist. However, to Henry George, the resulting contrast between wealth and misery was intolerable.

From this observation followed the remedy he prescribed; it was to tax away the unearned gain in land values that did not derive from the effort or intelligence of the owner but came in effortless fashion from the general advance of population and industry. The revenues that were collected, George believed, would more than cover the operating expenses of the State; all other taxes would be redundant. Thus his great reform was given the name of, the "single tax."[6]

Needless to say, there were a very large number of wealthy landowners, who strongly motivated and politically powerful, were in opposition to the single tax idea. However, even today the beliefs of Henry George can be found in less formal conscious thought. The real estate developer or speculator encouraged by and encouraging an increase in land values is, quite possibly, the least praised of American entrepreneurs.

## Thorstein Veblen (1857-1929)

Thorstein Veblen

Of the early twentieth century economic writers, Thorstein Veblen is perhaps still the most notable. Just south of the small city of Northfield, Minnesota are 290 acres of land where Thorstein Veblen spent his childhood. From that background, Veblen went on to study at Johns Hopkins University and Yale, where among his principal mentors was William Graham Sumner.

Veblen established himself as a critic of the classical system, at first in a series of short papers published at the turn of the century. In these papers, Veblen argued that the central ideas of the classical system did not reflect a search for truth and realty; rather they were and are a celebration of approved belief. In Veblen's view economic institutions change; so does economic subject matter; there can be understanding only if one is in tune with change.[7]

A further Veblen contribution which was presented in "The Theory of Business Enterprise," published in 1904, identified a powerful conflict in the modern business organization between the engineers and scientists, who were professionals of great skill and productive potential, and the profit oriented businessmen. The businessmen, according to Veblen, keep the talents of the scientists and engineers under control and suppressed them as necessary in order to maintain prices and maximize profits. Today product managers and marketing people have continued this argument. Also, this argument can be extended to compare the propensity of many U.S. companies to manage in the short-term, i.e., from quarter to quarter, versus the Japanese propensity to manage for the long-term and to seek market share as their main goal.

From this view of the business firm Veblen developed his conclusion. If the business community could somehow release those who are technically and imaginatively proficient from the restraints imposed by the system, there would be unprecedented productivity and wealth in the economy.

Veblen's views on two other matters are also worthy of comment. First is his emphasis on the ordinary worker's concern for the quality of his performance, i.e., "I take pride in my work." This statement can be found in Veblen's "The Instinct of Workmanship," published in 1914. This attitude can be seen today in such things as:

- The Japanese team approach to management and process engineering.

- The new emphasis on service as a major part of a product.

Secondly, and in addition to his other contributions, Thorstein Veblen remains a resonant voice nearly a century after his most memorable book was published. This work was his superb examination of the manners and motives of the rich in "The Theory of the Leisure Class," published in 1899.

The two phrases that Veblen coined; "Conspicuous Leisure," and "Conspicuous Consumption," have permanently entered the American language and culture. They have affected the economic and social attitudes and behavior of countless thousands who have never heard of Veblen. As a consequence of Veblen's work, leisure for the affluent in the United States has come "to lack repute." No one is spared the question, "What do you do for a living?" Even more specifically, no forms of entertainment and no house, if sufficiently expensive or grand, are safe from the denigrating description "Conspicuous Consumption."[8]

## Joseph A. Schumpeter (1883-1950)

Joseph Schumpeter

During the early decades of the twentieth century the classical tradition, was now above any challenge in England. Also, because of the influence of such disciples as Harvard's Frank W. Taussig (1859-1940), classical economics was fully accepted in the United States. Prices adjusted to marginal costs; costs, including that of labor, adjusted downward as necessary to ensure the employment of available plant, materials, and above all, workers. Say's Law, which states that supply creates its own demand, was widely accepted.

Although Alfred Marshall ruled in these early years, his system did receive some influential amendments. Joseph Schumpeter added a major dimension to the Marshallian equilibrium. This came from the central figure of Schumpeter's system, the entrepreneur, who aided by bank credit, challenges the established equilibrium with a new product, a new process or a new type of productive organization. The tendency then is to a new equilibrium; a new stability in what Schumpeter saw as a circular flow with production moving in one direction, and the money to fund the production in the other. This new equilibrium would inevitably be disturbed and broken by the next innovator. Therefore, economic life would continue and expand; for this is the nature of economic development.

Joseph Schumpeter was born in Austria in 1883. He studied law at the University of Vienna and attended lectures by the leading economist of the day. These economists included some of the founders of the Austrian school of economics. The Austrian school traces its origins to Karl Menger and Friedrich von Wieser who worked in Vienna in the latter part of the nineteenth century. In the twentieth century the Austrian tradition was brought to the United States by Ludwig von Mises and Friedrich von Hayek among others. Today the Austrian school continues to have a strong following in the United States partly because of the theories of one of its close cousins, the Public Choice School of economics, which will be described in a later chapter.

In the view of the Austrian economists the spontaneous order of the marketplace is best viewed in terms of a market process that takes place continuously. The central player in the market process is the entrepreneur. It is the entrepreneur's efforts to move resources from less valued to more valued uses that is the source of profit for the capitalist.

In 1912 Schumpeter published his first book on economics entitled "The Theory of Economic Development." The book is about the way in which capitalism develops its propensity toward growth. The book starts with a description of a capitalist economy that lacks capital accumulation and growth is totally absent. Schumpeter's model pictures a society whose flow of production is perfectly static and absent of change, reproducing itself in a "circular flow" that never expands its ability to create wealth. Also, in the static flow of production, competition among the capitalists will remove all earnings that exceed their opportunity costs. In other words, economic profit would be zero with the economy in a static state. Workers would receive wages, landlords rent, and the capitalists would receive only their wages as managers.

Historically many economists had attempted to explain the source of profits in an economy. Schumpeter argued that profits did not arise from the exploitation of labor as Karl Marx had claimed, or from the "abstinence" of capitalists that was proposed by John Stuart Mill. Profits appeared in a static economy when the circular flow failed to follow its routine course. From the starting point of the circular flow some new force is required to break the inertia and this force is the introduction of technological or organizational innovations into the circular flow. As a result of these innovations, a flow of income arises that does not come from the contributions of the workers or the resources of the capitalist.[9]

A new product that obtains an initial monopoly position in the marketplace or a new manufacturing process that reduces unit costs can result in a profit for the capitalist that is substantially greater than their opportunity costs. In economic terms the capitalist receives an economic rent for his innovation. An innovation requires an innovator who is responsible for combining the factors of production in new ways. Schumpeter held that innovators do not necessarily come from any social class. He took an old word from the economic lexicon and used it to describe these revolutionists of production and product innovation. He called them entrepreneurs. Entrepreneurs, according to Schumpeter and their innovating activity were the source of profit and growth in the capitalist system.[10]

## THE THEORY OF MARKET STRUCTURE

The structure of a market is a term that refers to the conditions under which firms compete in it. The key traits of a market include the number and size of firms, the nature of the products, the ease of entry and exit from the market, and the information available to the competing companies.

Monopoly is a market structure in which there is a single supplier of a product. A monopolistic firm is the only supplier of a particular product. In addition, a monopoly firm must sell a product for which there are no close substitutes. The price of the product is set by the company. A monopoly is a price maker in the marketplace. An electric and gas utility is an example of a monopolistic firm.

Perfect competition is characterized by a large number of small firms, none with a significant share of the market; a product that is standardized, little or no barriers to either entry or exit from the business, and that all buyers and sellers have complete information about the price of the products, the inputs used to produce them and equal knowledge about industry production technology. A company in a purely competitive industry takes whatever price is established by the market. Purely competitively firms are price takers. Agricultural products are a good example of pure competition.

An oligopoly is a market structure with a few firms, at least some of which are large in relation to the size of the market. The product may be either standardized or differentiated; there may or may not be significant barriers to entry, and buyers and sellers do not have equal access to available information. The industry consists of both price makers and price takers as the firm with the largest market share often takes the lead in product pricing while the other companies follow the dominant firm. The automobile industry is an example of an oligopoly.

Monopolistic (differentiated) competition resembles perfect competition in that there are many small firms with easy entry and exit, but under this market structure, the various firms' products are differentiated from one another. Firms in this market structure invest additional amounts of money into expanding the features of their products to add value for their customers. Also these companies usually spend large amounts on advertising to create a favorable image of their products with potential distributors and retail customers. Companies that can successfully differentiate their products in the eyes of the consumers are price makers as they can usually charge a premium for their output. The restaurant industry is an example of monopolistic competition.

**The Trend Toward Oligopoly in Manufacturing**

In 1933 two economists working separately developed the theory of oligopoly. They were Edward H. Chamberlin (1899-1967) of Harvard and Joan Robinson (1903-1983) of Cambridge. Chamberlin and Robinson both argued that between the general case of competition in the classical system and the exceptional case of monopoly, there was an array of intermediate possibilities. The most important case as an intermediate between pure competition and monopoly, was that of small numbers of participants in the same industry. This market structure they called oligopoly, which is a term that promptly entered the language of economics. The American automobile, petroleum, steel, chemical, rubber tire, machine tool and farm equipment industries, with a few giants in each industry, are cases in point.[11]

The intelligent oligopolist would, in setting his price, give thoughtful consideration to what would be most advantageous for all; so would the others in their industry. Therefore, the price and profit that would be arrived at by an oligopolist, would be somewhere between that of pure competition and monopoly.

The concept of oligopoly was considered a lesser threat to competition than that of the monopoly, and therefore, entered classical thought without any great difficulty. The large modern corporate sector of the economic system, where oligopoly ruled, was the dominant sector, and, monopoly or not, one could not declare it illegal. Also, while oligopoly was, in principle socially unjust, in actual performance, it aroused no great consumer resentment. While economists might argue that oligopoly was wrong in principle; in practice, it produced a whole spectrum of new and lower cost products. Therefore, economists came to view oligopoly with theoretical concern, but they dismissed the necessity for practical action in dealing with it. Although monopoly was still considered the one great flaw in the system oligopoly was accepted as a common business practice.

## PRODUCTIVITY AND COMMUNISM

Just as the latter half of the nineteenth century saw the growth of formalized education for engineers, the twentieth century witnessed a great acceleration of formalized education for businessmen. Between 1900 and 1910 alone, 240 volumes of business management books were published, and in 1908, Harvard University founded its Graduate School of Business Administration.[12]

Therefore, what effectively ended the long run potential threat to Capitalism from Communism or more moderate forms of Socialism was the increase in the productivity of the workers. Increased output for man-hour meant increased profit for the owners of business.

However, increased productivity through training created skilled knowledgeable workers who could command more wages. Also, labor unions began to gather some strength during the twentieth century which gave the workers the ability to control the supply of skilled labor. The result of these changes was an increase in the amount of the price received for a unit of production that went to the worker. In summary, there eventually was no need for a revolt because the skilled worker was becoming the Bourgeois, the middle class or in today's economy, the favorite target of the tax collector.

**NOTES:**

**Chapter 10**
**Neoclassical Economics**

1.   Buchholz, Todd G., <u>New Ideas From Dead Economists</u>,   New York, NY, The Penguin Group,   1987, p. 152.
2.   Marshall, Alfred, <u>Principles of Economics, 9th Edition,</u> London,  England, 1961, p. 316.
3.    Buchholz, p. 160.
4.    Marshall, p. 3.
5.   Keynes, John Maynard, "<u>Alfred Marshal</u>," in Essays in <u>Biography,</u> London, England, Macmillan, 1972, p. 164.
6.   Galbraith, John Kenneth, <u>Economics in Perspective</u>, Boston, MA, Houghton Mifflin Company, 1987, p. 167.
7.   Galbraith, P. 171.
8.   Galbraith, P. 176.
9.   Heilbroner, Robert L. <u>The Worldly Philosophers</u>, New York, NY, Simon & Schuster, 1986, p. 295.
10.   Heilbroner, P. 296.
11.   Galbraith, P. 183.
12.   Krooss, p. 362.

# CHAPTER 11

---

# SCIENTIFIC MANAGEMENT, MASS PRODUCTION AND WORLD WAR I

*"We were going to build one model. The chassis would be exactly the same for all cars. Any customer can have a car painted any color he wants so long as it is black." —Henry Ford*

## THE PRODUCTIVITY REVOLUTION

According to Peter Drucker, Capitalism has gone through three distinctive phases; the Industrial Revolution, the Productivity Revolution and the Management Revolution. Within one hundred years, from 1750 to 1900, capitalism and technology conquered the globe which led to the creation of a civilized world. What made capitalism different from previous transformations was its speed of diffusion and its global reach across cultures, classes, and geography. This speed and scope converted capitalism into a system of consistent technical advances called the industrial revolution.

This transformation was driven by a change in the meaning and the use of information. Historically knowledge had always been applied for the purpose of intellectual pursuit, i.e., to the process of being. What made the industrial revolution different is that information was applied to making things, i.e., knowledge was applied to tools, processes and products. This change in the use of knowledge created the industrial revolution.

In its second phase, starting at the beginning of the twentieth century, knowledge gained a new meaning as it began to be applied to the work itself. This ushered in the Productivity Revolution, which in seventy-five years converted Marx's proletarian into a middle-class with an income level that was close to the upper class.[1]

## Frederick W. Taylor (1856-1915)

Frederick W. Taylor

History has proven Karl Marx to be a false prophet, in fact, the very opposite of what he predicted has happened. However, in the late nineteenth century many of his contemporaries shared his view of capitalism, even if they did not share his prediction of the outcome. Even those who spoke out most strongly against Marx's views accepted his analysis of the inherent contradictions of capitalism. Some of the industrialists, such as J.P. Morgan, were convinced that the military would keep the proletarian in check. Almost every intellectual of the late nineteenth century shared with Marx the conviction that capitalist society was a society of inevitable class conflict. However, as we have encountered throughout the history of economics, something developed to overcome the "inevitable contradictions of capitalism," the "alienation" and "immiseration" of the laboring class. The answer according to Peter Drucker, one of America's most prolific modern day writers, was the Productivity Revolution.[2]

The Productivity Revolution began in America in 1881 when Frederick Winslow Taylor first applied knowledge to the study of work, the analysis of work, and the engineering of work. This new field of study was soon to be called Scientific Management; a term that was first used in 1910 at hearings before the International Commerce Commission.

Scientific management represented the utilization of research as an approach to the solution of management problems. Scientific management stressed standardization of product and process; better organization, coordination and control of workers, materials, and machines. It also meant rigid production planning in factories, time and motion studies, incentive plans and selection and training of workers.

What got Taylor to start on the study of work was his shock at the mutual and growing hatred between capitalists and workers, which had begun to dominate economic discussion in the late nineteenth century. Taylor saw in these class conflicts what Marx and others saw, but he also saw what they failed to see; that the conflict was unnecessary. Taylor then set out to make workers more productive so that they would earn increased wages. Taylor's motivation was not efficiency in production or the creation of more wealth for the owners. His main motivation was the creation of a society in which owners and workers, capitalists and proletarians could share a common interest in productivity and could build a harmonious relationship on the application of knowledge to work.[3]

In the 1880's, Taylor began to make his initial experiments. At that time he was employed as the assistant foreman in the machine shop of the Midvale Steel Company. Taylor started by studying each job in order to ascertain scientifically the "one best way" of performing it. After determining the best way to do a job, he developed a set of rules for each worker to follow. Taylor's initial goal was to measure and specify a proper day's work for each operation. On the basis of this goal, he began to experiment by controlling all the variables in the actual production process in order to discover the most productive working conditions for one group of workers in one particular task.

Taylor almost immediately achieved success with his method as output began to increase without any additional effort on the part of the workers. After succeeding in increasing the productivity of a single group of workers, Taylor began to broaden his horizon. He perceived that jobs in all work places could be standardized and that operations behind the worker could be coordinated in order to facilitate the flow of work. This standardization meant that the output for each job could be measured against a predetermined benchmark and that operational flows could be coordinated so that men and machines would no longer be inactive between job operations. To implement his theory, Taylor instituted special training in order to secure the most effective performance and coordination of all operations at each work station. Thus planning, preparation, training and cooperation was added to measurement and standardization as elements of managerial technique.[4]

In its initial stages scientific management, as developed by Taylor, was basically concerned with the production function. However, after World War I, the movement broadened and began to aim for more rational utilization of all the elements in the factors of production, i.e., materials, labor and machinery. The various problems of management were approached analytically and studied in more detail than ever before. Business enterprise began paying more attention to functions such as sales forecasting, cost accounting, statistical quality control, and budgeting and personnel administration.

## PRODUCTIVITY AND THE AUTOMOBILE

One of the major changes brought about by the productivity revolution was its effect on the American worker. The industrial revolution concentrated on improving productivity by substituting machines for labor. The productivity revolution concentrated on making people themselves more productive. Many industries would serve as an example of the increase in manufacturing growth, but no case offers a better illustration of the sweep, the dynamics and the effects of industrialization and technological development than the history of the American automobile industry.

The automotive industry began in the late nineteenth century, and within a single generation, expanded into a giant of mass production. To describe how this change was accomplished is to describe the basics of industrialization; the factors that made industrialization possible, the long lasting process of invention, the fulfillment of mass production, the development of scientific management and the adaptation of these changes to the business enterprise.

The basis for the gasoline-driven automobile came in 1876, when a German inventor patented the four-cycle engine. Gottfried Daimler applied the new technology to motorcycles in 1885 and Karl Benz built a motor car in the same year. The United States adopted the contributions made to the automobile by foreigners, modified them and added the "American System" of mass production. Shortly after the turn of the century, America became by far the largest producer of automobiles. The vast area of the United States lent itself ideally to the use of the automobile, and a road system would soon be developed to take advantage of this new method of transportation. The American middle class was greater in number than that of any European nation. This offered the potential supplier of automobiles a mass market especially if the price could be brought in line with the purchasing power of this group. Also, the raw materials necessary for automotive manufacturing either were available in the United States or could be purchased abroad.[5]

The initial phase of this industry is analogous to a household industry with automobiles being produced in an individual's garage or small business establishment, and usually by a mechanic. Ransom E. Olds was the first man to attempt to manufacture rather than build automobiles. Olds believed that the principles used in manufacturing carriages could be applied to automobiles. This meant buying automotive parts in quantity and assembling them into a finished product. In 1899, Olds opened an automotive assembly plant in Detroit. However, after one year in Detroit, Olds moved to Lansing, Michigan, and in 1901 he began mass producing a $650 Oldsmobile by buying parts in quantity and assembling them on a moving assembly line. Olds was the first person in the automobile industry to use the division of labor, the first to use the moving assembly line, and the first to bring the materials to the worker instead of the worker to the materials. With this new process of assembly, Olds sold 5,000 cars in 1904.

By 1903, the pioneer work in mass production had been accomplished. The assembly line, interchangeable parts, precision instruments, machine tools, material routing, and machine layout had all been developed. The automobile industry was ready to expand into mass production.[6]

At the turn of the century, substantial progress was being made in incorporating mass production methods into the production of engines, bodies, and parts. Ransom Olds bought most of his engines from the Leland Faulconer Manufacturing Company in these years. The company's owner, Henry M. Leland believed that manufacturing a standardized engine with interchangeable parts was possible and practical. In 1903, Leland took over the Henry Ford Company and began to manufacture the Cadillac. This was the first automobile that adopted interchangeable parts successfully.

## Henry Ford (1863-1948

Henry Ford

While Olds and Leland were the pioneers in introducing mass production methods in the automobile industry, Henry Ford carried mass production much further. Ford's great contribution was the emphasis he placed on a combination of timeliness and accuracy through such improvements as standardization, the moving assembly line, material handling, and the careful timing of the manufacturing process. By 1908, most automobile manufacturers were producing high-priced cars. Ford decided that there was a greater opportunity for profit in the mass production of low-priced cars. As an example of his philosophy, Ford once said, "We were going to build one model. The chassis would be exactly the same for all cars," and he continued, "Any customer can have a car painted any color he wants so long as it is black."[7]

Ford began to manufacture the Model-T, which was a completely standardized automobile that retailed well within the price range of the middle class worker. Ford's Model-T completely dominated the market in these early years, but competition was beginning to develop. W.C. Durant had bought the Buick Company in 1904 and, in 1908 he combined Buick, Olds, Cadillac and several other manufacturers into a holding company which he named "General Motors." The competition between Ford and General Motors was intense, but at first Ford prevailed. In 1915 the Ford motor company produced 35 percent of the nation's total output of 880,000 motor vehicles, and by 1923, he produced 57 percent of the four million cars and trucks that were sold.

Led by Ford, the automobile business embarked upon the most spectacular mass production operation in history. This was the heroic age, the era of the industrial capitalist and an untapped market, a period of rapid plant expansion, extensive technological innovation, and substantial increases in productivity. In less than 20 years, the automobile industry emerged from nowhere to become by far America's leading industry. Only 200,000 automobiles were registered in 1908. By 1927 there was over 23 million automobiles registered.[8]

By 1923, it was apparent that the heroic age of the automobile business was clearly ending. Durant's strategy was to increase production to the point of growth for growths' sake. Ford was obsessed with production, to the exclusion of all other aspects of the business. Each, it was said, ran his company in a state of anarchy. However, by the early 1920's the style of management began to change as Alfred P. Sloan, Jr. took over the direction of General Motors, revised its objectives and reorganized its structure and administration. Sloan enlisted his executives in a real partnership. The entrepreneurial decision makers in General Motors were concerned with long-run objectives rather than the day-to-day activity of the firm. The whole managerial hierarchy attempted to approach problems in a systematic, orderly fashion. In summary, Sloan was the first industrialist to bring management techniques to the automotive industry. Ford had nothing but contempt for this new style of management, but the times were changing and Ford was not keeping up with the changes.

Twenty years of high-volume production in the automotive industry had ravished the virgin market that Ford had originally envisioned. At first automobiles had been price elastic that is total revenue would increase when prices were decreased as a result of an even larger increase in demand. However, the evolution of the used-car market, development of installment credit, and a market that was becoming saturated began to make prices inelastic. When the price becomes inelastic, corporations must adjust their strategy to emphasize the differences in product features and the quality. Product differentiation through advertising and promotion, and credits become more important in a market structure that had become what economists refer to as "Monopolistic Competition." As the industry matured, it became much more concentrated. During the period of

1903 through 1926, there were almost 180 companies that produced cars. Only 11 companies survived the entire period. Thus, by the end of the decade, the automotive industry was well on its way to becoming the country's largest oligopoly.

## THE FIRST LARGE MERGER WAVE (1898-1906)

The years around the turn of the nineteenth century marked a period of business consolidation that was considerably different from the previous decades. Business firms continued to grow at a fast pace, but they increased their size more through mergers than internal growth. Many more corporations went public in these years and new methods were developed for dealing with the competition. By the outbreak of World War I, the large, bureaucratic, and oligopolistic corporation, had become the dominant institution in the marketplace. By the beginning of the twentieth century the importance of the industrial capitalist was reduced and their type of business system could clearly not continue without a serious modification. By 1900, most of the flamboyant, owner-entrepreneurs who were the catalysts for the growth that began in the 1870's, had retired from active business life.[9]

The old industrial capitalist was slowly being replaced by the new business managers and steps were being taken to change the existing corporate structure and to overcome some of its weaknesses. Frequently the catalyst for this change was the investment banker of the era. These bankers had previously participated in the railroad and textile businesses, but as the nineteenth century came to an end, that intervention became more frequent. The investment bankers brought with them a management philosophy that was quite different from the industrialist. The investment bankers spread their influence over many industries instead of concentrating on just one industry. As a result, investment bankers were more interested in financial policy than in any other aspect of business activity. These bankers were, in a sense, portfolio managers who were not interested in production or distribution techniques.

Because the bankers and industrialists were so different, they tended to dislike and distrust each other. For example, J.P. Morgan is said to have once stated that Carnegie was a dangerous man who had demoralized the steel industry. For his part, Carnegie abhorred promoters and is said to have boasted that he could operate a steel business better than a lot of "stock-jobbers" who paid more attention to security manipulation than to steel making. However, whether the industrial capitalist liked the investment bankers was almost immaterial as far as economic growth was concerned, for the bankers controlled very large amounts of funds and with these dollars they acted as the catalytic agent in the development and growth of large business concerns in the early 1900's.

In American history, mergers occurred in three great waves; the first between 1898 and 1906, the second in the 1920's and the third following World War II and into the 1970's. The first of these merger waves, however, was the most important of the three to American economic history. All of the giant corporations that appeared in the early 1900's were for the most part a result of these mergers. During these years, more than 3,200 mergers took place in the manufacturing and mining industries and twenty-two firms including such names as United States Steel, American Tobacco, American Smelting and Refining and American Can, grew to massive size as a result of merger.[10]

Overall, business mergers were the result of the same basic causes that had produced vertical combinations in the previous decades. The major objective of these mergers was to gain control over the market and to eliminate competition. By 1900, concentration had gone far enough to alter the basic structure of the market. Sporadic price cutting still occurred, but, overall, prices were beginning to conform to the goals of the new business leaders. That is, prices were not set high enough to encourage competitors to expand or new firms to enter the market, and prices were not low enough to set off a destructive price war.

Businessmen also used mergers in an attempt to stop declining profit margins. These business leaders often assumed that large-scale enterprises created by mergers could gain substantial economies that were not available to smaller businesses. It was commonly believed that the economies of mass production were endless. These "economies of scale," as economists called them, could be achieved both in production and administration. The large firm had decided advantages in buying raw materials and in distribution of goods. The advantages achieved through economies of scale resulted in large companies having lower unit costs than smaller competitors.

Today, after the third wave of mergers and consolidations, we have learned that being bigger does not always mean operating more efficiently. Most probably, the initial growth of business firms in this era, lowered the unit costs of production. However, once an individual plant had passed its optimum size, further opportunities to reduce unit cost, were not available. The multiple plant organizational structure sometimes enabled firms to achieve further economies, but this too would end as firms, as well as the individual plants, passed beyond the point of diminishing returns.

Some businessmen who participated in these mergers were empire builders whose purpose was growth for growths sake. Others were motivated by the prospect of making financial profits on security transactions, but when economic logic took a back seat to financial analysis or growth, mergers often turned out disastrously. In fact, about half of the major mergers that were completed during this period, ended in failure. The reason for many of these failures is that the companies were put together as conglomerates not as diversified companies. The common link, in most conglomerates, is financial performance. In other words, there is no "synergy" between the separate companies within the organization. Once the economies of scale are depleted, there is no common bond between the units that make up the conglomerate. For example, if a conglomerate made up of two companies, was to each show a profit of $100, then the combined profit will be $200. In a diversified company where synergy exists, common functions such as selling, advertising, and research and development can often be combined in a way that will result in the profit of the entire company being greater than the contribution of its individual parts. Therefore, with diminishing returns from production and the lack of synergy between the individual units, the act of combining these companies into a conglomerate, serves no economic purpose. This is the basic reason that in the early 1900's, so many of these business combinations failed.

# WORLD WAR I AND THE INTERNATIONAL ECONOMY

Compared with the Civil War, considerably more armaments, munitions, and armored vehicles were used in World War I. Because it was far more mechanized than the Civil War, World War I required a greater industrial effort and much more government planning. New industries had to be created, old industries converted, and new facilities were built to provide the necessary tools of war. The federal government for the first time engaged in economic planning and set up elaborate controls to regulate the economy. The whole civilian population was affected to a far greater extent than in any previous war in American history.

When war broke out in Europe in 1914, it was almost a surprise to the nations involved. A conflict between the industrial countries of Europe was thought to be extremely improbable or at worst, if one did occur, it would be short. This was because the costs of a worldwide war would be too great. However, even the most pessimistic forecasts of the length and cost of World War I, was apparently drastically underestimated. One of the major awakenings brought about by the hostilities was the realization that the belligerents at one time were the other's best customers. The war shattered the network of international trade and monetary agreements that were critical to Europe's industrial development.

The Germans had originally planned to defeat the French before they could receive aid from Britain and Russia. However, this strategy failed because Russia mobilized much faster than the Germans expected. Consequently, the war in Western Europe became a bloody stalemate. The war soon became a conflict of endurance. The nation that could sustain its military efforts longest would have the best chance of winning the war. Once this was determined, the European belligerents attempted to divert their productive capacities towards producing more military equipment and destroying their enemy's military efforts.

All of the combating nations soon found their ability to produce was inadequate for both consumer requirements and the war's enormous demands. By 1916, the British Naval blockade became so effective that trade between Germany and North America was almost nonexistent. However, as the war needs rose, the allied nations (Britain, France and Russia), began looking to the United States (the only major industrial nation that was not at war), for economic assistance. By 1916, the flood of orders from the Allies began to overwhelm even the American productive capacity. The United States Administration was hesitant to assist the European Allies at first as Woodrow Wilson wished to remain neutral. However, Wilson eventually relaxed his opposition and let American manufacturers respond to the European demand. American exports began to rapidly increase to meet the European demand and to supply traditional European export markets such as Latin America. From 1914 to 1917, total United States exports to Europe, in current dollars, rose from $1,486 million to $4,062 million, an increase of 173 percent, while imports from Europe during the same period actually declined. This created a large negative merchandise balance of trade between the United States and Europe.

**Financing World War I**

In international trade and finance, a negative balance of trade must be financed through what is known as a country's international capital account. A negative balance of payments can only be financed through the reduction of a country's assets or by borrowing. Europe had traditionally made up its deficit in direct trade with the United States by running surpluses with nations from which America was a net importer. However, by 1916, this method of financing their trade deficit was no longer available. Europe had few goods to export to any region because most of their production capacity was devoted to the war effort. Therefore, to finance their imports, the Allies had to liquidate their American assets by shipping gold to the United States and selling their portfolios of American securities. As their assets became depleted, the Allies turned to the only means left to finance their imports, to borrow from America.

To finance their imports from America, British and French bonds were sold directly to private citizens in the United States. The firm of J.P. Morgan & Co. was active in purchasing war material on behalf of the French and British governments. In total, the Allies sold their holdings of United States securities worth $4 billion, shipped over $1 billion in gold, and borrowed almost $5 billion from private sources in America, to finance the war. After America entered the war, the U.S. government loaned the Allies another $9.5 billion. From a large-scale debtor through most of the nineteenth century, the United States had been transformed, in just a few years, into the world's largest international creditor.[11]

## The Wars Impact on the American Farmer

Because European demands for meat and grain were increasing, American farmers had to increase their agricultural production. The high demand for agriculture products was supplemented by government guaranteed prices after the United States entered the war in April of 1917. The combination of increased demand and higher farm prices encouraged farmers to expand production by putting less productive land to use. Farmers also purchased additional amounts of machinery that enabled them to produce more with less labor. A great deal of this expansion was financed by borrowing, which appeared to be a safe investment, while farm prices were rising. However, increases in real production in farming require time and agricultural production had shown only slight increases before 1918, but prices for most farm products had nearly doubled since 1914.[12]

World War I brought the farmer unprecedented prosperity, despite the fact that he had greatly expanded production. However, the farmer's new prosperity could only last as long as prices of agricultural products remained high. The additional cost of new machinery, placing less productive land into use and the interest on borrowed funds resulted in a large increase in farm production costs. An industry can only continue to operate in this way as long as demand is strong and prices are high.

Immediately following World War I, European demand for agricultural products fell substantially as they resumed their own production. Domestically, consumers began to spend a smaller percentage of their income on food as more durable goods became available. In the face of declining demand, farmers were unwilling or unable to reduce production sufficiently enough to prevent prices from falling drastically. Thus, the combination of high fixed costs, reduced demand and low prices resulted in some serious problems for the farmers after World War I.

## April 1917, the United States Enters the War

After 1916, the United States industry was operating at almost full capacity. Therefore, increased output of military goods could only be achieved by diverting resources from the production of consumer goods to the production of military goods. The task was further complicated by the diversion of labor into the armed forces. The prewar military strength of the United States had been about 165,000 men, but by 1918, the Army and Navy alone expanded to nearly three million.[10] This military expansion required almost 7 percent of the American labor force. Unemployment in the United States had almost vanished by 1918. This was because a large portion of the labor force was now employed by the military, and the demand for goods and services from the Allies had substantially increased.

Since the demands of the American and Allied military and those of the civilian population, far exceeded the available production capacity, a system of priorities was necessary. To meet this requirement, a series of government boards was established. Because of the strain of a huge increase in traffic traveling mostly to the east coast, the Federal government took over the management and operation of all United States railroads. Food purchases for the Allies were consolidated under the Food Administration with Herbert Hoover in charge. The Shipping Board and the Emergency Fleet Corporation took over the building of merchant ships and coordinated maritime traffic.

In total, the Wilson administration created several thousand Federal agencies in order to coordinate the war effort. The job of tying together the work of all these agencies was given to the War Industries Board, under the direction of Bernard Baruch. The War Industries Board made some progress in standardizing designs of tools and persuading some defense contractors to accept these modifications. However, the War Industries Board had two major problems in developing an effective plan for coordinating the war effort. First, there was little information available on the war needs as the United States had never fought in a major war on European soil, and secondly, there was a lack of industrial capacity to meet the war needs. Even when priorities were established, they were difficult to maintain, because the War Industries Board had no authority over prices, and many customers were far more concerned over output than prices. This was not a situation that encouraged producers to voluntarily comply with the Board by controlling prices for there was almost unlimited demand for their products.

In general, the success of the War Industries Board in controlling prices and allocating resources was at best only moderate. However, their success in achieving cooperation between the firms in some industries would be a factor in the trade association movement of the 1920's.

## The United States After World War I

When World War I ended, the United States had to assume a new global position. This new position was as the financial and the industrial leader of the world. However, the United States was totally unprepared for this was a role. In addition, the United States had accumulated some wartime legacies of its own; for example, inflation, over capacity in agriculture, shipbuilding, and the coal industry, plus a large war induced public debt. Yet in 1919, none of these problems seemed serious to most Americans especially when compared with the problems of the Europeans. However, signs were beginning to appear that the United States was almost as unprepared for their new role as the leader of the industrial world as they were prepared to enter a world war in 1916.

## NOTES:

## Chapter 11

## Scientific Management, Mass Production and WW I

1.    Drucker, Peter F., <u>Post Capitalist Society,</u> New York, NY, HarperCollins, 1993, p. 19.
2.    Drucker, p. 34.
3.    Drucker, p. 35
4.    Drucker, p. 32.
5.    Krooss, Herman, E. <u>American Economic Development</u>, Englewood Cliffs, NJ, Prentice-Hall,    1966, p. 380.
6.    Krooss, p. 382.
7.    Ford Henry, <u>My Life and Work</u>, Garden City, N.Y.,  Doubleday & Co., 1992, pp. 91-92.
8.    Krooss, p. 384.
9.    Krooss, p. 171.
10.   Nelson, R.L., <u>Merger Movements in American Industry,    1895 - 1956</u>, Princeton, NJ, Princeton  University Press,   1959.
11.   Puth, Robert C., <u>American Economic History, Third Edition</u>, Fort Worth, TX, The Dryden Press, 1993,   p.     492.
12.   U.S. Department of Commerce, Bureau of the Census, <u>Historical Statistics of the United States</u>, Washington, DC, Government Printing Office, 1975, Volume 1 - p. 511.

# CHAPTER 12

---

# THE ROARING TWENTIES -
# PROSPERITY AND DEPRESSION

*"The depression must be allowed to run its course. Recovery was something that always came by itself and our analysis leads us to believe that recovery is sound only if it does come of itself." —Joseph Schumpeter*

## THE CHANGING CORPORATE STRUCTURE

In the nineteenth century, both the internal business structure and its external environment were relatively simple. Most businesses, with the exception of the railroads, were small and were run by an owner-manager. Labor unions were weak and almost non-existent for non-skilled workers and government was friendly. In the twentieth century, the ownership of the large corporation changed and became increasingly more widely dispersed. The professional manager began to replace the entrepreneur and the investment banker as the person in control of large corporate enterprise. This, in turn, resulted in a whole series of new corporate problems such as the separation of ownership from control, the corporate hierarchy and the corporate bureaucracy.

The behavior of the marketplace was also very different in the twentieth century. The market changed because population growth slowed and consumers demanded more diversification in the products they purchased, and in the method of financing the purchases. In response to the changing market demands, corporations had to develop a whole new bag of selling tricks. Departments were developed in major companies with the responsibility of marketing products to consumers. Corporations began to intensify their advertising campaigns in an attempt to convince potential consumers of the quality of their products. They began to search for markets overseas. They created new products through research and development, and they diversified by branching out into entirely new businesses. Competition became more of a struggle between marketing departments to differentiate their products based on real or perceived differences and less emphasis was placed on pricing. Internally, the centralized organization of the industrial capitalist gave way to the decentralized organization of the career manager.[1]

By the 1920's, most large firms were still centrally organized and still dealt in a single product. However, to protect themselves against future business cycles and changing consumer demand, many businesses began to diversify. Some pioneering business owners began to recognize that diversification required an entirely different kind of managerial approach. The DuPont Company's reaction to the trend towards diversification can be used to illustrate how strategy and structure changed in this very successful firm.

Following World War I, DuPont's managers felt that further expansion in their main product explosives was not attractive because of decreased demand. The company, therefore, began to diversify its investments, which included the purchase of a substantial share of General Motors stock, and it began to manufacture and market new products through existing departments such as chemicals, paints, celluloid, dyestuff, and synthetic fibers. However, it was soon discovered that their existing department structure could not be used efficiently to produce and market many different products.

To resolve this problem, in 1921 DuPont adopted a new structure of five autonomous divisions, which were cellulose, paint, purolin, dyestuff and explosives. Each of these new divisions was run by a general manager, with its own staff and with the responsibility for day-to-day operations. This placed the responsibility of production and marketing at the division level. The central office was then given the responsibility of developing strategy for managing the firm in the long run.

During the 1920's, the second merger wave began. There were several differences between the mergers of the 1920's and those of the

1890's. In the 1890's, mergers were between very large corporations within the same industry. The goal of these mergers was monopoly. In the 1920's, mergers were usually between middle size companies and the goal was oligopoly. A second difference was that, in the 1920's, bank mergers, in addition to the mergers that had already taken place in manufacturing, mining and transportation, became popular. Finally, mergers for the purpose of diversification became one of the dominant reasons for combining corporations. In summary during the 1920's, the entrepreneur in large corporate business was replaced by the professional manager. Diversification into new products and markets became the dominant reason for corporate mergers, and the major form of corporate business became the oligopoly.

## THE NEW CENTRAL BANK - FEDERAL RESERVE SYSTEM

In the early part of the twentieth century money was still seen in these years as a largely neutral intermediary that facilitated the exchange process. Also, the Central Bank, the most elegant example being the Bank of England, was able to control any unduly liberal lending and deposit creation activities that might jeopardize the ability of the individual banks to redeem their deposits in gold. If lending and the resulting money creation seemed too liberal, government bonds from the portfolio of the Central Bank could be sold to reduce the money stock.

In 1913, after nearly 80 years, it had become possible to face down populist suspicion in the United States and establish a Central bank. The Federal Reserve Act of 1913, created the Federal Reserve System of twelve banks that were geographically placed throughout the country. Control over the system was given to the Board of Governors of the Federal Reserve System that was located in Washington, DC.

At first the Federal Reserve Board was primarily an administrative agency with little control over the system's operations. Even the power to rediscount was not centrally controlled but was dispersed throughout the 12 district banks. The original purpose of congress in creating the Federal Reserve System seems to have been to improve the commercial banking machinery, rather than to exercise a major influence over the economy. However, within a few years after its inception, the Federal Reserve System began to abandon its passive role as a mere helpmate for the commercial banks and took on a more active role in guiding the economy. During the 1920's the Federal Reserve developed another extremely important tool to help regulate the money supply and therefore, in theory, the growth of the economy. This tool was in the form of open market operations. When member banks did not find it necessary to borrow from the Fed because of the low level of business borrowing, the System, in order to maintain its revenue, began to buy government securities and found that this tactic had an important impact on member bank reserves. At first, each district bank carried on its own open market operations; but under the leadership of Benjamin Strong, the Governor of the New York Federal Reserve Bank, a committee was formed in April of 1923 to coordinate the activities of all the district banks. By 1923, the Federal Reserve had begun to develop a theory to control credit and the money supply. The general aim of the new policy was to provide credit freely enough to encourage business expansion, but not freely enough to encourage speculation.[2]

## THE PRIMARY CAUSES OF THE GREAT DEPRESSION

Historians have searched with little success for that one thing that caused the depression of 1929. Blame has been placed on the distortions caused by World War I, the problems of the farmers, the overproduction of consumer durable goods, the stock market crash of 1929 and the inappropriate policies of the federal government. However, the real cause of the great depression is most probably a combination of all of the above events. Therefore, each of these occurrences will be examined separately, while at the same time keeping in mind that it was a series of situations that contributed to the length and severity of the depression.

### The Distortions Caused by World War I

After World War I, the major problem that faced the American economy was inflation. The federal government did very little to plan for this situation and failed to act effectively to control inflation. The stored up demand for consumer goods and the increased expenditures for new construction created an economic boom after the war. However, the combination of new technology and new management techniques in manufacturing increased production to a rate that was greater than the current demand. The result of this over production was a buildup in manufacturing inventories that led to a mild downturn starting in January of 1920. The Federal Reserve acted to the mild contraction by reducing the growth of the money supply. This was the wrong policy as a reduction of the money supply leads to a reduction of the demand for consumer durable goods and a reduction in business investment in new plant and equipment. The result of the business contraction and the policies of the Federal Reserve was a sharp reduction in prices. Production declined especially in the fall of 1920 and as a result of this reduction in output, nearly 10 percent of the labor force was unemployed at the bottom of this depression.

The depression bottomed out  in July of 1921, some eighteen months after it had begun. Sales began to pick up and manufacturers began once again to build up their inventories. The recovery gathered strength and continued through the 1920's, with only minor pauses in 1924 and 1927.[3]

Although the American contribution to World War I was large both in financial and human costs, it was far less than the European belligerents. However, what was more important in the long run to the American economy were the structural changes that were brought about by the war. The most significant of these changes was the dramatic enhancement of America's position in the international economy. The war pushed America to a position of dominance so swiftly that serious international instability resulted. America was placed in the position of the world's leading economy, a position that it was totally unprepared to handle.

**The Problems in Agriculture**

For the farmers, favorable conditions had persisted for almost two decades, from the turn of the century through 1919. On the basis of past events, farmers began to expect continued strong demand for their products and rising prices. After World War I, American farmers, expecting continued prosperity made large investments in farmland. In so doing, farmers were behaving much like large scale manufacturers with large investments in additional, often marginal land, and machinery. This continuing investment in fixed assets caused farmers to become extremely vulnerable to a reduction in prices. Individual farmers control only a small percent of the marketplace for agricultural products. Therefore, they do not, for all practical purposes, have any influence over the price of farm products. Therefore, the only way they can maintain a level of income high enough to cover a large investment in fixed costs, is to increase production. The reason for this is based on the simple business formula of (Revenue = Price x Quantity). If the farmer has no control over price, then the only other option available to him is to increase quantity, or in this case production. However, if all farmers increased production at the same time, this will lead to an over supply of farm products, which in turn will result in prices being reduced even further.

In June of 1920, farm prices began to drop sharply and with it the dreams and fortunes of many farmers. Those farmers who had expanded production and increased their land holdings during the periods of prosperity now found themselves heavily in debt and in many instances were not able to cover fixed expenses. During the remainder of the 1920's, farm prices continued well below what they were at the turn of the century. This resulted in a reduction of purchasing power of farmers to about three-quarters of what they had experienced during World War I. Consequently, agriculture's share of the national income was also in decline. In summary, the American farmer was in a state of depression long before the great depression began, and they never recovered before suffering further blows in the 1930's.

## Overproduction of Consumer Durable Goods

The 1920's was a time when consumers shifted their household demands dramatically to the purchase of durable goods on credit. During the 1920's a host of new electrical household gadgets appeared. To purchase the new consumer durable goods, Americans began to use installment-plan buying, instead of saving for future purchases. However, when consumers buy items on credit, it increases the overall expense of the purchase because interest payments are added to the cost of the product. Buying on credit shifts consumption from the future to the present and at the same time reduces the consumers' long term buying power. For example, the extended use of installment-plan buying in the 1920's was so great that 75 percent of automobiles, 70 percent of furniture and 80 percent of household appliances were purchased on credit. A permanent new "American Way of Life" was born, financed by innovations in the country's financial institutions and a desire by consumers to enjoy now and pay later.

In addition to installment plan purchases, there was a housing boom during the 1920's. Mass production of automobiles brought their price within the range of the middle class worker and the improved roads led the way to the development of the suburbs. This led to a large increase in residential construction outside of the cities. The great building boom of the 1920's raised total income generated from construction by almost 80 percent. The value of new construction permits rose by almost 190 percent between 1919 and 1926. However, building construction in both residential and non-residential units is subject to long cycles of growth. A.F. Burns and Wesley C. Mitchell in the publication "Measuring Business Cycles," concluded that building cycles are regular, predictable and usually last, in America, from 18 to 22 years. When the construction boom stopped in 1926, it was not halted by rising building costs, demand simply dried up. It was not the case that the country was suffering from an excess of housing, but, given the existing distribution of family incomes, demand was exhausted.[4]

During the 1920's, as previously discussed, there was another wave of mergers that resulted in even more concentration in business. This concentration led to increased market power and a tendency for manufacturers to keep prices at a level that increased corporate profits but reduced consumer purchasing power. This resulted in an income distribution that was highly in favor of corporate executives, at the expense of the middle class workers. This along with the reduction in the rate of population growth was the reason that consumer demand for durable goods began to decline in the summer of 1929. However, the manufacturing sector did not react to the reduced consumer demand by decreasing production. This resulted in a large stockpile of inventories, which in turn, led to a reduction in economic growth, in the summer of 1929. A downturn in economic activity had begun. However, the reduction in growth, from the loss in demand in both the construction and consumer durable goods industries, would probably have resulted in a downturn that was similar in size and magnitude to the depression of 1921.

**The Stock Market Crash of 1929**

Since the latter part of 1927, the stock market prices had been seriously inflated. When choosing a corporate stock, an investor can use two different types of analysis; a fundamental analysis of the company's potential growth or a technical analysis based on charting the company's or markets past growth. During the latter part of the 1920's, the investing public began to ignore the fundamentals and began to bet on the future growth of the stock market based strictly on a technical analysis. In other words, investors feeling confident about the current level of stock market prices, became convinced that they would continue to increase in the future. However, there were at least three sources of weakness in the stock market that made it vulnerable to a potentially large correction.[5]

The first weakness was the makeup of the investment public and the method used to finance the purchase of stocks. Most of the additional money that was coming into the stock market was from those individuals and organizations that were new to the market. Their interest was not long term capital gains, but short term profits. Although some of the new investment originated in the commercial banking system, a greater portion of the investment was from foreign banking agencies, corporations with large cash balances, brokers, and individuals searching for short term profits. Adding to this potential problem was the method in which the stocks were purchased. Individual investors could invest on margin; that is they would borrow up to 90 percent of the price of the stock, in order to make the purchase. This method of funding a purchase is called financial leverage. Financial leverage will benefit the investor as long as the price of the stock increases at a rate greater than the interest paid on the loan. However, if the price of the stock goes down, financial leverage will greatly increase the size of the loss.

In addition, stock purchases on margin usually contain a call feature. The broker borrows the money that is lent to an investor from a bank with the provision that the bank can demand payment of the loan by the broker on very short notice. Also, the broker's loan to the investor requires that the purchaser of stock, on margin, maintain a certain portion of the price of the security, in an account with the broker. The market value of the stock is used by the broker as collateral for the loan to the investor. If the price of a stock goes down, the broker will request that the investor place more cash in the broker's account. Therefore, when an investor purchases stock on margin, he risks the loss of market value and the loss of cash, if the price of the stock goes down. In fact, if there is a major reduction in the value of all traded corporate stock, everyone involved in the margin purchase loses; the investor loses value and cash, the broker cannot pay off its loans with its banks and the banks must reduce their assets and equity by the amount of any loans that have to be written off.

A second source of weakness was a new financial institution called the investment trust. The investment trusts were similar in nature to our modern day mutual funds. They were non-operating companies that purchased stocks for their own account and offered its own stock to the small investor. Because of the newness of the investment trust, they were not subject to government regulation. Furthermore, these trusts relied heavily on debt financing. This made their own stocks very attractive in a bull market, but very risky in a down market. Consequently, these highly leveraged investment trusts were vulnerable to any hint of weakness in the market. The trusts contributed to the burst of unmatched growth in the late 1920's and, in the process, made the market even more top-heavy. In addition, because many of the investment trusts were owned and promoted by commercial banks, the stock market crash was a contributing factor to the coming crisis in the banking industry.

A final source of weakness was the activities of the stock market "insiders" and the lack of regulation of this group of investors. These insiders were usually made up of groups of exchange members who represented syndicates of large investors. They would choose a particular stock and bid up its price without regard to the fundamental earnings capacity of the company. Once the price of the stock rose significantly, the insiders would sell the stock short (betting that the price of the stock would go down) before the price returned to its natural value. The lack of regulation of brokerage firms allowed the insiders to feed the bull market of 1927-1929, which added a further measure of instability to the market. Also, lack of regulation jeopardized the capital of many investors who had been duped by the insiders and their brokers.

The stock market, during the late 1920's, had become the symbol of the nation's prosperity and economic strength. Also, the stock market was the embodiment, of the faith of millions, in the ability of corporations to sustain that well-being. When the stock market crashed all the frenzy that had stretched out over two years in sending stocks up was concentrated in a few incredible weeks, beating prices down. On Tuesday, October 29, 1929, an avalanche of selling crushed the stock exchanges. Goldman Sachs, a highly regarded investment trust, lost almost half of its market value on this day. In a single day, the increase in the value of traded stocks of the entire preceding year had been wiped out and millions of individual investors who, based on their previous paper gains, thought they were well off, were faced with the reality of being poor.

When the bubble burst in October of 1929, Americans' optimism changed and they became pessimistic about the future. The impact of the crash was to sharpen and prolong the crisis of confidence that grew worse as the depression dragged on between 1929 and 1933. The depression became self-perpetuating. The longer it continued, the more dismal were the prospects for recovery. The stock market crash contributed to the length and severity of the depression by providing tangible proof of the weakness of the American economy.

## Monetary Policy and The Federal Reserve

Monetary policy reached the height of its prestige during the 1920's. Many economists believed that the Federal Reserve System, with its ability to expand and contract the money supply, greatly reduced the potential for depression. During the 1920's, the Federal Reserve lowered the rediscount rate (the rate charged to commercial banks on loans from the Fed), and brought government securities in the open market during the mild recession of 1924 and 1927. These actions by the Federal Reserve tend to encourage economic expansion by increasing the money supply and lowering interest rates. However, during 1928 and 1929, the Federal Reserve instituted a tight money supply in an attempt to reduce the speculative boom in the stock market. The Federal Reserve executed its tight money policy by raising the rediscount rate to 5 percent in 1928 and to 6 percent in 1929. At the same time, the Federal Reserve reduced its holdings of government securities from $620 to $145. However, the Federal Reserve's action to tighten the money supply was badly timed. Changes in monetary policy have a lagging effect on growth as they have to filter their way through the banking system. Therefore, the Federal Reserve's tight money policy, that was implemented in late 1928 and 1929, probably started to affect economic activity in the summer or fall of 1929. Thus, the tight money policy that was designed to break the back of the stock market boom, probably accomplished that purpose, but in doing so, most certainly helped to push the economy into a depression.

As soon as the depression began, the Federal Reserve reversed its tight money policy and began to supply additional reserves to the banking system by buying government securities in the open market, increasing its holdings from about $450 million in late 1929 to $1.9 billion in late 1932. At the same time, in order to encourage borrowing, the Federal Reserve lowered its rediscount rate to 1.5 percent. However, by 1932 any act by the Federal Reserve to encourage borrowing was practically useless, as the economy was in such bad shape that there was almost no demand for bank loans.

Overall, the basic problem with the Federal Reserve was the bad timing of their monetary policy. However, in October of 1931, frightened by a drain on the gold supply, The Federal Reserve raised the rediscount rate from 1.5 percent to 3.5 percent, to protect the gold reserve. From this action to reduce the flow of gold out of the country, the Federal Reserve severely limited the ability of the nation's banking system to meet domestic demands for currency by making borrowing much more expensive. This action to tighten the money supply was taken in an economic environment in which there was almost no demand for loans. In total, as a result of the Federal Reserves policies, the stock of money fell by almost one third, from August 1929 to March 1933, when the economy reached the trough of the great depression.

When the money supply is reduced significantly, national income can only be sustained at the current level if the velocity of money increases, i.e., consumers would have to spend their money faster. However, Americans responded to the depression by deferring spending and withdrawing their deposits from their banks. The increased preference for holding their savings in cash was a result of the expectation that prices would continue to fall and because consumers did not believe that banks could guarantee the safety of their deposits.

The combination of poorly conceived and poorly executed monetary policy and the lack of public confidence turned financial panics into serious banking crises in October 1930, March 1931, and January of 1933. The heavy withdrawal of deposits in each crisis produced a wave of bank failures. The failures reinforced public distrust of banks, causing each crisis to become worse than its predecessor. The problem continued to become progressively worse until in March of 1933, the bank holiday and the Emergency Banking Act caused all banks to close for at least one week to protect the system from massive deposit withdrawals.[6]

**Fiscal Policy and the Hoover Administration**

The federal government's policies were no more effective than those of the Federal Reserve during the early years of the depression. The framework of international trade collapsed as most nations, now caught up in a world wide depression, attempted to export their unemployment by raising tariffs. The United States through the Smooth-Hawley Tariff of 1930, raised its import rates and extended the range of dutiable imports to levels comparable to the high tariff era which existed before 1900. However, this strategy only served to increase worldwide unemployment, because if all major trading nations increase their tariff, no country can gain in the long run, and the economic efficiency of international comparative advantage is lost to all countries.

As for the administration, President Hoover believed that the federal government was obligated to maintain a balanced budget and that to allow revenues to fall short of expenditures for any prolonged period was a prescription for national bankruptcy. Hoover, also believed that relief payment to the unemployed without some form of work expectation, would ruin the moral fiber of the recipients.

The immediate reaction of the Hoover administration to the depression was a cut in taxes and an increase in spending on public works projects. However, the budget surplus of 1929, soon became a deficit. The administration's response to the federal deficit was to reduce spending, but the deficits continued, and in 1932 a large tax increase was enacted. Since higher taxes could only reduce an already inadequate volume of private spending, this policy was misguided. Nevertheless, it was supported by both houses of congress.

In summary, there was probably no one singular culprit that was responsible for the great depression of 1929. The depression was the result of a series of events, each adding to the length and magnitude of America's longest and most devastating economic downturn.

**NOTES:**

**Chapter 12**
**The Roaring Twenties-Prosperity and Depression**

1.  K250ss, Herman E., <u>American Economic Development</u>, Englewood Cliffs, NJ, Prentice-Hall,    Inc., 1966, p. 176.
2.  Kroos, p. 244.
3.  Brownlee, W. Elliot, <u>Dynamics of Ascent, Second   Edition</u>, Belmont, CA, Wadsworth Publishing  Company, 1988, p. 380.
4.  Hughes, Jonathan, <u>American Economic History, Third Edition</u>, Evanston, IL, 1990, p. 450.
5.  Brownlee, p. 412.
6.  Brownlee, p. 415.

# CHAPTER 13

---

# THE GREAT DEPRESSION AND THE NEW DEAL (1929-1939)

*"The only thing we have to fear is fear itself." —Franklin Delano Roosevelt*

## CLASSICAL ECONOMICS AND DEPRESSION

A singular and significant feature of the classical system was the lack of a theory of depression. The equilibrium to which the economy adjusted itself was one of full employment. This was the result to which movements in wages and prices inevitably led.

From the classical theory there could not be a remedy for a depression, if depression had been ruled out by the theory. Consequently, when the great depression struck after the stock market crash in October of 1929, economists stood aside. This was something to be waited out.

Through what remained the presidency of Herbert Hoover, until March of 1933, the economic policy of the United States followed the classical design. Recovery was expected and compulsively predicted. There was no need for action to advance the inevitable. Herbert Hoover was, in fact, in complete accord with the accepted economic ideas of his time.

However, in 1933, there was a full fledged depression that had three undeniable features as follows:

- The first was the relentless deflation in prices, with its bankrupting effect on industry and agriculture. This was especially severe on any industry that had high fixed costs.

- The second feature was unemployment. By 1933 the unemployment rate was over one quarter of the working population.

- The third was the hardship depression brought for especially vulnerable groups of the old, the young, and those in poor health.

## FRANKLIN D. ROOSEVELT (1882-1945) AND THE NEW DEAL

F. D. Roosevelt

When Franklin D. Roosevelt became president in March of 1933, the first broad line of his policy addressed the problem of prices; the second sought to aid the unemployed by providing them with jobs; and the third attempted to mitigate the hardships of the vulnerable. In this last line of policy was the idea of the Welfare State, which had come earlier to Europe and was by this time on its way to the United States. However, Roosevelt did not develop a new approach to stimulating a depressed economy in a vacuum. Roosevelt received assistance from a new breed of economic advisors who were not restrained by classical beliefs.

In Roosevelt's gubernatorial (New York) years, a small group of scholars rallied to support him. The economic advisors among these new scholars were from Columbia University and were part of a group of Roosevelt's advisors, who were often referred to as the "brain trust." Two members of the Roosevelt brain trust, Rex Tugwell and Adolph Berle, were figures of particular distinction. Rex Tugwell was a key participant in developing strategy for Roosevelt's presidential election and later served in the administration. With his academic credentials, Tugwell was in a good position to persuade Roosevelt that he could break with the classical tradition.

The second economic figure in the brain trust was Adolph Berle, who like Tugwell, was a professor at Columbia University. A lawyer, not an economist, by profession, Berle was the author, along with

Gardner C. Means, a young economist at Columbia, of an attack on the classical system of economic analysis.

The Berle and Means publication was entitled "The Modern Corporation and Private Property." It was about the management and control of the large enterprise. Their book described the current concentration of business in America. According to Berle and Means, the professional managers were now extensively in control of the modern business enterprise and their objective was often self-enrichment. This is a subject that has been previously noted as one of the reasons why major industries in the 1920's produced more than could reasonably be sold.

In the imperfect or monopolistic competition of Joan Robinson and Edward Chamberlin, the capitalist or entrepreneur still ruled and profits were still maximized. The results were not socially optimal, but they could be adapted to classical thought. The views of Berle and Means could not.

Following Roosevelt's election to the presidency, Rex Tugwell and Gardner Means immediately took government posts. Berle joined the ranks a little later. By the time Roosevelt came to office, prices had been in a devastating three year slump, and from across the country there were appeals for government action to reverse the trend. One of the first reactions by the Roosevelt administration was an attempt to stabilize the economy. These actions took the form of declaring a bank holiday in March of 1933, suspension of gold payments to increase exports, and policies developed to stabilize prices.

## ACTIONS TO STABILIZE THE ECONOMY

### Stabilizing the Banking Industry

By 1921, there were over 31,000 separate commercial banks in the United States. That number was reduced considerably because over 14,800 of these banks had failed by 1934. In 1932, there was a decline in the rate of bank failures from the previous year, but as 1933 began, pessimism started to set in and a new wave of bank failures threatened the collapse of the entire system. When the depression began, demand deposits held with commercial banks or savings and loan associations, were not insured by the federal government. Because they feared a loss of deposits if their bank failed, large numbers of people were going, into banks and demanding their deposits. In a fractional banking system, such as ours, deposits are put to work making loans. This results in a balance sheet where deposits are vastly in excess of actual currency. Banking is based on the theory that all depositors will not want to withdraw their funds at the same time. However, if a majority of a bank's depositors demanded an immediate withdrawal of funds, the bank would become insolvent and therefore, would be required to stop doing business.

By March 4, of 1933, a run on the nation's banks caused such a financial panic that most of the banks in all thirty-eight states were forced to close. On March 6, 1933, President Roosevelt declared a "Bank Holiday," which specifically forbid the nations' banks to make any payments in cash. The major purpose of closing the banks was to give them the opportunity to liquidate some of their assets, especially government securities. The Federal Reserve banks attempted to assist the commercial banks with their liquidity problems by issuing more Federal Reserve notes against the government bonds that were held by the banks. The banks were audited by government inspectors who were instructed to take an optimistic view of the current values of bank assets.

As banks were found to be in satisfactory condition, they were issued licenses by the treasury and then allowed to reopen. About 2,000 banks never reopened their doors after the holiday; however, public confidence in the banking industry was restored and the outflow of currency was halted. Cash actually started to flow into the banks, and the wave of bank failures was over. As the banks began to reopen, the government began to take steps to improve the quality of their assets. Large volumes of bank loan assets were sold to federal government agencies such as the Reconstruction Finance Corporation, the Home Owners' Loan Corporation, and the Federal Farm Mortgage Corporation. These agencies also made loans to commercial banks, and purchased some of their debt and equity issues.

While all of the changes to the banking industry outlined above were important, the most important and enduring improvement, was the creation of the Federal Deposit Insurance Corporation and the

Federal Savings and Loan Insurance Corporation. These two federal agencies provided the commercial banks and savings and loan associations with federally backed insurance against individual bank deposits. All members of the Federal Reserve System were required to join the Federal Deposit Insurance Corporation, and nearly all of the state chartered banks became members on a voluntary basis. The result was a major improvement in the stability of the commercial banking system. Bank runs all but disappeared because depositors were assured of the safety of their deposits.[1]

## The Suspension of Gold Payments

In the first days of the New Deal, Roosevelt ordered the suspension of gold payments by the banks and forbade the hoarding of gold. This action suspended the gold standard in the United States. Also, the order prohibited the holding of gold, in anticipation of its appreciation in dollars. Although commodity prices stirred upward briefly in the summer of 1933, there was nothing in the president's action that added to purchasing power and demand.

In the autumn of 1933 the administration began to offer progressively higher prices for newly mined gold, which was brought to the treasury to be traded into dollars. The dollar fell on the foreign markets as foreign currencies, which were still on the gold standard, could now be exchanged for more dollars. This resulted in a depreciation of the dollar. As a result of the cheaper American money there were some improvements in exports. However, the results of this action to stimulate export were minimal as the United States in the 1930's was basically a domestic economy.

## ACTIONS TO RAISE PRICES

The first action to increase prices was a direct one that took place through the National Industrial Recovery Act. Under the provisions of this act, sellers were brought together to agree on minimum prices. They, in turn, were required to allow labor to bargain collectively and in good faith. Oligopoly, not competition, was now recognized as the industrial norm. Therefore, it was thought, that individual firms could strongly influence their own prices. The National Industrial Recovery Act provided the organizational framework of this program by instituting over 700 industrial codes that sought to stabilize production, employment, and prices. By agreement, the firms joining in an NRA code acted to arrest the downward spiral of prices. Market competition to reduce price was proclaimed by the NRA to be against the public interest, and monopoly; the conceded flaw in the classical system, was proclaimed acceptable. In fact, the NRA codes sought to create a monopoly pricing structure. At first, the ambitious effort at industrial coordination appeared to work; production, employment, and income grew during much of 1933. However, planning as a solution to the recovery problem never got a long-run test because the political difficulties of reconciling the conflicting interests of large manufacturers, small businessmen, and labor served seriously to reduce the effectiveness of the NRA. Then, on May 27, 1935, the Supreme Court invalidated the code making provisions of the National Recovery Act, thus bringing the experiment to an abrupt end.

The second major effort at price enhancement occurred in agriculture. Beginning in the last century, the United States government and the states, through land grant colleges and universities, had been supporting agricultural experiment and education. In the United States Department of Agriculture in Washington, there was a large and intellectually active center of research in the highly regarded Bureau of Agricultural Economics.

The Bureau of Agricultural Economics, in its examination of farm prices, agricultural credit, farm markets and farm management, was highly pragmatic. This method of operation was, at the time, necessary to assure funding from Congress. Because of their practical orientation, these economists were not committed to the classical system. From the 1920's on, the principle concern of the Bureau was with economic problems, particularly the low prices paid to the farmers. Various scholars from Minnesota, Massachusetts, Montana, and California began an intense discussion of how to raise farm prices. Government, not just the marketplace, it was thought, should have a role in determining farm prices.

With the arrival of Roosevelt in 1933, the agricultural economists also came to Washington. Under their direction, the Agricultural Adjustment Administration (The Triple A) was born. One major provision of this act was a policy that sets minimum prices for most agricultural products, reduced farm production, and provided for the storage of any production that exceeded the established limit.

## ACTIONS TO IMPROVE EMPLOYMENT

Most of Roosevelt's "New Deal" programs were aimed at treating the symptoms of the depression and not at finding a cure. While the cause of the depression was greatly reduced demand, for both industrial and consumer goods and services, the result was severe unemployment. The Roosevelt administration, unlike the Hoover administration, accepted responsibility for easing the plight of the unemployed. In May of 1933, the Federal Emergency Relief Administration, with Harry Hopkins as its director, officially came into existence. The purpose of the FERA was to assist the unemployed. The federal government decided that federal efforts to aid the unemployed would be concentrated on finding jobs. The Federal Emergency Relief Administration was empowered to make grants to the states to support their work relief efforts. Such FERA programs as the Civil Works Administration, the Works Progress Administration, and the Civilian Conservation Corps provided several million people with jobs each year.[2]

While some of these programs were said to be mere excuses to provide income to the unemployed, the basic concept was a response to the obvious hardships caused by the depression. The programs for the most part were designed to provide employment and income; however, many times the resulting products were not of a material consideration. The exception to this was the Public Works Administration. The responsibility of the PWA was not just to create jobs but to invest in public infrastructure, such as roads and dams. The primary emphasis of the PWA, under Secretary of the Interior Harold Ickes, was on the importance of the projects themselves. Every effort was made to complete these projects as efficiently as possible, regardless of the employment effects.

Although the PWA provided about seven hundred thousand jobs in 1936, this was far below the nearly five million employed under FERA programs at their maximum in 1934. However, many important and lasting improvements to our infrastructure such as the Hoover Dam on the Colorado River, was a direct result of the projects completed under the Federal Emergency Relief Administration. In total, during the depression years, federally funded employment programs, were directly responsible for creating more than eight million jobs. While FERA projects were not a cure for the headache of unemployment, for those employed by the program, it was certainly a great aspirin.

## ACTIONS TO RELIEVE THE HARDSHIPS OF THE DEPRESSION

One of the most significant responses to the Great Depression in the United States was the creation of the welfare state. It would be the creation of the welfare state that would endure from the Roosevelt administration. However, the welfare state was not conceived in America. The welfare state was born in Germany of Count Otto Von Bismarck (1815-1898). In the Prussian and German tradition, the state was competent, beneficent and highly prestigious. In 1884 and 1887, welfare legislation was passed in the Reichstag. The legislation provided for accident, sickness, old-age, and disability insurance.

A more comprehensive step in this process came in Britain twenty-five years after Bismarck's great initiative. Under the sponsorship of Lloyd George, the Chancellor of the Exchequer, legislation was passed in 1911 that provided for sickness and invalidism insurance and then unemployment insurance. A non-contributory system of old-age pensions had previously been written into law. In a very real sense, the success of Lloyd George in 1910 and 1911 paved the way for the American action a quarter of a century later. John R. Commons, of the University of Wisconsin, is the American companion to Bismarck and Lloyd George on the development of the welfare state.

John Commons' greatest achievement was in assembling and leading a group of colleagues who set out in a highly practical way to redress the evident social problems of the time. Their initiative began with the Wisconsin State Government in Madison. The Wisconsin Plan included a pioneer state civil service law, the effective regulation of public utility rates (a monopoly), a limit on usurious interest charges, support to the trade unions, and a state income tax. Also, an unemployment compensation system was developed in 1932. This had a penetrating effect on economic and political attitudes. This was the most important contribution to the federal legislation on the subject of welfare reforms that came three years later.[3]

## The Social Security Act

The Social Security Act of 1935 provided three types of relief from the hardship caused by the depression. First, there was direct aid to those unable to work: the old, handicapped, and dependent children. Secondly, it provided a system of accumulating income for retired workers; and finally, the act provided for unemployment insurance. The portion of the social security program that provided direct money payments to the needy was the forerunner of our current welfare system. The Social Security Act was the first explicit recognition in the United States that, in a market economy, there may be persons unable to provide for themselves.

The Social Security Act, which provided pensions for retired workers, was to be financed by taxes on both individual incomes and employers' payrolls. The contributions to fund worker pensions were to be shared equally between the employers and employees. However, since a payroll tax increases production costs, this expense would eventually be passed on to the consumer in higher prices. Social Security, however, did remove some of the hardships of old age. No longer was it necessary for people to work until they were almost dead. Prior to the Social Security Act the elderly who lacked adequate savings, often wiped out by the depression, faced a rather poor assortment of choices. They could depend on their children or turn to the public authorities for support. The Social Security Act provided a system of forced savings, with a federal government guarantee that the potential benefits could not be taken away by future depressions.

Another part of the Social Security Act was a system designed to provide income to the unemployed. A tax was levied on employers' payrolls and used to establish a fund from which payments could be made to those out of work. The length of time over which payments would be dispensed was limited for the purpose of providing incentives for the unemployed to seek work. The plan was designed to encourage each state to set up its own program and to ensure conformity among the various state programs.

The principle that the Social Security (old-age pensions) accounts must be sustained by their own tax levies has remained nearly unchallenged ever since. The response from classical economists to the Social Security Act was relatively mild. Unemployment and economic disabilities of age did exist; perhaps these flaws should be remedied. The old-age pensions paid their own way; they were insurance, not a radical thing.

In total, the changes made by the Roosevelt administration during the depression years, in the basic workings of the American economy, were modest. The emphasis was largely on saving the market system, rather than replacing it with a socialist system. Although the changes were modest at first their effects remain well into the twenty-first century. Social welfare programs such as social security, unemployment insurance have been greatly expanded and have eased the burden of many of the people that receive the benefits of these programs. And these achievements were made against the advice of the leading economists of the time. Academics may argue who was the greatest president, but for those who elected him to four terms in office, Franklin D. Roosevelt was the greatest president of the twentieth century.

**NOTES:**

**Chapter 13**
**The Great Depression and the New Deal (1929-1939)**

1.  Puth, Robert C., <u>American Economic History, Third Edition</u>, Fort Worth, TX, The Dryden Press, 1993, p. 569.

2.  Chandler, L., <u>America's Greatest Depression, 1929- 1941</u>,  New York,  N.Y., 1970, p. 196.
3.  Galbraith,   John   Kenneth,   <u>Economics   in   Perspective</u>, Boston, MA, Houghton Mifflin Company, 1987, p. 215.

# CHAPTER 14

---

# KEYNESIAN ECONOMICS

*"In the long run we are all dead."--John Maynard Keynes*

## ECONOMICS IN ANTICIPATION OF KEYNES

In 1936, the fourth year of the Roosevelt administration's "New Deal," a very temporary recovery developed. However, 17 percent of the American labor force was still unemployed, and real gross national product was only 95 percent of the 1929 level. In 1937, there was another sharp slump. Since there was already a depression, a new name had to be found, and it was called a recession. Classical economic theory continued relentlessly to predict an eventual recovery from the depression. However, by this time a large portion of the population was beginning to wonder if the economy would ever return to normal. What was needed was a new theory to explain why the economy was not adjusting to lower wages and lower interest rates and therefore, returning to a level of full employment as the classical economists had promised. The public, in general, was just running out of patience. A new economic theory was required to explain the current circumstances. The new economic theory was developed by the distinguished British economist John Maynard Keynes in his 1936 publication, "The General Theory of Employment, Interest and Money." The essentials of Keynes' case were designed to release the fiscal policies of the British treasury and the Roosevelt administration from its classical economic constraints. The modern economy, Keynes held, does not necessarily find its equilibrium at full employment; it can find it with unemployment, i.e., the underemployment equilibrium.[1]

According to Keynes, it is not necessary to wait for the economy to adjust itself to a depression. The government can, and should, take steps to overcome a shortage of aggregate demand. In a depression the desire of the federal government to balance their budget must give way to the need to stimulate aggregate demand. However, there were economists, who, by their actions, expressed the need for government intervention to stimulate demand well before Keynes. The most notable was the case of Sweden. Here for two generations, an alert group of economists took part in critical discussions of economic ideas as they were related to public affairs.

The independent minded Swedish scholars were men such as Gunnar Myrdal, Bertil Ohlin, Erik Lundberg, and Dag Hammarskjold. Dag Hammarskjold was later appointed to be the Secretary General of the United Nations. While these men all had full knowledge of the classical theory, they were more concerned with the practical problems of the Swedish economy. Instead on being constrained by a theory that just was not working, they advocated the deliberate use of the government budget to sustain demand and employment. The worldwide depression of the 1930's led the Stockholm economists to abandon hope that actions of the Central Bank to lower interest rates would materially expand investment expenditure and, therefore, aggregate demand. Instead, they held that in good times the public budget should be balanced, but in depression the budget should be unbalanced deliberately so that the excess of expenditure over income would sustain demand and employment. All of this was being done in Stockholm in the 1930's, well in advance of Keynes. By the middle of the decade, word of developments in Sweden was finding its way to Britain and to the United States. Sweden, with its now well developed social welfare system, was being pictured as the "Middle Way" between the classical economic system and Socialism and Communism.[2]

Finally, in anticipation of Keynes, there was a highly practical application of government deficit spending going on in the United States. Through most of the 1930's, the federal government ran a substantial deficit. Beginning in 1933, this was increased by expending for direct relief, public works, and other public forms of employment. This type of employment was managed through such agencies as the Federal Emergency Relief Administration, the Public Works

Administration, and the Works Progress Administration. By 1936, the federal revenue receipts were only 59 percent of government expenditures. The deficit was four and two tenths of a percentage of the current gross national product. The hardships brought about by the depression had already made what Keynes was to urge necessary.

## JOHN MAYNARD KEYNES: THE MAN BEHIND THE THEORY

Early advocacy of Keynesian policy included strong attempts at persuasion by Keynes. However, none of this earlier effort ranked in importance with the publication of "The General Theory," as his book began to be known, in 1936. It was, as Keynes had intended it to be, a lethal blow at the classical conclusions as to demand, production and employment and the resulting policy. Say's Law was dead, and a new theory developed by John Maynard Keynes had arrived to take its place.

The General Theory owed much of its acceptance to the Great Depression and to the failure of classical economics to contend with the problems brought about by that unsettling event. However, the acceptance that this book received owed much to Keynes' ability and reputation. No economist is ever more highly regarded than he regards himself or followed with more certainty than that which he himself manifests. The affect that The General Theory had in changing economic analysis owed much to the background, reputation and prestige of its author.

### John Maynard Keynes (1883 - 1945)

John Maynard Keynes was born in 1883 into a Puritanical Victorian home. John Neville Keynes, his father, was a well-known economist at Cambridge University; but Keynes, unlike his parents, had little use for puritan values. Keynes attended King's College at Cambridge where he developed friendships and liaisons with other intellectuals and was invited to join the university's most select and secretive society, the Apostles. Later, Keynes and many of the other Apostles, formed the Bloomsbury Group, whose Anti-Victorian, and

John Maynard Keynes

Bohemian attitudes powerfully affected the evolution of British culture.[3]

Keynes originally attended Cambridge to study mathematics. His introduction to economics was through Alfred Marshall's "The Principles of Economics." After a brief departure from Cambridge, Keynes returned to accept Marshall's offer as a lecturer in economics. In his early years at Cambridge, his economic beliefs did not extend far beyond those of Marshall and the classical tradition. During the 1920's, Keynes continued to teach, edit, write, and advise the British government. He corresponded with most of the prominent politicians, academicians, and artists of his time. A lot of skill and a little bit of luck assisted him as he accumulated a fortune trading in stocks and commodities. There is a question that is often asked of economists, which is; "If you know so much why aren't you rich?" Only David Ricardo would rank higher than Keynes in becoming rich and most other economists would flunk this test miserably.

## Keynes on Savings and Investment

In economics, Keynes originally focused mostly on monetary policy, especially in his "Treatise on Money," published in 1930. The Treatise tied together much of Keynes' earlier work on investment, with some new discussion of the connection between savings and investment. The Treatise examined the question of what made the economy operate so unevenly. The question had received the attention of economists for decades. Malthus had considered that savings could somehow result in a general economic glut, but most other early nineteenth century economists rejected the idea. In the world of Ricardo and Mill, virtually the only people who could save were the wealthy and their savings were usually invested in their own businesses. Therefore, saving was properly called accumulation for it represented the amassing of a sum of money and the immediate use of those funds in purchasing new capital equipment.

After the American Civil War, the structure of the American and European economies changed. The distribution of wealth improved as those who had the technical skills required to operate the new factory machines could demand higher wages. At the same time, business organizations became larger and were increasingly searching beyond their owners for more investment capital. Commercial banks also entered the equation by performing the function of funneling consumer savings into business investment. Hence savings and investment became divorced from each other as they became separate operations carried out by different groups of people. However, this separation of savings and investing often led to economic problems because the funneling of savings into investment is not automatic. Business firms usually need savings to fund the expansion of their operations. This is because business cash flows are not sufficient to provide it with enough capital to build a new factory or to purchase an expensive piece of equipment. Consumer saving is not spending, because it reduces national income. If businesses invest the savings of consumers the economy usually grows; however, if these savings are not invested it could lead to depression. The Treatise was a masterful analysis of this seesaw of savings and investment and its potential effect on economic stability.

## The Fall of Classical Economics

The early 1930's brought challenges to economics so perplexing that Keynes soon began to realize that he could not rest on his previous publications. From 1929 to 1933 in the United States, Adam Smith's invisible hand of the free market kicked prosperity in the backside. Unemployment went from 3 percent to 25 percent, national income was reduced by almost half and the economy came to a screeching halt. The popular song writer Yip Harburg echoed the frustration and disparity of the nation in his song "Brother, Can You Spare a Dime?"

The British treasury and the American government, especially under Hoover, prescribed patience and promised recovery in the long run. However, Keynes blasted the treasury view as he wrote in his "Tract on Monetary Reform." What is the point of having such a government? "In the long run we are all dead." Keynes justified the advice he gave to politicians in his 1936 masterpiece. The General Theory smashed the classical theory of economics and presented a new framework for a new field of study to be called macroeconomics.[4]

## THE ECONOMICS OF JOHN MAYNARD KEYNES

In the General Theory, Keynes denounces the classical model of a self adjusting economy. According to Keynes, the most nincompoopish belief was in Say's Law that, as previously discussed, states that the production of goods and services generates enough income to workers and suppliers for all the products to be purchased. However, if someone believes in Say's Law, according to Keynes, they cannot believe in long-term unemployment or depressions. The simultaneous occurrence of a self adjusting mechanism to prevent long-term unemployment, and the great depression of 1929 is, by definition, mutually exclusive. Only a schizophrenic could believe in both. Even Keynes would not accuse his colleagues of being schizophrenics. He gave them the benefit of the doubt and called them stupid.[5]

Keynes developed a two-pronged attack against the prime positions of the classical system. According to Keynes, the self adjusting system of classical economics did not work because there was no link between savings and investment and wages were not flexible. On the subject of savings and investment, Keynes held that consumers and businesses save and invest for entirely different reasons. Households save for many different reasons, but what determines how much they are able to save is their disposable income. Interest rates have very little to do with the amount that consumers save. Businesses may invest more if interest rates are low because some projects may become profitable with low interest rates. However, a business invests in fixed assets based on future expectations. If a business believes that there is no market for its products, they will not invest to increase production capacity. This business decision will be made without regard to the rate of interest.

If household savings exceed business investment, a decline in aggregate demand will result. Business inventories will increase and production will decrease as a result of reduced demand for the company's products. Companies will react to the reduced demand by reducing the size of their work force, leading to even less consumption. As income falls, consumers, especially those out of work, will start to liquidate their savings. Savings will eventually drop enough to equal investment, but not necessarily at full employment.

The central ideas of Keynes' theory are that the decisive problem of economics is how the levels of output and employment are determined. Keynes argued that there is a direct relationship between income and savings. As consumer disposable incomes increase, savings increase, and as incomes decrease, the portion of total income saved decreases. Keynes assumed that each time a consumer gets an additional dollar of income they have two choices; they can spend or save the income. Keynes calls the part spent the marginal propensity to consume, and the part saved the marginal propensity to save. When analyzing the U.S. gross domestic product, it becomes apparent that the largest portion of expenditure, i.e., 70 percent of total GDP in 2010, is personal consumption. Therefore, if incomes are reduced, as a result of a reduction in employment, consumption will also fall. In addition, since households make up the largest portion of total expenditures, a reduction of consumer expenditures will have the greatest effect on aggregate demand.

Businesses also buy goods and services. By investing in fixed assets and additions to inventory, businesses account for another substantial part of aggregate demand, i.e., 12.5 percent of GDP in 2010. However, the most important reason that businesses change their investment plans is their future profit expectations. Businessmen do not change their investment plans in response to short run changes in interest rates, and they especially do not increase their investment in production capacity when there is a reduced demand for their products.

Therefore, in order for an economy to operate to its potential production capacity with full employment, households must provide consumption and businesses must expand their investment in fixed assets and inventory. The expansion must be adequate for sales of goods to be brought into equilibrium with the amount of items produced. Thus, if people were to spend all of their income, the marginal propensity to consume would be one. If all income is consumed, then the economy would function according to the classical economist self adjusting model. However, since people save some of their income, business investment must make up for the lack of personal consumption. If business investment does not equal savings, output will be greater than sales, inventories build, and employers will lay off workers. Therefore, according to Keynes, depressions are caused by a drastic reduction in demand and one of the main culprits is savings.

In addition to his views of the relationship between savings and investment, Keynes did not agree with the classical theory on the flexibility of wages and prices. When unemployment occurred in the classical context, the accepted cause was wages that were too high or too rigid. With Keynes, this was no longer so; what was true for the individual employer was not true for all. If all employers were to lower wages in a time of unemployment, the flow of purchasing power, the aggregate of effective demand, would diminish. The result of this reduced purchasing power would be that consumers would not have enough income to buy the products produced. Therefore, unemployment could not be blamed on high wages or on the supply controlling effects of labor unions. Unemployment is a result of decreasing aggregate demand. Thus, according to Keynes, the equilibrium situation in the economy is not necessarily at full employment; it can be at different and even severe levels of unemployment. This new theory by Keynes became known as the Underemployment Equilibrium.

**The Keynesian Solution**

In the past, critics of the capitalist system angrily pointed their finger at the robber barons. Keynes suggested that consumers, who insist on increasing their savings, especially in times of recession, do more harm than the nefarious industrialist. In addition, this wicked deed of savings has a tendency to compound itself through what Keynes called the "Multiplier." This theory states that an increase or decrease in spending has an affect on the economy that is greater than the original change in expenditures. This multiplier affect occurs because as money is spent on goods and services, those who receive the revenue now have additional income, part of which they spend.

Keynes provided a simple formula to calculate the multiplier with the key being the marginal propensity to consume:

Multiplier = 1/[1-MPC] or 1/MPS

According to Keynes, the higher the degree of consumption, the higher the multiplier affect would be. On the basis of this formula, Keynes concluded that small reductions in investment may severely pressure the economy as a whole. Also, if deficient demand is the cause of a recession, the cure must be to stimulate more spending. However, if the MPC is known, spending can be injected into the economy, which will multiply throughout and end the recession by filling the original gap between output and consumption.[6]

Keynes estimated the United States multiplier to be about 2.5 times, and based on this estimate, he advocated massive federal spending programs. His recommendations were made in letters written directly to Roosevelt as well as publishing articles in magazines. According to Keynes, the United States could stimulate its economy directly through government spending projects. However, the amount of the injection could be less than the shortfall of consumer and business spending. For example, with a multiplier of 2.5, if the difference between the potential output and the actual output of an economy was $1 billion, the government would only have to inject $400 million in new expenditures to fill the output gap. Therefore, Keynes urged Roosevelt to raise the level of government spending. This meant that the federal government would have to run a deliberate deficit in order to pull the economy out of a depression. This alone would break the underemployment equilibrium, by increasing aggregate demand, through investing the savings of the private sector. It was a powerful affirmation of the wisdom of what was already being accomplished by the Roosevelt administration in order to relieve the hardships caused by the depression.

## Keynes and Mars the God of War

For the Keynesian system World War II had major consequences. First, it brought a younger breed of economists into positions of power in Washington. Secondly, World War II demonstrated beyond comparison the power of Keynesian economics. In addition, these young Keynesian economists had the support of such established authority as Alvin Hansen, who came to the Federal Reserve Board, and John Maynard Keynes, who arrived from England to represent the British government.

The final contribution of World War II to the propagation of Keynes' beliefs was that it showed what his economics could accomplish through fiscal policy. Fiscal policy was defined as the actions of the federal government in changing expenditures and tax collections for the purpose of stimulating or slowing down an economy. From 1939 to 1944, the wartime peak, gross national product in constant dollars (1972 dollars adjusted for inflation), increased from $320 billion to $569 billion. Personal consumption expenditures increased from $220 to $255 billion. Unemployment was approximately 17.2 percent of the civilian labor force in 1939; in 1944 it was a nominal 1.2 percent. Overall, in the last full year of the war, Americans were living better than ever before. This was the result of the upward pressure of public demand on the economy. The federal government purchases of goods and services, in these years, increased from $22.8 billion in 1939 to $269.7 billion in 1944. No one could seriously doubt that Mars the God of War, had demonstrated how fiscal policy, could be used to stimulate an economy.

Also, World War II had a great and everlasting effect on the tax system of the United States. Taxes, by modern standards, had been insignificant before 1941. In 1939, federal revenues were just under $5 billion; by 1945, they were in excess of $44 billion. With the war, and in justification of these taxes, came the notion of an approach to the equity of sacrifice: the poor would pay with their military service or their toil; the affluent, especially the non-serving rich, would pay with their taxes. The principle of a strongly progressive tax, effectively income redistribution, is still a major topic of political debate in the 1990's.

As the World War II had affirmed Keynes, so it had dealt a heavy blow to classical laissez faire. In the economics profession a new view of government and a new reliance on its intervention would be one of the major economic consequences of the war.[7]

## KEYNES AFTER KEYNES

After the war the Keynesian economists retained their power in Washington and had found allies in the business world. Full employment would no longer be considered the autonomous consequence of the competitive economy. Keynes proved that the underemployment equilibrium was possible, and in the future it would be the responsibility of the federal government to ensure full employment.

The quarter century following the end of World War II, was very good in economic performance. In only three of these twenty-five years did the American gross domestic product fail to increase. Reinforcing domestic expenditures in the United States was an inflow of purchasing power from abroad as the country had a strongly favorable trade balance. After World War II, the United States was the only major industrial power that remained intact. This put America in a position of economic leadership that had no comparison in the twentieth century.

The World War II demands required a sizable advance in the growth of the economy and an enormous transfer of resources from peacetime to wartime needs. The average level of federal expenditure from 1942 through 1945 amounted to roughly one half of the net national product. The federal government, in contrast to its performance during World War I, made a determined effort to control inflation. Roosevelt initiated a program of price controls and rationing in January of 1942 and the Truman administration maintained it until June of 1946. The primary vehicle for implementing price control was the Office of Price Administration (OPA). As a result of the efforts of the OPA, price increases averaged only 6.4 percent, from 1939 to 1948. This was the result of an effective enforcement campaign, the popularity of the general war effort, and the unusual willingness with which Americans accepted price controls and rationing.

One of the curiosities of the postwar expansion was that it defied a restrictive government fiscal policy. The curtailment of government expenditures that began in 1946 continued throughout 1948, with expenditures declining to about one third of what they had been in 1945. However, government tax receipts decreased by less than 10 percent. This resulted in a government surplus of $8.4 billion by 1948.

After World War II, there was a great deal of concern in the United States that the nation would return to the depression of the 1930's. However, during the war two major things occurred to prevent a continued depression. First, there was the elimination of unemployment, and secondly, an expansion of the total number of persons employed. The war effort required a tremendous expansion of the production of military equipment. With the bulk of the young men recruited to fight the war, it was necessary to recruit millions of women to work in the factories that produced military equipment. In addition, government rationing programs restricted the supply of consumer goods that were available to purchase. This pattern of increased revenue and reduced products to purchase resulted in a large increase in savings. The end of World War II brought with it a release of pent-up consumer demand following the lifting of wartime restrictions, especially with regard to consumer durable goods and housing. The combination of pent-up consumer demand and the lifting of wartime restrictions resulted in a large increase in consumer demand that eliminated any possibility of a renewed depression. Because of the large accumulation of money and other highly liquid assets to support this demand, the public would have spent a great deal more on peacetime goods and services had the government not run a surplus.

Another expansive force was the increase in the stock of money, which grew at a rate of slightly more than 4 percent per year between January 1946 and August 1948. The weakness of policy during the late 1940's and the 1950's was more in the management of fiscal policy than in the use of monetary mechanisms. The Federal Reserve Board maintained a rather consistent posture throughout the period, in effect, working to keep the nation's money stock growing at a reasonable stable rate, one upon which other institutions and individuals could depend.

In 1964, There was a deliberate attempt to use Keynesian economics to prevent the economy from entering into a recession. It was the tax reduction of that year. This idea to stimulate demand was begun earlier by President Kennedy, and signed into law after Kennedy's death by President Lyndon Johnson. The highest rate on the personal income tax was reduced to 70 percent. Also, there was a reduction in other lower income brackets and the basic rate on the corporate income tax was reduced. This tax reduction was deliberately designed to expand consumer purchasing power which would stimulate aggregate demand and avoid a budget surplus at full employment. Also, the Federal Reserve accommodated fiscal policy by instituting a moderately simulative monetary policy. The results of the federal government's use of fiscal policy to stimulate the economy, was that the unemployment rate declined from 6.7 percent in 1961 to 3.8 percent in 1966. The first attempt by the federal government to use fiscal policy to increase aggregate demand and therefore, to reduce unemployment was a success and resulted in only a slight increase in the rate of inflation.

**NOTES:**

**Chapter 14**
**Keynesian Economics**

1.  Galbraith, John, Kenneth, <u>Economics in Perspective</u>, Boston, MA, Houghton Mifflin Company, 1987, p. 222.
2.  Galbraith, p. 225.
3.  Buchholz, Todd, G., <u>New Ideas From Dead Economists</u>,    New York, N.Y., Penguin Books, 1989,
    p. 205.
4.  Buchholz, p. 206.
5.  Buchholz, p. 207.
6.  Buchholz, p. 212.
7.  Galbraith, p. 249.

# CHAPTER 15

---

# ECONOMIC MEASUREMENT AND FORECASTING

*"Forecasting is very difficult, especially if it's about the future." —Edgar Fielder.*

## NATIONAL INCOME ACCOUNTING

Once the concept of macroeconomics was developed by John Maynard Keynes in the "General Theory," it became essential to create a terminology to describe its aggregate elements. During the 1940's, many of those who had been converted to Keynesian economics set out to develop a terminology and to measure the entire system of final output in the United States. Their work was the starting point for what today is called National Income Accounting. Simon Kuznets and Richard Stone received a Nobel Prize in Economics for their efforts to define a set of rules and definitions for measuring total economic activity.

National income accounting provides a way of measuring the total output of an economy over a designated period. The Department of Commerce, which gathers the necessary statistics, provides a measurement of economic activity each quarter called the Gross Domestic Product (GDP). GDP is widely reported in the media each quarter as an annualized figure. For example, if GDP grew by 1 percent in the first quarter of 2012, this would equate to a projected growth of 4 percent for the entire year. In national income accounting, aggregate economic production is broken down into two kinds of output, consumption and investment.

Consumption consists of goods and services bought by households for their personal use, such as new cars, and household goods and services. These various goods and services are often referred to as consumer goods. Investment goods are those purchased by business firms to start or to increase their production, by individuals to purchase new homes and by the government to build public infrastructures such as highways and bridges.

Accounting by definition is based on certain identities. For example, in a business, revenue must equal the total cost of producing plus a profit or in some cases a loss. All costs and revenue are kept track of through the use of double entry bookkeeping. In the national income accounts, whenever things are produced, income goes to the people who participated in the production of those goods and services. In other words, individual wealth is created by the production of goods and services. In financial accounting terms, for every use of funds in producing a product, there must be a source for those funds. In the national income accounts, we can define GDP as expenditures as a use of funds and GDP as income as a source of funds. GDP as expenditures, is divided into four main categories: Consumption expenditures, gross private investment, government purchases, and net exports

## GDP as Expenditures

Consumption expenditures are the total of all goods and services that are purchased by households during the course of a single year. This category is further broken down into durable and non-durable goods. Durable goods are those products that last for periods greater than one year; for example, automobiles and household furniture. Non-durable goods are those that usually last for a period of less than one year. Consumption expenditures are by far the largest category of GDP.

Gross private investment expenditures are made by businesses and households for capital goods. When economists use the term investment, they refer to the nation's stock of capital assets. Financial assets such as corporate stocks and bonds are not considered capital assets. Gross private investment is broken down into two sub-categories called, fixed investment and changes in business inventory. Fixed investment is by far the largest portion of investment and includes investment in residential buildings, buildings used by business and government, and equipment such as machinery and computers. Inventory investment is the change in the aggregate value of the current stocks of finished goods that businesses have produced and have not yet sold.

Government purchases are divided into federal expenditures and state and local government purchases. Government purchases involve consumption and fixed investment as they can buy both bridges, highways, and pay their employees. The state and local government purchases combined are greater than the federal governments. However, the budget of the federal government is much larger than their total purchases. For example, for total year 2013, total federal expenditures were $3,793 billion and total purchases in the GDP accounts were $1,246 billion. The reason is that the largest part of the federal budget is mandated payments such as transfer payments or entitlements. For 2013 mandated payments totaled $2,349 billion. The remainder of the expenses for 2013 was for disaster expense and interest on the federal debt. Transfer payments take money from some Americans and transfer it to others, for example, from tax payers to Medicare recipients. However, the government does not spend the money on purchases and therefore transfer payments are not part of the GDP.[1]

Net exports are the final value of all goods and services that are sold to foreign individuals, businesses and governments less the amount of goods and services that are purchased from foreign sources. If we sell more goods and services abroad than we buy there is a positive balance of trade and as in recent years, if we buy more than we sell, a negative net export figure is entered into the GDP accounts.

## GDP As Income

Domestic income is the total income earned by the residents and businesses in a country. However, the United States' federal government does not report domestic income in the GDP accounts. The government instead reports national income. National income is the total income earned by the citizens and businesses of a country. Since GDP is based on domestic income an adjustment to account for the foreign income that is paid and received must be made to reconcile the two methods of accounting. To move from domestic income to national income, you must add the difference between investment income received from abroad minus the income earned by foreigners. This adjustment to domestic income is called the net foreign factor and is necessary to convert gross domestic product to gross national product so that national income and expenditures can be compared.

National income consists of, compensation paid to employees, rents paid to individuals, interest payments paid by businesses to individuals, and business profits. Compensation paid to employees consists of wages and fringe benefits paid to individuals, adjusted for government income taxes, social security and unemployment insurance deductions. Compensation to employees makes up the largest category of GDP as income.

Rents are the income that is received by individuals for letting other people use their property. Rents received by business firms are not considered here because they are a part of the income and therefore the profit of businesses.

Interest payments are the income that businesses pay to households that have purchased financial assets from the firms. The largest providers of interest payments to households are the financial institutions that hold individual demand and time deposits.

Profits are the amounts left over after a business makes payments to the factors of production. Corporate profits are either paid out to shareholders in the form of dividends or held by the corporation as retained earnings. However, both dividends and retained earnings are owned by stockholders. Therefore, for national income accounting purposes, both are considered to be household income.[2]

To equate national income to gross national product, two additional adjustments must be made. GDP as income reflects net investment and GDP as expenditures show gross investment. To reconcile the two accounts, depreciation expenditures must be subtracted from gross investment. Also, GDP as expenditure contains indirect business taxes. Indirect business taxes include retail sales taxes, excise taxes, business property taxes, customs duties and license fees. These are all expenses of doing business, but they are not income flows to the factors of production and therefore, is not considered as part of the GDP as income accounts.

**Table 15-1**

**National Income Accounting Source and Use of Funds**
**Statement Year 2013 (Dollars in Billions)**

| Source of Funds | | Use of Funds | |
|---|---|---|---|
| GDP as Income | $ Billions | GDP as Expense | $ Billions |
| ----------------------- | ------------ | ----------------------- | ------------ |
| Wage and Benefits | 8,860 | Durable Goods | 1,263 |
| Rental Income | 591 | Non-Durable | 2,623 |
| Interest Income | 553 | Services | 7,615 |
| | | | |
| Household Income | 10,004 | Consumer Exp. | 11,507 |
| | | Residential Invest. | 517 |
| Corporate Profits | 2,102 | Business Invest. | 2,047 |
| Non-Corp. Profits | 1,349 | Inventory Changes | 106 |
| | | | |
| Business Income | 3,451 | Investment Expense | 2,670 |
| Business Taxes | 1,088 | | |
| | | Government Purchase | 1,246 |
| National Income | 14,543 | Federal | 1,246 |
| | | State & Local | 1,880 |
| Adjustments | | | |
| | | Total Government | 3,126 |
| Depreciation Exp | 2,647 | | |
| Net Foreign Factor | (256) | Exports | 2,260 |
| Statistical Error | (134) | Imports | 2,757 |
| | | | |
| Total Adjustments | 2,257 | Net Exports | (497) |
| | | | |
| Total Sources | 16,800 | Total Uses | 16,800 |

**Source: Bureau of Economic Analysis Table 1.1.5, March 2014.**

Table 15-1 is a source and use of funds statement for the year 2013. This statement shows in detail how the two accounts are reconciled. However, in calculating GDP using two different methods, there are bound to be some slight differences. These differences are reconciled by an account that is called statistical discrepancies. These discrepancies are caused by the different methods that the Department of Commerce uses to calculate GDP.

## THE ROLE OF SAVINGS AND INVESTMENT

Growth is the norm in a capitalist economy. This is a function of the desire of businesses to expand by constantly seeking new markets, new products, and new ways to reduce the cost of production. As detailed in Table 15.1, gross domestic product as expenditures has four major economic sectors. The table below shows these sectors as a percent of total GDP for 2013 and 2012.

| Description | % of | Total | GDP |
|---|---|---|---|
| | 2012 | 2013 | Change |
| Consumer Expenditures | 70.9 | 68.4 | (2.5) |
| Investment Expenditures | 13.2 | 15.9 | 2.7 |
| Government Expenditures | 19.5 | 18.6 | (.9) |
| Net Exports | (3.6) | (2.9) | .7 |
| | | | |
| Total GDP | 100 | 100 | 0.0 |

Household expenditures on consumer goods are by far the largest section of GDP at 68.4 percent. The change from 2012 to 2013 shows a 2.7 percent increase in investment expenditures. This was due to business investment and an improving housing market in 2013.

A key factor in an expanding economy is the ability of the private sector to invest in new structures, both residential and business, and new factory equipment. Business expansions are funded by both internally generated retained earnings and personal savings.

Personal savings and undistributed corporate profits are reported in the National Income and Product Accounts. Table 15-2 details the relationship between National income, personal income and personal savings.

**Table 15-2**

**National Income Accounts Personal Income and Savings**

| National Income Accounts | 2012 | 2013 |
|---|---|---|
| | ($ in billions) | ($ in billions) |
| National Income | 13,849 | 14,543 |
| Less Corporate Profits | 1,951 | 2,102 |
| Business taxes | 1,069 | 1,088 |
| Other transfer payments | 1,547 | 1,660 |
| Plus | | |
| Personal income receipts on assets | 1,750 | 1,998 |
| Personal current transfer receipts | 2,375 | 2,444 |
| Equals Personal Income | 13,407 | 14,135 |
| Less  Personal current taxes | 1,476 | 1,658 |
| Equals Disposable personal income | 11,931 | 12,477 |
| Less: Personal outlays | 11,460 | 11,914 |
| Equals: Personal Savings | 471 | 562 |
| Personal savings as a percent of disposable income. | 3.9 | 4.0 |

**Source: Bureau of Economic Analysis – Table 2.1 Personal Income and its Distribution, March 2014.**

For 2013 the personal savings rate averaged 4.0. Percent of disposable income compared to 3.9 percent for 2012. The size of consumer expenditures is predictable based on existing demand and future demand for household purchases. Therefore, the major question about GDP growth is what happens to the percent of consumer's disposable income that is saved.

Just as households buy their goods and services mainly out of earnings, the business sector funds its short-term operations from the cash it generates from sales. The major difference is that the business sector does not normally save a large portion of its cash receipts. Most companies that wish to expand their operations through capital investment expenditures must borrow at least a portion of the total cost of large expansion projects.

Household savings are borrowed by the business sector to finance the building of new capital goods and this becomes a primary means by which an economy increases its productivity. This leads to an explanation of how GDP grows and why it fluctuates as follows:

1. Gross domestic product grows because savings are converted into investment for capital equipment.
2. The savings that originate in the household sector are invested by the business sector.
3. GDP fluctuates because the process of transforming savings into investment is not always smooth or steady.[3]

## THE GOVERNMENT SECTOR

Governments' in most industrialized countries share three economic goals: economic growth, full employment, and price stability. In order to achieve these goals, a government often redistributes income to social projects and to individuals. This government does through a system of taxing its citizens. The economic rational a government often uses for its redistribution of their citizen's income would fall into the categories of either positive or normative economics. Positive economics is based on the theory of economic efficiency or the distribution of the goods and services that an economy produces to its most productive resources. Normative economics is based on a question of fairness or who should receive the goods and services produced. Normative economic theory suggests that income should be redistributed from those who have more than they need to those that have less. The redistribution of income from those who are working to those who are not working in the form of Social Security, Medicare and Welfare are examples of normative economics. Therefore, a major role of government is to tax its citizens in order to fund this redistribution and to setup the mechanism, which will require administrative cost, to run the system.

An example of a government using positive economics is where, the market system does not allocate all resources in a way that the citizens of a country desire. A country requires a system of laws that direct its business activity. Without a dependable legal system a market economy could not operate. Also, a market economy may not properly allocate resources to train and educate its people. Without an educated work force a county would not be able to compete with other industrialized economies. And finally, a modern economy needs to provide its citizens with protection from foreign invasion, criminal actions against its citizens and unsafe and the unfair practices of individual businesses. Therefore, the question is not; do we need government, but how much government and at what cost? An additional question is how can a government use both fiscal and monetary policy to help achieve its goals of full employment, price stability and economic growth? The government's use of fiscal policy was introduced in chapter 13 "Keynesian Economics." Monetary and fiscal policy will be covered in more detail in later chapters.

## BUSINESS FLUCTUATIONS

In order to make the mass amounts of historical economic data useful it is helpful to categorize the various forms of fluctuations and to develop techniques of analyzing them. Economists usually classify business fluctuations by the trend, cycles, and seasonal variations. Each of these fluctuations is a result of a different class of factors, and discovering the nature of these causes is important to economic forecasting.

Seasonal variations occur because of changes in business conditions from one season of the year to the next. A seasonal variation exists when there is a regular pattern of variation in the series and this change occurs over a period of time that is usually one year. The trend is the persistent underlying movement that has taken place in a series of data over a period long enough to cover several business cycles. The long-term trend in real gross domestic product (GDP adjusted for inflation), has been gradually rising at a fairly constant rate. Economic growth is the result of increasing the quantity and/or the quality of a country's factors of production. For example, in order to increase the size of the labor force either the population must grow and/or the quality of the labor force must improve.

A business cycle is the movement of some aggregate measure of economic activity upward or downward over time. The length of time of the cyclical movements will vary, and the magnitude of the movement upward or downward will differ over time. A business cycle can be divided into four phases as the economy fluctuates around the long-term growth trend. The peak of the cycle is the point which real output reaches a maximum. The period during which real output falls is known as the contraction phase. At the end of the contraction, real output reaches a minimum known as the trough of the cycle. After the trough, real output begins to grow again and the economy enters an expansion that lasts until a new peak is reached.

Joseph Schumpeter drew on the work of other economists and concluded that there were three distinct cycle lengths. He named the cycles after the economist that was most associated with these cycles. The Kondratieff cycles consisted of long waves averaging fifty-four years and oscillated around the economic trend. The second of these cycles, Schumpeter called Juglar cycles. These cycles oscillate around the Kondratieff waves and are nine to ten years in duration. Schumpeter named the third cycle, Kitchin cycles which lasted about forty months. The forty month cycle approximates the average length of most post World War II short term business cycles. The principle reason for the Kitchin cycles is the accumulation and eventual reduction of business inventories as aggregate demand changes. However, longer cycles are affected more by the level of investment in long-term fixed capital and business innovations.

Innovations, according to Schumpeter, can be put into five classes, which require the introduction into the economic system of one or more of the following:

•   New products, capital goods or consumer goods.

•   New methods of producing goods or services.

- New markets for commodities.

- The exploration of newly discovered sources of raw materials.

- New means of organizing business activity.

According to Schumpeter, the first Kondratieff wave started in the late 1780's and was associated with the industrial revolution and the development of steam power, iron and cotton textile mills. The second wave started in the late 1840's as a result of the expansion of the railroads. This expansion of railroad transportation created opportunities for mass marketing. The third Kondratieff cycle, started around the turn of the twentieth century. This cycle marked the introduction of electricity into the homes and factories and with the mass assembly of automobiles.[4]

In modern times, we can make a good case for the fourth Kondratieff wave in the invention of the jet airplane and the microcomputer. The invention of the microprocessor in 1971 by Intel has changed the organization of every business from the small establishment to the giant multinational corporation. The jet airplane brought with it tourism, which by the 1960's was the largest single industry in the world and made multinational giants out of several American corporations.

An examination of economic history reveals periods of great prosperity, often lasting a decade or more, followed by equally long periods of very slow, zero or even negative growth. The most accepted explanation of this phenomenon is that technology and innovation opens up a whole level of opportunities for economic growth. Therefore, improving technology as a result of capital investment and innovation must be considered when developing an economic or business forecast.

## ECONOMICS AND BUSINESS FORECASTING

Prior to 1970, economics was basically used to explain current events. There was, for all practical purposes, no attempt to forecast economic events into the future. However, there were two developments in this period that changed the future value and use of economic data. The first was the Input/output analysis of Wassily W. Leontief. The Leontief tables showed the value of what each industry and subsections of each industry sold to each other and received from each other. The resulting great complex, showed how any given change is distributed through the economic system. For example, what an increase in automobile production would mean in extra sales to the steel industry.

The second development was a product of the great engineering advances in data storage. This was the development of the econometric or computer models of the economy. Going beyond Keynes, and Leontief, these economic models seek to emulate the effects of all major changes in the economic system. Changes in public expenditures, taxes, interest rates, wages, profits, industrial production by individual industries, and housing construction were captured. With this data the changes that were measured were associated with other changes that were occurring throughout the economy.

From the models came forecasts and more specific information relevant to corporate decisions. Each day, business executives and government officials, make decisions that require assumptions about the future. The modern large business enterprise must plan. Planning always involves the future. The forecasts help establish probable magnitudes of demand for a firm's products and keep decisions within the range of plausibility.

However, when preparing a forecast, the business or government planner would be wise to use the rules of forecasting that were first developed by Edgar Fiedler.[5]

- Forecasting is very difficult, especially if it's about the future.

- The moment you forecast you know that you are going to be wrong: you don't know when and in which direction.

- The forecasters best defense is a good offense, so; if you have to forecast, forecast often.

- But if you're ever right, never let 'em forget it!

**NOTES:**

**Chapter 15**
**National Income Accounting and Forecasting**

1.  Colander, David, C., <u>Economics</u>, Burr Ridge, IL, Richard D. Irwin, Inc., 1994, p. 166.
2.  Colander, p. 171.
3.  Valentine, Lloyd M., <u>Business Cycles and Forecasting</u>, Cincinnati, OH, South-Western Publishing Co., 1991, p. 126.
4.  Heilbroner, Robert, Thurow, Lester, Economics explained, NYC, NY, Simon & Schuster, 1994, p. 89.
5.  Fiedler, Edgar, <u>Across The Board</u>, New York, N.Y., The Conference Board, 1977.

# CHAPTER 16

---

# INFLATION AND MONETARISM

*"His [Keynes] disciples, as disciples will, went much farther than the master. The view became widespread that money does not matter." -- Milton Friedman*

## THE ECONOMICS OF INFLATION

Gross Domestic Product can be defined as the aggregates of all revenue that is received for the sale of goods and services that are produced in an economy in one year. In addition, GDP can be represented using the simple equation of: "R = P x Q," where:

R = Total Revenue = GDP,
P = Aggregate prices of all goods and services,
Q = Aggregate quantity of all goods and services
    produced.

Nominal GDP is the total value of goods and services reported at current prices. Real GDP is the term that economists use to describe the total amount of goods and services produced, adjusted for price level changes, i.e., nominal GDP = P x Q, and real GDP = Q.

For example, between 2009, the year currently used by the Department of Commerce as the base year, and 2013 the U.S. gross domestic product, measured in nominal terms, increased from $14,418 to $16,800 billion, an increase of $2,382 billion or 16.5 percent. However, a major portion of the dollar value of GDP reflected an increase in the prices at which goods and services were actually sold. For comparison, the Department of Commerce sets the base year, in this case 2009, at 100. The GDP deflator is then used to adjust nominal

GDP to real GDP. The GDP deflator is used to adjust gross domestic product to account for the effects of inflation because it is the most broadly based measure of price changes in the U.S. economy. For 2013, the GDP deflator was 106.588 or 6.588 percent higher than it was in 2009. To adjust nominal GDP to real GDP, nominal GDP is divided by the GDP price deflator as follows:

### Table 16-1 Nominal and Real GDP

| Description | | ($ in Billions) | ($ in Billions) | ($ in Billions) |
|---|---|---|---|---|
| Nominal GDP | | | $16,800 | |
| ----------------- = | Real GDP | | --------- = | $15,761 |
| GDP Deflator | | | 1.06588 | |
| | | | | |
| Description | | 2009 | 2013 | Increase |
| Nominal GDP | | $14,418 | $16,800 | $2,382 |
| Real GDP | | $14,418 | $15,761 | $1,345 |

Therefore, the increase in GDP from 2009 through 2013 can be broken down into its two fundamental elements as follows:

| Increase due to | $ (Billions) | % Increase |
|---|---|---|
| Price (P) | $ 1,037 | 7.2 |
| Quantity (Q) | $ 1,345 | 9.3 |
| | --------- | -------- |
| Total Increase | $ 2,382 | 16.5 |

During this five-year period, GDP increased by an average of 3.3 percent. The average increase due to price changes was 1.4 percent and the increase in real output averaged only 1.9 percent. This is an indication of a period of slow growth in output and a moderate rate of inflation.

Inflation is defined by economists as a long-term sustained increase in the general level of prices. The most often used measures of changes in the price level are the GDP deflator, the producer price index and the consumer price index. The GDP deflator, used in the above example, is a weighted average of the prices of all final goods and services produced in the economy in one year. The producer price index is a ratio of a composite of prices based on a sample of goods and services bought by business firms. Economists use the PPI as an early indication of the future direction of inflation. This is because many of the producer prices are those of the raw materials used as inputs in the production of consumer goods.

The most widely reported measure of inflation is the consumer price index. The CPI is often used to index wages in labor contracts and is also used by the federal government to decide the yearly increase in social security payments and the salaries paid to many government workers. To determine the CPI, the government records the prices of approximately 90,000 different consumer purchases in seven different groups each month. The major groups of consumer purchases are entertainment, medical care, housing, food and beverage, transportation, apparel, and other goods and services. The data is collected and compiled by the U.S. Department of Labor Statistics that has about 680 workers and 360 part-time collectors who survey prices in eighty-five cities. The annual budget for developing the CPI on a monthly basis is about $35 million.

## THE ROOTS OF INFLATION IN AMERICA

The result of the simultaneous use of expansive fiscal and monetary policies that was started in 1964, was the achievement of an exceptionally low rate of unemployment. However, the low unemployment rate came at the expense of future price increases. At the beginning of 1966, unemployment moved below 4 percent for the first time since 1957 and remained below that level until the first quarter of 1970. However, the increasing aggregate demand that reduced unemployment, also placed pressure on the economy's production capability. The combination of increased consumer disposable income and the expansion of the money supply created a situation where there was more marginal money available to spend than products available for purchase. This occurrence of "too much money chasing too few goods," as economists called it, accelerated the rate of price increases and created a widespread anticipation of further price increases. This created a psychology of inflation among American businesses who became more concerned with increases in revenue than with controlling operating expenses. The attitude of many producers and even commercial banks was that, if they could pass along price increases to consumers, why should they worry about controlling costs.

In the Keynes system deflation and unemployment called for higher public expenditure and lower taxes, which were politically acceptable actions. Price inflation, on the other hand, called for lower government expenditure and higher taxes, which were far from politically agreeable. Therefore, the economics of John Maynard Keynes, while acceptable in theory, was not effective in controlling inflation. Keynesian policy was a one-way street, an avenue that presented a politically pleasant remedy for curing a recession, but a politically unpalatable solution to the problem of inflation. After 1966 the rate of inflation began to accelerate; it went up more than 6 percentage points between 1969 and 1970, nearly 8 percent between 1972 and 1973 and nearly 14 percent from 1974 to 1975. In 1975 the phrase "double digit inflation," was introduced to American economic terminology.

A further and yet more serious problem in all the industrial countries was the new form of inflation. This was price and wage increases coming from the interaction in the modern economy and its large corporate organizations. With industrial concentration, corporations had achieved a very substantial measure of control over their prices. Also, trade unions, by controlling the supply of labor to large manufacturing corporations, had achieved substantial authority over the wages and associated benefits paid to their members. From the interaction of these entities came a new and powerful inflationary force. This was the upward pressure of wage settlements on prices, and the upward pull of living costs on wages. This was the interacting dynamic that came to be called the "wage-price spiral."[1]

In 1965, with the economy running at nearly full capacity, President Lyndon Johnson instituted his "Great Society" social welfare program. At the same time America had begun a military involvement in the civil war between North and South Vietnam. However, based on excessively optimistic forecasts of military and domestic expenses, the total cost of this joint program was badly underestimated. The Johnson administration began to realize that taxes would have to be raised to prevent further inflation. However, no tax increase was enacted until 1968, when inflation was already well established. The new taxes were introduced as a surcharge rather then a part of the permanent tax tables. The reaction of consumers to a temporary increase in tax rates was a decrease in savings. The decrease in savings increased the marginal propensity to consume which offset the effects of the tax increase. This change in consumer spending habits made the tax increase totally ineffective.

## Policies of the Nixon and Ford Administrations

In 1969, Richard Nixon became the thirty-seventh president of the United States. The Nixon administration found it necessary to maintain the tax surcharge throughout 1969, and then the surcharge was removed in stages. After all, politicians do not like to give up increased taxes. Meanwhile, the Federal Reserve began to implement policy designed to tighten the money supply. The result of the Feds policy was a sharp reduction in the growth of the nation's money supply and an end to the economic expansion that had begun in 1962. By 1970, a recession had replaced the long economic expansion in the United States and recessions bring about an event that often puts fear in the heart of politicians, i.e., unemployment.

A combination of 6 percent unemployment and 5 percent inflation created a real problem for politicians about to launch a reelection campaign. The problem for the administration was how to reduce unemployment and inflation at the same time. Remember, both monetary and fiscal policies, which are designed to effect recession or inflation, work on one side of the problem at a time. President Nixon's answer to this dual problem was the announcement of a "New Economic Policy." The most important part of the new economic policy was an immediate freeze on all wages and prices. Although the price controls received widespread political support when they were announced, they proved mostly ineffective. Employers and workers quickly found ways to limit the effect of these controls. Many goods that were normally sold domestically were exported to avoid the price controls. Companies found ways to avoid the wage controls by promoting key employees or by changing job titles.

The result of the first peacetime attempt to establish wage and price controls was, for the most part, a failure. The controls were designed to cure inflation by treating its symptoms, while at the same time other government policies exacerbated the causes of the inflation. Most wage and price controls were dropped in mid-1973. However, since the factors that cause inflation had not been addressed, the result was an increase in inflation after the controls were lifted. Finally, beginning at the end of 1973, there came the large increase in oil prices, the results of the cartel action of the Oil Producing States (OPEC). Between 1972 and 1981, the index of prices of household fuels in the United States climbed from 118.5 (1967=100) to 675.9, an increase of almost 600 percent.

In 1975, President Gerald Ford called into conference some of the country's better known economists to prescribe for inflation (There was a 13.5 percent increase in the consumer price index in that year). The full group agreed on only one remedy: government should remove any impediments to market competition. For practical effect, this was no better than the president's own prescription, which was the wearing of buttons inscribed with the insignia (WIN - Whip Inflation Now). The Keynes system of using fiscal policy while theoretically logical, was in practice of limited value. Congress was not going to vote to increase taxes or to reduce expenditures to decrease inflation. This is because most congressmen run for office on a platform emphasizing the amount of increased government programs that they can obtain for their district. The way that politicians get elected to office in the United States, was found to be mutually exclusive with the requirements of Keynes economics, during periods of inflation. Consequently, there remained only one viable course of action: to use monetary policy to control inflation.[2]

## MONETARY POLICY

In 1979, President Jimmy Carter appointed Paul Volcker as the Chairman of the Federal Reserve System. Under Volcker, the Federal Reserve began a policy that was determined to control inflation.

However, before we examine the effects of this new policy, it would be beneficial to explain just how monetary policy works and to illustrate how the Fed uses its monetary tools to implement the policy.

Monetary policy operates against inflation by raising interest rates. As interest rates increase, consumer durable goods such as new homes and automobiles become too expensive to purchase and business organizations reduce investment spending as the expected return on investment for new projects does not meet the companies' minimum return on investment requirements. This, in turn, reduces bank lending, the resulting deposit of funds and the creation of money.

## Monetary Policy and the Federal Reserve System

Monetary policy is executed by the Federal Reserve System in the United States. The Federal Reserve System is divided into twelve district banks that are directed by a nine-person board of directors with three coming from commercial banks, three from non-banking business interest and three appointed by the Federal Reserve Board. The Federal Open Market Committee is the official policy making body of the Federal Reserve System. The committee is made up of the seven members of the Board plus five of the twelve district bank presidents. Since the New York Federal Reserve Bank actually carries out monetary policy, the president of the Federal Reserve Bank of New York, is a permanent member of the committee.

The major responsibility of the Federal Open Market Committee is to set monetary policy goals that, in theory, would lead to long-term economic growth and stable prices. The Fed controls the money supply, which in turn, affects the nation's gross domestic product and the level of prices. The Federal Open Market Committee sets monetary targets and then implements them through the Federal Reserve Bank of New York. Each FOMC directive outlines the conduct of monetary policy over a six to eight weeks period.

The Federal Reserve controls the money supply by changing the reserves of its member banks. There are three ways that Federal Reserve action can affect the money supply. These tools are an adjustment to banks reserve requirements, changes in the Federal

Reserve Discount Rate and Open Market Operations. These tools work as follows:

## Reserve Requirement

The Fed requires banks to hold a fraction of their deposits on reserve. This fraction is the required reserve and was last changed in 1992 to 10 percent of demand deposits. Legal reserves are the sum of a bank's vault cash and deposits in the Federal Reserve Bank. When legal reserves equal required reserves, the bank has no excess reserves and can make no new loans. If the Fed lowers the reserve requirement, as it did in 1992 from 12 to 10 percent on transaction accounts, a portion of what was previously required reserves becomes excess reserves. Excess reserves can be used by commercial banks to make loans and in turn, to expand the money supply. Also, if the Fed wants to fight inflation, it can increase reserve requirements which will reduce excess reserves and reduce the money supply.

## Discount Rate

The Discount rate is the interest the Fed charges its member banks who borrow directly from the Federal Reserve. When the Fed raises the discount rate, it raises the cost of borrowing. This action reduces the amount of reserves borrowed by member banks. If the Fed reduces the discount rate the excess reserves at commercial banks will tend to increase. This, however, is not a very effective tool for controlling the money supply, for banks usually borrow from the Fed only to satisfy seasonal needs and as a last resort.

## Open Market Operations

This is the major tool of monetary policy. If the Fed wants to Increase bank reserves, the Federal Open Market Committee issues a directive to the bond trading desk at the New York Fed, to buy bonds. The bonds are purchased from private bond dealers. The dealers are paid with checks drawn on the Federal Reserve, which then are deposited in the dealers' accounts at commercial banks. As bank deposits and reserves increase, banks are able to make new loans. To the extent that the banks use these new reserves to make loans, the money supply expands. If the Fed wants to decrease the money supply, it sells bonds.

The expansion of the money supply depends on the amount of new purchases of securities by the Fed and the banking system's willingness to make new loans. If the banks choose to use excess reserves to buy securities for their own portfolio, then the money supply is not increased.

Also, when the Fed talks of controlling the money supply, they are not just referring to cash in consumers' pockets. The Fed defines money in terms of M1 and M2. M1 is called the money stock and is defined as Federal Reserve notes in circulation plus transaction deposits. Transaction deposits are made up mostly of demand deposits kept with commercial banks. M2 is defined as M1 plus short term liquid assets that cannot be used directly as a medium of exchange but can be easily converted into cash or checkable deposits. The money supply, referred to as M2, includes M1 plus money market demand deposits at banks, money market mutual fund accounts, savings accounts and certificates of deposit that are under one hundred thousand dollars. When the Federal Reserve announces that they are targeting the money supply they are referring to the monetary items in M2. What the Fed normally targets is a range of yearly growth of the money supply, for example, between 4 and 8 percent per year.

## Monetary Policy and Inflation

As the 1970's passed, inflation persisted. The administration of President Jimmy Carter initiated a strong monetarist action. During the early 1980's another word was added to the economist's vocabulary, "Stagflation," that describes a stagnant economy in association with continuing inflation. In the early 1980's, interest rates were brought to unprecedented levels, in the United States. This resulted in the unwanted combination of double-digit inflation and double digit interest rates. Double digit interest rates curtailed demand for new housing construction and for automobiles and other credit supported purchases. In 1982 and 1983, they brought a sharp restriction in business investment expenditure. The sharp reduction in business investment resulted in a large increase in unemployment, i.e., 10.7 percent in late 1982. Further, the high interest rates brought in a strong flow of foreign funds, which bid up the value of the dollar, curtailed American exports, and strongly encouraged imports, especially from Japan. The overall result of the use of monetary policy to curtail inflation was the deepest economic recession since the Great Depression of the 1930's. [3]

However, by the end of 1984, the consumer price index was nearly stable. Inflation had been substantially reduced. Monetary policy had worked to control inflation, by producing a severe economic slump. There remained a question as to rather the cure was worst than the disease. One way to answer this question is to analyze the results of the 1980 in the form of GDP growth. Gross domestic product increase from $ 3,131 billion in 1981 to $5,489 in 1989 an increase of over 75 percent an average increase of over 9 percent.  In comparison, by 1988 the CPI index had fallen to 4.1 percent.

## MILTON FRIEDMAN AND MONETARISM

Many economists believe that the equation of exchange provides important insights into the way the economy functions and the way monetary policy can affect price levels in the long run. Monetarism is a theory of long-term macroeconomic equilibrium based on the equation of exchange. According to the equation of exchange, shifts in the velocity of money are reasonably predictable. The equation of exchange was first introduced into economics in 1911, by Irving Fisher of Yale University. The most popular version of the equation of exchange is the "Quantity Theory of Money" with its simple equation of MV=PQ. The M in this equation represents the money stock and the V is the velocity of money. The velocity of money is defined as the amount of times money is spent during the course of one year. The P in the equation represents the general price level and the Q is the amount of goods and services actually produced by an economy in one year. Therefore, according to the equation, the stock of money multiplied by the number of times money turns over equals the dollar value of all goods and services produced in that year.

## Monetary Economics

The basis for the monetarist theory is as follows:

- Velocity of money is constant or at least predictable.

- The amount of goods and services that can be produced in the short run is fixed because organizations require time to increase their production capability.

- Increases in the supply of money, in the long-run, will only result in an offsetting increase in price levels. The quantity theory essentially eliminates velocity and quantity from the equation, and concludes that any change in the money stock will be felt only in the price level.

Monetarists usually agree that short term changes in the supply of money can affect economic activity. For example, the Federal Reserve can increase the money supply that will lower interest rates. In times of recession, the lower interest rates will stimulate additional consumer purchases of durable goods and increases in business spending. The reason for the increased spending is because many consumer items that are purchased on credit become more affordable with lower interest rates. Also, business projects that did not provide an acceptable rate of return under assumptions of high interest rates, may be approved when the cost of funding the proposed projects is reduced. There is one other key ingredient that determines whether monetary policy will be effective. Monetary economics works through the extension of bank credit. Therefore, the commercial banking systems must be willing to make loans if monetary policy is to have any influence on economic growth.

While monetarists concede that the Federal Reserve System can affect economic growth, they argue that these benefits are only short-term. In the long-term, they hold, changes in the money supply can only change price levels. Assuming the velocity of money is constant, the classical quantity theory of money implies that, over the long-run, rapid inflation can be caused by growth of the money stock, if that growth is in excess of the long-term growth rate of the gross domestic product. This implies that monetary policy can keep inflation under control over the long-run by making sure the growth rate of the money stock does not exceed the growth rate of an economy's ability to produce.

## Milton Friedman (1912-2006)

Milton Friedman

Milton Friedman was a diligent advocate of the policy that was to fill the post-Keynesian void. Friedman was the leading American exponent of the classical competitive market, which he claimed still exists, except as it suffered from ill-advised government intrusion. He is a powerful opponent of government regulation and government in general. According to Friedman, the key to a healthy, stable economy is for the money supply to expand, at a constant rate, in accordance with the growth of an economy's production capability. He is a believer in laissez faire capitalism and a fan of Adam Smith. For his work, he received the Nobel Prize in Economics in 1976. Friedman's books include "A Monetary History of the United States, Capitalism and Freedom, and Free to Choose." Friedman taught at the University of Chicago for 30 years. He retired in 1977 and currently works out of the Hoover Institute at Stanford University.      In a series of studies Friedman rescued the quantity theory of money from the attacks of Keynesian economists. In 1956, Friedman published a set of essays that were designed to test the quantity theory. According to Friedman, demand for money and in turn the velocity of money is stable. The demand for money depends on long-term factors such as health, education, and individual income expectations. Since consumers do not vary their long run expectations very often, the amount of times each year that they spend their money does not vary widely. In other words, velocity remains constant in the long-run. Consumers will not let a bad week or month or even a year alter their spending patterns. They will simply use up some of their savings.[4]

To test his theory of long-run stable velocity of money, Friedman, with Anna J. Schwartz, published "A Monetary History of the United States, 1867-1960." This publication pointed out that between the years 1929 and 1933, the quantity of money available in the United States, had plunged by one-third. According to Friedman and Schwartz, one of the major causes of the Great Depression was the refusal of the Federal Reserve to provide liquidity to the nation's banks when panic stricken depositors demanded redemption of their deposits. In summary, Friedman claimed that poor policy execution by the Federal Reserve has accompanied every severe recession and every significant inflation that occurred in the twentieth century.

In addition to explaining the power of money and breathing new life into the quantity theory, Friedman attempted to challenge Keynes' claim that government spending could spur the economy. However, to prove this point, monetarist had to show that the Keynesian expenditure multiplier did not exist. Monetarist, when analyzing the Keynesian prescription for stimulating an economy, ask one simple question: Where does the money come from? If the money supply remains constant and the government increases its expenditures, then either consumers or businesses must spend less. Therefore, increased government spending must take the place of business or consumer spending. Economists refer to the replacement of consumer and business expenditures with government spending as the "Crowding Out" effect.

Keynesians do not deny that crowding out takes place. However, they propose that crowding out does not completely offset government spending, especially during a recession. Therefore, the debate between the monetarist and Keynesians revolves around the question of the size of the multiplier and whether it is consistent during different levels of economic growth and recession. Data Resources Corporation has developed a large computer model of gross domestic product and its many components. According to the DRI model, the multiplier is estimated to be about 1.6 the first year of the increased government expenditures and steadily dropping after that.[5]

By the late 1970's, the monetarists were no longer receiving the butt of jokes from the economics' profession. Many of the views of Milton Friedman and the monetarist were being recognized. Central Banks throughout the world began to closely monitor their country's money supply. Main-stream economists absorbed many of the monetarists' views and began to shed their insistence on the use of fiscal policy alone. An even congress was rescued, as the Federal Reserve provided them with a set of tools for fighting inflation without the difficult task of having to reduce their spending habits.

## NOTES:

**Chapter 11**
**Inflation and Monetarism**

1.    Galbraith, John Kenneth, <u>Economics in Perspective</u>, Boston, MA, Houghton Mifflin Company, 1987. p. 267.
2.    Galbraith, p. 270.
3.    Galbraith, p. 275.
4.    Buchholz, Tod, G. <u>New Ideas From Dead Economists</u>,      New York, N.Y., Penguin Books, 1989, p. 231.
5.    Buchholz, p. 234.

# CHAPTER 17

---

## RONALD REAGAN AND THE 1980's

*General Secretary Gorbachev, if you seek peace, if you seek prosperity for the Soviet Union and Eastern Europe, if you seek liberalization: Come here to this gate! Mr. Gorbachev, open this gate! Mr. Gorbachev, tear down this wall—Ronald Reagan*

### RONALD REAGAN (1911-2004)

Ronald Reagan

The 1980s will be remembered in America as the era of conservative politics with Ronald Reagan as its chief advocate. Ronald Reagan was not merely a successful president, he was a great president. Not all intellectuals agree with this statement, however, the majority of American voters who overwhelming elected him to two terms in office would agree. Reagan dominated American politics in the second half of the twentieth century in much the way Franklin D. Roosevelt dominated the first. Clare Booth Luce once said that history will remember each president by a single line: "Lincoln freed the slaves," or "FDR brought the country out of depression" for example. Margaret Thatcher, the British Prime Minister during the 1980s, came close to composing Reagan's legacy when she said, "Ronald Reagan won the cold war without firing a shot."

When Reagan came to office in 1981, America was on a downward spiral in economic well-being and global influence. He faced several problems including rapid inflation, the energy crisis, unemployment, and government over-regulation.

Inflation had been accelerating since the 1960s and reached double digits in the 70s. At a rate of 12 percent in 1979-1980, inflation would double the prices of basic goods and cut in half the value of savings and pension plans in just a few years. The energy problem, with rising gasoline prices and fuel shortages, also contributed to higher prices. Gasoline prices had soared from about 35 cents a gallon in 1970 to more that $1.50 in 1980.

Interest rates had peaked at 21 percent in 1980, making it difficult for most families to buy homes and for companies to fund the purchase of long-term assets such as new factories and equipment. Unemployment and poverty rates were high, and industrial productivity was down to about 1.5 percent per year. Consumer confidence was low and economic growth had ground to a halt resulting in the worst economy since the great depression.

A policy analysis study by the Cato Institute highlighted some of Reagan's economic achievements during the years 1981 through 1989. The average annual growth rate of real gross domestic product (in 1987 dollars) from 1981 to 1989 was 3.2 percent per year, compared to 2.8 percent from 1974 to 1981. Real median household income rose by $4,000 in the period, from $37,868 in 1981 to $42,049 in 1989. From 1981 through 1989 the U.S. economy produced 17 million new jobs, or roughly 2 million jobs per year. When Reagan took office, the unemployment rate was 7.6 percent. In the recession of 1981-82, that rate peaked at 9.7 percent. When Reagan left office, the unemployment rate was 5.5 percent. In 1980 the consumer price index (CPI) rose to 13.5 percent. By Reagan's second year in office, the inflation rate fell by more than half to 6.2 percent. In 1988, the CPI had fallen to 4.1 percent. In 1981 the prime rate (lending rate to high credit quality businesses) was over 18 percent. By 1987 the prime rate had fallen to 8.2 percent. The stock market as reflected in the Dow Jones Industrial Index, doubled in value and the United States reaffirmed its position as the world's preeminent economy.[1]

Reagan's achievements on stopping the advance of communism were even more amazing. When Reagan was elected president democracy was on the retreat in much of the world. Soviet Premier Khrushchev's boast that the Soviets would "bury the West" seemed a real possibility. In South and Central America, guerrilla revolutions, fueled by popular discontent against the old dictatorships led to a socialist rebellion in many parts of the region. For the first time, the Soviet nuclear arsenal surpassed that of the United States.

During the Reagan administration, the communist influence in the region began to decline as dictatorships collapsed in Chile, Haiti, and Panama. In addition eight more Latin America countries, Bolivia, Honduras, Argentina, Grenada, El Salvador, Uruguay, Brazil and Guatemala, elected democratic leaders. Fewer than one-third of the countries in Latin America were democratic in 1981: more than 90 percent of the region developed democratic governments by 1989.[2]

The freedom revolution soon penetrated into the Soviet countries. Poland held free elections, and Lech Walsea, the president of the country's largest labor union, was elected president. The march toward democracy continued until the majority of the countries in the Soviet bloc declared their freedom, and in 1989, the Berlin Wall, long the symbol of communist domination, came down.

In 1991, the Soviet Union abolished itself, and Boris Yeltsin became the first freely elected president of Russia. An era of friendship between the United States and Russia was made possible by the diminished nuclear rivalry between the two nations as Russia strives towards democracy and the century old debate between Capitalism and Communism was resolved.

Reagan did not achieve this success alone, others such as Margaret Thatcher, Pope John Paul II, Vaclav Havel, Lech Walesa, and especially Soviet General Secretary Mikhail Gorbachev, played a key role. However, Reagan was the catalyst; he was the chief architect of this change.

Dinesh D'Souza, a domestic policy analyst in the Reagan administration, in his book "Ronald Reagan: How an Ordinary Man Became an Extraordinary Leader" summarized his and many others' opinions as to Reagan's achievements by writing "Reagan's greatness derives in large part from the fact that he was a visionary, a conceptualizer who was able to see the world differently from the way it was. Reagan understood Soviet Communism with the same moral clarity that Lincoln had in understanding slavery. Both men were fundamentally motivated not by political calculation but by a basic sense of right and wrong."[3]

## SUPPLY SIDE ECONOMICS

In the 1970s and early 1980s, two economist revised the classical economic system and refurbished it to fit the modern would. The two men were Robert Mundell and Arthur Laffer. The economic system was named supply side economics. Robert Mundell was the first economist to predict the rise in inflation that occurred in America and the rest of the world during the 1970s. Keynesian economic theorists during the 1970s were baffled by the recurring combination of high inflation and high unemployment. They couldn't solve the problem of stagflation. Mundell turned the Keynesian demand model upside down. Instead of the philosophy that taxes should be raised to curb excess demand, Mundell argued that inflation is a monetary problem that can only be cured by an increase in dollar purchasing power value. Mundell wrote that only tax-rate reduction would restore the necessary worker rewards and investment incentives to increase the supply of new jobs, production capital formation and growth. Robert Mundell, currently a professor at Columbia University, received the Nobel Prize in Economics in 1999.

Arthur Laffer, a protégé of Mundell's, extended the theory by developing what became known as the Laffer curve. The Laffer curve suggests that there is an optimal tax rate that maximizes government revenue from taxation. Laffer argued that as taxes increased from fairly low levels, tax revenues received by the government would also increase. However, he stated that as tax rates rose, there would come a point (on the curve he designed) where people would regard it as not worth working so hard. Essentially, the marginal returns to working harder would become lower because tax rates are higher at higher incomes. Therefore, Laffer suggested that, if high tax rates were decreased, this would provide increased incentives for people to work harder and, thereby, increase total tax revenues for the government.

The basic premise of supply-side economics is that it places supply over demand in the hierarchy of economics and, therefore, deals with enhancing economic production, efficiency, and growth within the context of the marketplace. Supply-side economics focuses largely on relative prices, such as incentives for working, saving, investing, and risk-taking. Supply-side economics falls under the broader category of free-market economics. Therefore, supply-siders hold the same skepticism of government, as do their free-market cousins, such as public choice, monetarists, and Austrian economists. They argue that production for the sake of production is fruitless. Production must meet current demands or create new ones. Value must be created. Supply-side economists recognize that government lacks the requisite experience, knowledge, and incentive to make resources allocations that create value.

## REAGANOMICS

In 1981 Reagan advisors such as Arthur Laffer, Norman Ture, Martin Anderson and Jack Kemp, urged him to implement supply-side tax cuts. This change in economic policy became known as Reaganomics and consisted of four key elements designed to reverse the high-inflation, slow growth economic record of the 1970s. The key elements were as follows: (1) A restrictive monetary policy engineered through Federal Reserve Chairman Paul Volker; (2) The Economic Recovery Tax Act of 1981 including a 25 percent across-the-board tax cut designed to spur savings, investment, work, and economic efficiency; (3) A promise to balance the budget through domestic spending restraint; (4) An agenda to roll back government regulation.

### Fiscal Policy Achievements

The economic achievements of the Reagan years as previously outlined were impressive. The fiscal record of the 1980s was not as impressive. The national public debt in real dollars (adjusted for inflation in 1987 dollars) doubled from $1,004 billion in 1981 to $2,028 billion in 1989. The rise in the national debt imposed significant repayment costs to future generations. Nominal federal revenues doubled in the 1980s from $518 billion to $1,031 billion. As a share of GDP, however, federal tax revenues fell by 1 percent during the period. The federal budget was not cut under Reagan. In fact, it was 69 percent larger when Reagan left office than when he entered it. As a share of GDP, federal outlays declined by less than 1 percent. Overall domestic spending growth was relatively constrained during the Reagan presidency. Domestic outlays as a share of GDP fell from 15.3 percent to 12.9 percent from 1981 to 1989. However, the reductions in domestic spending as a percent of GDP were much smaller than the amounts needed to balance the federal budget, cut taxes and finance a military build-up.

Analysis of the data from 1981 points a finger directly at the defense build-up as the main reason for the deficits of the Reagan era. The cumulative increase in defense spending from 1981 to 1989 was $809 billion. The commutative buildup in the deficit for the same period was $779 billion. If the defense spending had been held to an inflation rate of 3 percent during the period of 1981 to 1989, the total real deficit would have fallen rather than risen.[4]

In conclusion, when the facts are analyzed a case can be firmly stated that the Reagan tax cuts were not a primary cause of the expansion of the deficit in the 1980s. The two main causes were an unexpectedly sharp reduction in inflation in the early 1980s that led to large real increases in federal spending, and a nearly $1 trillion military build-up during the last phase of the cold war. If the entire accumulation of debt in the 1980s went to finance the Reagan defense build-up, the key policy question would shift to whether it was appropriate to borrow for those large military expenditures. Was the Reagan administration justified in paying for the one-time increase in "public investment" spending through debt rather than taxes? Or, put another way; was it appropriate to have asked our children and grandchildren to help defray the cost of defeating the Soviet Empire? The answer to that question rests to some extent on the issue of whether the defense build-up materially contributed to the collapse of the Soviet Union. If the Reagan defense buildup contributed to the fall of the Soviet Union, and many Soviet leaders, including General Secretary Mikhail Gorbachev, have indicated that it was a major factor, than the value to our children of establishing an economic partnership with the new Russia and presidents Boris Yeltzin and currently Vladimir Putin should far out way any cost.

## Deregulation

Reagan reappointed Paul Volker chairman of the Federal Reserve Board and later appointed Alan Greenspan who remains the current chairman. He gave them both the authority to do what it took and encouraged them to deregulate the economy. Reagan also turned around the labor situation in the Federal government by standing up to the air traffic controllers union (PATCO) and settled their dispute firmly as he refused to allow a materialistic union to strike against the American public. Reagan's first official act as president was, by executive order, to immediately terminate oil price controls, a policy that instantly reenergized America's domestic exploration and production of oil. Virtually every energy policy in the 1970s exacerbated the energy crisis, from the windfall profits tax to energy price controls. Reagan hastened the end of the energy crisis by repealing virtually all of these policies. Reagan was instrumental in deregulating the transportation industry and the banking and financial services industry. He was instrumental in setting loose the forces that led to the deregulation of telecommunications, and more recently, utilities. It was Reagan who engineered a free trade agreement with Canada, which was later, under President Clinton, expanded to include Mexico to form the NAFTA agreement. Reagan also floated the notion of hemispheric free trade where, at some point in the future, Canada, the United States, Mexico, and all of Latin America would be linked into a free trading zone. Creating a free America trade zone is still a topic for discussion among the many countries of the Americas.5

## THE FALL OF COMMUNISM

At the end of World War II, there were two military superpowers, the United States and the Soviet Union. However, there was only one economic superpower, the United States. In any economy, certain items can be produced at the expense of other products. When the Reagan administration increased its defense spending in the middle 1980's, the Soviet Union had to increase their spending on defense in order to maintain military equity. Since the Soviet Union was not an economic superpower, their increased defense expenditures had to be funded through a decreased investment in civilian consumption. However, the reason for the fall of communism in the Soviet Union was even more fundamental than the trade-off between civilian and defense spending. The reason that Communism failed is due to the faults of the system itself.

The Soviet system, unlike capitalism, did not evolve gradually over time. The system came into being after the revolution of 1917. A semi-feudal society was taken over by a group of revolutionaries who were driven by the philosophy of Karl Marx. According to Marx, after the revolution, a temporary regime known as the "dictatorship of the proletariat," would take over the transition from capitalism to socialism. Once government was organized, a planned socialist economy would emerge that would set up the organization that was necessary for the production and distribution of goods and services. However, the revolution presented, Lenin, Trotsky and the other leaders of the new Soviet Union with problems far more complex than Marx's utopian design. One of the major problems of the new government was how to distribute food from the farms to the factory workers.

In 1927, Joseph Stalin became the new leader of the Soviet Union. Stalin decided to solve the food distribution problem by taking over the farms. While the process of collectivizing both agriculture and industry solved the distribution problem, there was a tremendous social and economic cost. Many peasants slaughtered their livestock rather then hand them over to the new collective farms and others just refused to cooperate with the new system. In reprisal, Stalin acted with brutal force. Farmers that would not cooperate were executed or put in labor camps. In the cities, factory workers were given tasks by the central authorities. The right to strike was forbidden and trade unions were eliminated. Under Stalin, the Soviet Union was transferred from a utopian form of socialism, as advocated by Karl Marx, to a dictatorship.

Economists often define socialism as a system where the productive resources are owned by government. In a capitalist system, the market through the price system is used to produce and distribute goods and services. In the absence of a market, direct orders from a central planning agency must be used to distribute society's products. In a socialist economy, planners not consumers determine the demand for products. In a totally planned economy, every item that goes into the final plan must be in great detail. Schedules of production are needed down to the smallest items. Supplies of labor must also be planned. Thus, the master plan must be accompanied by a whole hierarchy of smaller plans in order to achieve the smallest of objectives. Even one little planning error can have disastrous affects, if it is part of the strategic link in the chain of production and distribution. In short, to effectively run a socialist system, the leaders of the system would have to know all of the possible available alternatives. The probability of success of such a system approximates the possibility that one group of people knows all the answers to all of the problems inherent in an economy. While it is possible to develop strategy for even a large economy, it is the execution of the plan that requires an ability greater than that, which could be possessed by a small group of people.

With all of its improbabilities, central planning worked in the years following World War II. However, after the war, the inherent problems of a socialist system began to appear. The problem of developing and implementing the basic framework of a modern industrial state became increasingly difficult. Under Stalin's successors Nikita Khrushchev and Leonid Brezhnev, the Soviet system began to show signs of failure. The system was becoming bogged down with a large bureaucracy. Consumer goods were produced in sufficient quantity, but they were of such poor quality that warehouses bulged with unusable shoes and shoddy clothes. Although the Soviet Union produced almost twice as much steel per capita as the United States, there was a chronic steel shortage because the material was used so wastefully. In summary, by the time that Mikhail Gorbachev began to speak of "Glasnost" (openness) and "Perestroika" (the fundamental restructuring of the economic system) in 1985, the Russian system was apparently becoming an economic failure.

According to Margate Thatcher, The meeting between Soviet General Secretary Mikhail Gorbachev and President Reagan at Reykjavik in October of 1986 was the turning point in the cold war. Finally, Gorbachev realized that he had a choice: continue a no-win arms race, which would utterly cripple the Soviet economy, or give up the struggle for global domination and establish peaceful relations with the West. In December 1987, Gorbachev visited Washington, DC to sign the INF treaty in which the superpowers agreed to reduce their intermediate-range nuclear missiles to zero. For the first time in history, the United States and the Soviet Union had agreed to eliminate an entire class of nuclear weapons.

On June 12, 1987, Reagan made a trip to the Brandenburg Gate in Berlin, Germany. The purpose of the trip was to encourage Gorbachev's reform efforts. Reagan used this speech to drive Gorbachev into an awkward political position, to compel him to prove his sincerity before the world. The most memorable part of the speech was when Reagan said: "General Secretary Gorbachev, if you seek peace, if you seek prosperity for the Soviet Union and Eastern Europe, if you seek liberalization: Come here to this gate! Mr. Gorbachev, open this gate! Mr. Gorbachev, tear down this wall."

The collapse of the Soviet empire in Eastern Europe occurred shortly after Reagan left office. The revolt began in Poland, where the Communists were routed in a public election and Lech Walesa became president of Poland. Next, Hungary claimed itself to be a free republic. On November 9, 1989, shortly after Reagan left office, demonstrators in East Germany removed the communist dictator Eric Honecker and the Berlin Wall were torn down.

In November of 1994, Reagan revealed to the world that he was suffering from the memory destroying neurological illness known as Alzheimer's disease. There is a bitter irony in the fact that Reagan, once a brilliant storyteller who was so delighted in entertaining friends and aides with stories of his past, had been robbed of the ability to access those tales. The man, who left the White House with the highest approval rating of any modern president, reportedly had little memory of having lived there. In a touching epistle to the citizens who twice elected him their leader, Reagan wrote, "I now begin the journey that will lead me into the sunset of my life."

Ronald Reagan Died at his home in Bel Air, California on June 5, 2004 of pneumonia as a complication of Alzheimer's. Reagan's body would lie in repose on Monday and Tuesday at the Reagan library. His casket would lie in state in the U.S. Capitol in Washington and he was buried at the Reagan presidential library in Simi Valley, California on Friday June 11th.

All week long the world sent praise for America's 40 president. Below is just a sample:

- **Former Soviet Mikhail Gorbachev**: "I deem Ronald Reagan a great president, with whom the Soviet leadership was able to launch a very difficult but important dialogue."
- **Former Prime Minister Margaret Thatcher**: "He will be missed not only by those who knew him and not only by the nation that he served so proudly and loved so deeply, but also by millions of men and women who live in freedom today because of the policies he pursued."
- **Senate Majority Leader Bill Frist**: "President Reagan's bold leadership in difficult times provided Americans with tremendous strength and inspiration."
- **Senate Minority Leader Tom Dashle**: "America has lost an icon. Ronald Reagan's leadership will inspire Americans for generations to come. His patriotism and devotion to our country will never be forgotten."
- **Lt. Col. Oliver North**: "Ronald Reagan was easily the greatest president of my lifetime—and he will be regarded as one of the greatest leaders this country has ever had."
- **Former President George H.W. Bush**: "We had been political opponents and became close friends. Reagan could take a stand and do it without creating bitterness or creating enmity on the part of other people.
- **Former President Bill Clinton**: "It is fitting that a piece of the Berlin Wall adorns the Ronald Reagan Building in Washington."
- **President George W. Bush**: "Ronald Reagan won America's respect with his greatness, and won its love with his goodness. He had the confidence that comes with conviction, the strength that

comes with character, the grace that comes with humility, and the humor that comes with wisdom."

- **Nancy Reagan:** "I think they broke the mold when they made Ronnie. He had absolutely no ego, and he was very comfortable in his own shin; therefore, he didn't feel he ever had to prove anything to anyone."

## NOTES:

## Chapter 11
## Ronald Reagan and the 1980s

1.  Niskanen, William A. & Moore, Stephen, <u>Supply-Side Tax Cuts and the Truth About the Reagan Economic Record</u>, Washington, DC, The Cato Institute, 1996, p. 3-5.
2.  D'Souza, Dinesh, <u>Ronald Reagan: How an Ordinary Man Became an Extraordinary Leader,</u> New York, NY, Touchtone, 1999, p. 26.
3.  D'Souza, P. 28
4.  Niskanen & Moore, P. 9.
5.  Kudlow, Lawrence, <u>Reagonomics: What Worked? What Didn't,</u> Presentation to the Center of the American Experience, Washington, DC, 1997, p. 2.

# CHAPTER 18

---

# NATIONAL DEBT AND INTERNATIONAL TRADE DEFICITS

*"There are two ways to conquer and enslave a nation. One is by the sword and the other is by debt." - John Adams*

## THE TWIN DEFICITS

During the severe recession of the early 1980's in the United States the production of goods and services declined over a broad range. With the exception of adequate housing, no one was thought to suffer because of what was not produced. All suffering was identified with the interruption in the flow of income, i.e., with the loss of employment. That, not prices or the unequal distribution of income, is demonstrably the prime social anxiety of our time. In the modern industrial economy production is of first importance not for the goods it produces but for the employment and income it produces. Economics in the 1980's concerns itself with the elements of national income (wages, rents, interest and profits), more than national product. Say's Law has, for all practical purposes, been reversed. That is demand creates its own supply.

Unemployment, in the past, has been seen as a macroeconomic problem. Unemployment was something caused or remedied by the overall design and management of fiscal and monetary policy. This also will cease to be so; increasingly it will be seen that unemployment arises from the non optimal performance and the changing competitive position of particular industries. In the United States, coal mining, steel making, automobile, and textile and apparel manufacturing are examples of industries that are losing market share to foreign competitors. While macroeconomic policies can increase or decrease general unemployment, they cannot remedy it, given the specifics of these industries.

Money spent abroad for goods and services and travel by American residents in excess of what foreigners were spending in the United States had an economic effect precisely opposite from the expansive public deficit of the Reagan administration. The Keynesian effect of economic stimulation through increased government spending was thus to a large extent offset in the 1980's by the negative effect of the large trade deficit.

## The Trade Deficit

The world may change, but the need for economics to explain the change remains. The world of the 1990's and beyond will be almost as different from the world of the 1950's as the industrial revolution was from merchant capitalism. The United States has gone from a point where they were the world's largest creditor after World War II to the world's largest debtor in the 1990's. From 2009 through 2013 the United States has run a huge current account deficit with the four Asian countries shown in Table 18-1.

Table 18-1
U. S. Asian Trade ($ in billions)

| Trade Deficit | 2009 | 2010 | 2011 | 2012 | 2013 |
|---|---|---|---|---|---|
| China | 264 | 302 | 318 | 333 | 327 |
| Japan | 49 | 75 | 81 | 94 | 91 |
| South Korea | 6 | 6 | 5 | 8 | 11 |
| Taiwan | 12 | 10 | 15 | 11 | 15 |
|  | ------- | ------- | ------- |  |  |
| Total | 331 | 393 | 419 | 446 | 444 |

As a comparison, the current account balance, for the United States in the year 2013, was a negative $379 billion. Of this total, $444 billion or over 100 percent of the trade deficit was with the above Asian Countries. Another way to examine the trade deficit is by region. For 2013 the trade deficit by geographical region was as follows:

| Geographic Region | 2013 Current Account Balance |
|---|---|
| Asian Countries | $444 |
| European Union | $ 2 |
| NAFTA (Canada & Mexico) | $ 39 |
| OPEC Countries | $ 47 |
| Remainder of the World | $-153 |
| Total Current Account | $379 |

**Source: Bureau of Economic Analysis Tables: March 2014**

Four geographic regions account for $532 of the total current account deficit of $379 or over 100 percent. The OPEC current account deficit was 12 percent of the total deficit in 2013 compared to 18 percent in 2012. This was a reduction of 6 percent from 1012 as the U.S. has become less dependent on OPEC oil. In addition OPEC countries are large purchasers of goods and services from the U.S.

## The International Balance of Payments Accounts

One way to help understand the international balance of payments accounts is to start with an analysis of the basic components of GDP as expenditures. The last component in the GDP as expenditures account is net exports.

The net export's component of GDP is derived from a country's balance of payments account. The balance of payments is a record of a country's trade in goods, services, and financial assets with the rest of the world. There are two basic categories in the balance of payments account; the current account and the capital account.

| GDP As Expense By Component | Dollar Amount | ($ in billions) |
|---|---|---|
| | **2012** | **2013** |
| Personal Consumption Expenditures | $11,150 | 11,502 |
| Gross Private Domestic Investment | $ 2,475 | 2,670 |
| Government Purchases | $ 3,167 | 3,125 |
| Net Exports | $ (547) | (497) |
| Total GDP | $16,245 | 16,800 |

The current account is the sum of the balances in the merchandise, services, net investment and net transfer receipts accounts. The merchandise account records all transactions involving goods. U.S. exports of goods are merchandise credits; U.S. imports of foreign goods are merchandise debits. The services account includes travel and tourism, royalties, transportation costs, and insurance premiums. The sum of the total merchandise and services accounts is equal to the GDP net exports. One of the largest components of the current account is the return on investments. The income earned from investments in foreign countries is a source of funds and the income paid on foreign-owned investments in the United States is a use of funds. The final component of the current account is net transfer receipts, which include foreign aid, gifts, and other payments to individuals that are not exchanged for goods or services.

The capital account is where trade involving financial assets is recorded. The capital, in this account, refers to financial flows such as bank deposits, purchases and sales of stocks and bonds, and loans. A source of funds is the sale of an asset to a foreign resident or a loan from a foreign organization such as a commercial bank. A use of funds is a purchase of assets that are owned by a foreign citizen or a loan to someone in that country. The total of source and use of funds must agree in order to balance the books between countries. A simple example, of an international sources and uses of funds statement, is shown below:

| Sources of Funds | Uses of Funds |
| --- | --- |
| Sale of an asset | Purchase of an asset |
| Borrowing from a country | Lending to a country |
| **Total Sources** | **Total Uses of Funds** |

When countries import more than they export, the difference must be made up in the capital account. In order to finance net imports, a nation has only two basic choices; that is to either sell some of its assets or to borrow from a country that has a positive position in net exports. Because of its propensity to consume more foreign goods than it sells, the United States has been forced to accumulate large amounts of foreign debt or to sell large amounts of its assets to foreigners. From 1990 through 2013, the United States has imported more than it exported every year. The resulting negative net export data from the Commerce Department is detailed in Table 18-2. In addition, Table 18-3 provides an example of an international sources and uses of funds statement. The difference between the net exports on a GDP basis and the current account balance is that the current account adds financial transfers to the Net Exports shown in the GDP accounts. For example, for 2013 (Net Investment Income minus Unilateral Transfers totaling = $118 + Net Exports of $-497) = Current Account Balance of $-379.

From 1990 through 2013 the United States accumulated $8,428.6 billion dollars in negative net exports on a current account basis. This is dollars that is owed from American businesses to the rest of the world.

## Table 18-2
## Net Exports from 1990 through 2013  ($ in Billions)

| Year | Exports | Imports | Net Exports |
|---|---|---|---|
| 1990 | $557.1 | $628.5 | $ -71.4 |
| 1991 | $601.5 | $621.1 | $-19.6 |
| 1992 | $640.5 | $671.5 | $-31.0 |
| 1993 | $660.1 | $725.8 | $-65.7 |
| 1994 | $722.0 | $818.4 | $-96.4 |
| 1995 | $818.6 | $902.8 | $-84.2 |
| 1996 | $875.2 | $963.1 | $-87.9 |
| 1997 | $966.4 | $1,055.8 | $-89.4 |
| 1998 | $964.9 | $1,116.7 | $-151.7 |
| 1999 | $989.8 | $1,240.7 | $-250.9 |
| 2000 | $1,069.0 | $1,438.0 | $-369.0 |
| 2001 | $1,050.3 | $1,380.1 | $-329.8 |
| 2002 | $1,014.9 | $1,438.5 | $-423.6 |
| 2003 | $1,049.0 | $1,543.9 | $-494.9 |
| 2004 | $1,147.0 | $1,764.0 | $-617.0 |
| 2005 | $1,740.9 | $2,545.8 | $-804.9 |
| 2006 | $2,096.2 | $2,907.7 | $-811.5 |
| 2007 | $2,410.6 | $3,149.2 | $-738.6 |
| 2008 | $2,591.3 | $3,264.6 | $-673.3 |
| 2009 | $2,115.9 | $2,535.8 | $-419.9 |
| 2010 | $2,496.6 | $2,966.8 | $-470.2 |
| 2011 | $2,843.8 | $3,317.2 | $-473.4 |
| 2012 | $2,936.5 | $3,411.5 | $-475.0 |
| 2013 | $2,927.3 | $3,306.6 | $379.3 |
| Total  21 Year | Accumulated | Trade Debt | **$8,428.6** |

## Source Bureau of Economic Analysis Tables March, 2014

## Table 18-3
## U.S. Balance of Payments for 2013 ($ in Billions)

| Balance of Payments | Sources | Uses | Balance |
|---|---|---|---|
| Current Account Merchandise Balance | | | |
| Exports | $1,590 | | |
| Imports | | $2,294 | |
| Balance of Trade | | | $-704 |
| | | | |
| Service Balances | $682 | $453 | $229 |
| GDP Net Exports | $2,272 | $2,747 | $-475 |
| Investment Income | $789 | $560 | $229 |
| Unilateral Transfers | | $133 | $-133 |
| | | | |
| Total Current Account | $3,061 | $3,440 | $-379 |
| Capital Account | | | |
| Capital Inflows | $906 | | |
| Capital Outflows | | $553 | |
| Capital Account Transactions | | $2 | |
| Statistical Error | $28 | | |
| Total Capital Account | $934 | $555 | $379 |
| Total Sources and Uses | | | 0 |
| | | | ==== |

**Source: Bureau of Economic Analysis – U.S. International Transactions Table 1, March 2014.**

Note: Net Exports in National Income Accounts totaled $497 billion. The small difference is the result of different survey techniques.

## Gross Federal Debt Outstanding

Federal debt managed by the Bureau of the Public Debt (BPD) comprises debt held by the public and debt held by certain federal government account, the latter of which is referred to as intragovernmental debt holdings. As of September 30, 2013 and 2012, outstanding gross federal debt managed by BPD totaled $16,732 and $16,059 billion, respectively. The increase in gross federal debt of $673 billion during fiscal year 2013 was due to a decrease in gross intragovernmental debt holdings of $33 billion and an increase in gross debt held by the public of $706 billion. As table 18-4 illustrates, both intragovernmental debt holdings and debt held by the public have increased since fiscal year 2006. The primary reason for the increases in intragovernmental debt holdings is the excess annual receipts (including interest earnings) over disbursements in the Federal Old-Age and Survivors Insurance Trust Fund, Civil Service Retirement and Disability Fund, Military Retirement Fund, and DOD Medicare-Eligible Retiree Health Care Fund. The increases in debt held by the public are due primarily to total federal government spending exceeding total federal revenues. As of September 30, 2013, gross debt held by the public totaled $11,976 billion and gross intragovernmental debt holdings totaled $4,756 billion.

As of September 30, 2013 the statutory debt limitations was $16,699. A delay in raising the statutory debt limit existed at the end of fiscal year 2013 and lasted until October 17, 2013 when the Continuing Appropriations Act of 2014 was enacted. This act established a process that resulted in an increase of the statutory debt limit on February 8, 2014.

## Table 18-4-A
## Total Federal Debt Fiscal Years Ending Sept. 30, 2006 – 2013

| Year | Deb Held by Public | Intragovernmental Debt Holdings | Total Federal Debt Outstanding |
|------|------|------|------|
| 2006 | 4,843 | 3,650 | 8,493 |
| 2007 | 5,049 | 3,944 | 8,993 |
| 2008 | 5,809 | 4,202 | 10,011 |
| 2009 | 7,552 | 4,346 | 11,898 |
| 2010 | 9,023 | 4,528 | 13,551 |
| 2011 | 10,127 | 4,654 | 14,781 |
| 2012 | 11,270 | 4,789 | 16,059 |
| 2013 | 11,976 | 4,756 | 16,732 |

### Interest Expense

The primary components of interest expense are interest paid on the debt held by the public and interest credited to federal government trust funds and other federal government accounts that hold Treasury securities. The interest paid on the debt held by the public affects the current spending of the federal government and represents the burden of servicing its debt (i.e., payments to outside creditors). Interest credited to federal government trust funds and other federal government accounts, on the other hand, does not result in an immediate outlay of the Federal Government because one part of the government pays the interest and another part receives it. However, this interest represents a claim on future budgetary resources and hence an obligation on future taxpayers. This interest, when reinvested by the trust funds and other federal government accounts, is included in the programs' excess funds not currently needed in operations, which are invested in federal securities. For fiscal year 2013, interest expense incurred totaled $425 billion, interest expense on debt held by the public was $247 billion, and $178 billion was interest incurred for intragovernmental debt holdings.

As Table 18-4 indicates, total interest expense increased from fiscal year 2007 to 2008. However, due to the economic conditions, there was a significant increase in the demand for government backed securities during fiscal year 2009, which resulted in lower average interest rates and interest expense for that year. For example, the average interest rates on Treasury bills outstanding as of September 30, 2009 and 2008 were 0.3 percent and 1.6 percent, respectively. Interest expense increased for fiscal years 2010 and 2011 due primarily to an increase in Treasury notes and bonds outstanding, which have higher average interest rates than Treasury bills. Interest expense decreased for fiscal year 2012 due primarily to a decrease in the average interest rates for Treasury notes, bonds, and Treasury Inflation-Protected Securities. For fiscal year 2013 interest expense was $425 billion a decrease of $7 billion from 2012

**Table 18-4-B**
**Interest on Federal Debt Fiscal Years Ending September 30, 2004 – 2013**

| Year | Debt Held by Public | Intra-Govt. Debt | Gross Federal Debt |
|------|---------------------|------------------|--------------------|
| 2004 | $158 | $164 | $322 |
| 2005 | $181 | $174 | $355 |
| 2006 | $221 | $183 | $404 |
| 2007 | $239 | $194 | $433 |
| 2008 | $242 | $212 | $454 |
| 2009 | $189 | $192 | $381 |
| 2010 | $215 | $198 | $413 |
| 2011 | $251 | 203 | $454 |
| 2012 | $245 | $187 | $432 |
| 2013 | $247 | $178 | $425 |

## Holders of the Federal Debt

Federal Debt Held by the Public includes federal debt held by U.S. citizens, corporations and government agencies and federal debt held outside of the U. S. government by individuals, corporations,

Federal Reserve Banks, state and local governments, and foreign governments and central banks. A continuing trend is the increase in reported foreign ownership of Treasury securities.

Treasury reporting shows that foreign ownership of Treasury securities represents a significant portion of debt held by the public. As of June 30, 2013, the reported amount of Treasury securities held by foreign and international investors represented an estimated 47 percent of debt held by the public. This percentage is slightly lower than the 48 percent as of June 30, 2012, but remains considerably higher than the estimated 30 percent of debt held by the public as of June 30, 2001. Treasury estimates that the amount of Treasury securities held by foreign and international investors has increased from $983 billion as of June 30, 2001, to $5,594 billion as of June 30, 2013—an increase of $4,611 billion. Estimates of foreign ownership of Treasury securities are derived from information reported under the Treasury International Capital reporting system.

**Debt Held by the Public**

Debt held by the public primarily represents the amount the Federal Government has borrowed to finance cumulative cash deficits. During fiscal year 2013, Treasury primarily used the existing suite of securities to meet the borrowing needs of the Federal Government while its offerings of long term securities extended the average length of maturity. As a result, Treasury notes increased by $635 billion, bonds by $156 billion, respectively. Treasury bills outstanding decreased by $85 billion in fiscal year 2013. As of September 30, 2013, gross debt held by the public totaled $11,976 billion an increase of $706 billion over 2012. This increase was primarily the result of borrowings needed to finance the government's fiscal year 2013 deficit.

The Federal Reserve Banks (FRBs) act as fiscal agents for Treasury, as permitted by the Federal Reserve Act. As fiscal agents for Treasury, the FRBs play a significant role in the processing of marketable book-entry securities and paper U.S. savings bonds. For marketable book-entry securities, selected FRBs receive bids; issue book-entry securities to awarded bidders and collect payments on behalf of Treasury; and make interest and redemption payments from

Treasury's account to the accounts of security holders. For paper U.S. savings bonds, selected FRBs sell, print, and deliver savings bonds; redeem savings bonds; and handle the related transfers of cash.

## Intragovernmental Debt Holdings

Intragovernmental debt holdings represent balances of Treasury securities held by over 239 individual federal government accounts with either the authority or the requirement to invest excess receipts in special U.S. Treasury securities that are guaranteed for principal and interest by the full faith and credit of the U.S. Government. Intragovernmental debt holdings primarily consist of balances in the Social Security, Medicare, Military Retirement and Health Care, and Civil Service Retirement and Disability trust funds. As of September 30, 2013, such funds accounted for $4,376 billion, or 92 percent, of the $4,756 billion intragovernmental debt holdings balances.

As of September 30, 2013 and 2012, gross intragovernmental debt holdings totaled $4,756 billion and $4,789 billion, respectively a decrease of $33 billion. The majority of intragovernmental debt holdings are Government Account Series (GAS) securities. GAS securities consist of par value securities and market-based securities, with terms ranging from on demand out to 30 years.

The Social Security trust funds consist of the Federal Old-Age and Survivors Insurance Trust Fund and the Federal Disability Insurance Trust Fund. The Medicare trust funds are made up of the Federal Hospital Insurance Trust Fund and the Federal Supplementary Medical Insurance Trust Fund. The Military Retirement and Health Care Funds consist of the Military Retirement Fund and the DOD Medicare-Eligible Retiree Health

## Changes to the Statutory Debt Ceiling

On August 2, 2011, the Budget Control Act of 2011 was signed into law raising the statutory debt limit by $400 billion to $14,694 billion, and by $500 billion to $15,194 billion on September 22, 2011. The Budget Control Act of 2011 also enacted caps on discretionary spending for fiscal years 2012 through 2021 and created the Joint

Select Committee on Deficit Reduction, which was tasked with proposing legislation for additional deficit reduction over the same period. As of January 27, 2012 the statutory debt limit was increased to $16,394 trillion. Gross Federal Debt outstanding was $16,059 as of September 30, 2012. On May 19, 2013 the debt limit was raised to $16,699 billion which was the amount of qualifying federal debt securities outstanding on that date. A delay in raising the statutory debt limit existed at the end of fiscal year 2013 and lasted until October 17, 2013 when the Continuing Appropriations Act of 2013 was enacted. The Act established a process that will result in and increase of the statutory debt limit on February 8, 2014. In its February 2014 report the Congressional Budget Office predicted a federal deficit for fiscal year 2014 of $514 billion. The CBO also projected the debt held by the public to be $12,717 trillion by the end of 2014. If debt held by the government remained the same as in 2013 that would result in a debt limit requirement of $17,473 trillion by the end of fiscal year 2014.

## Historical Perspective

Federal debt outstanding is one of the largest legally binding obligations of the Federal Government. Nearly all the federal debt has been issued by the Treasury with a small portion being issued by other federal government agencies. Treasury issues debt securities for two principal reasons, (1) to borrow needed funds to finance the current operations of the Federal Government and (2) to provide an investment and accounting mechanism for certain federal government accounts' (primarily federal trust funds) excess receipts. Total gross federal debt outstanding has dramatically increased over the past 25 years from $2,125 billion as of September 30, 1986, to $16,732 billion as of September 30, 2013. Large budget deficits emerged during the 1980's due to tax policy decisions and increased outlays for defense and domestic programs.

Through fiscal year 1997, annual federal deficits continued to be large and debt continued to grow at a rapid pace. As a result, total federal debt more than doubled between 1986 and 1997. By fiscal year 1998, federal debt held by the public was beginning to decline. In fiscal years 1998 through 2001, the amount of debt held by the public fell by $476 billion, from $3,815 billion to $3,339 billion. However, federal debt held by the public began to increase in fiscal year 2002, primarily as a result of higher federal outlays. From fiscal year 2009 through fiscal year 2013, federal debt held by the public increased by $4,424 billion. For the same period, intra-government holdings increased by $410 billion. This resulted in an increase in total federal government debt outstanding of $4,834 trillion.

## Figure 18-1 Gross Federal Debt Outstanding

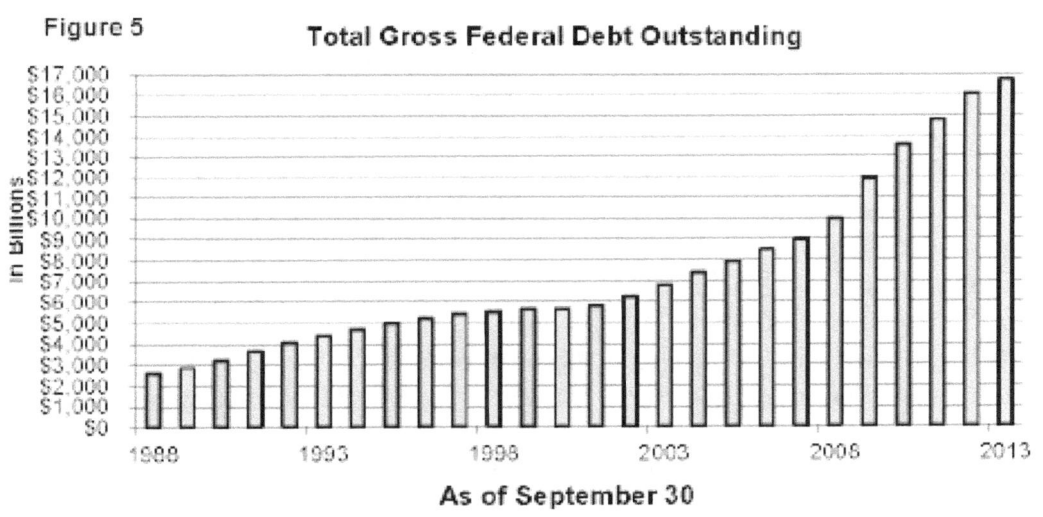

**Source: GAO United States Government Accountability Office Report to the Secretary of the Treasury, Nov. 2013**

## The Size of the Federal Debt

Many economists and politicians have pondered the question about the size of the gross federal debt in the United States. One of the major questions that are asked about the gross national debt is its size. One way to answer this question is to compare the debt with something. The best vehicle available for comparing a nation's gross accumulated debt is that country's ability to produce goods and services, i.e., their gross domestic product. Table 18-5 shows the gross federal debt compared to the gross domestic product from 1990 through 2013. The gross domestic product data for 2013 is first estimate of GDP and is subject to revisions. The gross federal debt is for the federal government's fiscal year ending September 30, 2013.

The gross federal debt increased as a percentage of gross domestic product from 1991 through 1996 as the federal government produced deficits in each of these years. The gross domestic product continued to increase after 1996, however, the federal debt was reduced as a percent of GDP in 1996 and the deficit was turned into a surplus in 1998.

In 1990 gross federal debt was 61.1 percent of gross domestic product. In 1995 the gross national debt reached a high point of 67.1 percent of GDP. By 1996 the ratio of gross national debt to GDP had stabilized at 65.1% and started on a steady downward trend as the federal deficit was reduced to $78.7 billion in 1997. In 1998 the federal government actually showed a surplus of $24.4 billion. The surplus increased to $251.4 billion in fiscal year 2000 but retreated to $127.0 billion in fiscal 2001. In fiscal year 2002 the previous year's surplus turned into a deficit of $ 159 billion, in 2003 the deficit increased to $373 billion and in 2004 the deficit increased to $412. The deficit was reduced to $297 in 2005, to $237 in 2006 and to $162 billion in 2007.

In 2008 the American economy descended into a recession. This reversed the recent trend of reduced deficit spending and resulted in a deficit of $760 billion. In 2009 the deficit increased to new historical levels of $1,417. For fiscal year 2010 the deficit was slightly reduced to $1,294 billion and in 2011 the deficit was further reduced to $1,104 billion. In fiscal year 2013 the deficit increased by $673 billion. The ratio of gross federal debt to gross domestic product increased to 101.7 percent in 2013. The ratio increased in 2013 over 2012 as a result of the GDP growing by $816 billion over 2012 while the gross federal debt for fiscal year 2013 grew by $673 billion. To determine rather the United States has begun to manage its debt we can look to the European Union for guidance. Under the terms of the Maastricht Treaty, by 1999 European Union countries would have to reduce their gross national debt to GDP ratio to 60 percent to qualify for the new European common currency. Based on its gross federal debt to gross domestic product ratio of 99.6 percent in 2013, the United States might not qualify for admission to the European common currency. However, this European guide of 60 percent gross federal debt and gross domestic product will probably increase as most of the European economies were still recovering from recession in 2013.

**Table 18-5**

**Gross National Debt Percent of GDP ($in Billions)**

| Year | Gross Nat. Debt | GDP | GNP/GDP |
|------|-----------------|-----------|---------|
| 1990 | $3,233 | $5,802 | 55.7% |
| 1991 | $3,665 | $5,986 | 61.1% |
| 1992 | $4,063 | $6,319 | 64.3% |
| 1993 | $4,411 | $6,642 | 66.4% |
| 1994 | $4,693 | $7,054 | 66.6% |
| 1995 | $4,974 | $7,401 | 67.2% |
| 1996 | $5,245 | $7,813 | 67.1% |
| 1997 | $5,413 | $8,318 | 65.1% |
| 1998 | $5,526 | $8,781 | 62.9% |
| 1999 | $5,656 | $9,269 | 61.0% |
| 2000 | $5,674 | $9,873 | 57.3% |
| 2001 | $5,807 | $10,082 | 57.4% |
| 2002 | $6,198 | $10,446 | 59.3% |
| 2003 | $6,760 | $10,988 | 61.5% |
| 2004 | $7,355 | $11,735 | 62.7% |
| 2005 | $7,905 | $12,487 | 63.3% |
| 2006 | $8,451 | $13,254 | 63.8% |
| 2007 | $8,951 | $13,841 | 64.7% |
| 2008 | $10,011 | $14,441 | 70.1% |
| 2009 | $11,898 | $14,256 | 83.3% |
| 2010 | $13,551 | $14,660 | 92.0% |
| 2011 | $14,781 | $15,094 | 97.9% |
| 2012 | $16,059 | $15,797 | 101.7 |
| 2013 | $16,732 | $16,800 | 99.6 |

The major portion of the net public debt is the internal debt. The internal debt is the portion of the debt owed to the citizens of the United States. The remainder is the nation's external debt, that portion of the debt that is owed to citizens of other nations. Payment of interest on the debt to a country's own citizens is a redistribution of income and therefore does not directly decrease total demand. However, 47 percent of the net public debt or $5,594 billion is owed to foreign banks, individuals, businesses and governments. As the portion of the debt held by foreigners' increases, greater amounts of interest are paid out each year to foreign citizens. Payment of interest on debt held by foreigners sends money out of this country, which could contribute to a reduction in aggregate demand sometime in the future.

Will the Federal Government go bankrupt if it continues to increase its debt? There is very little risk of this happening because the Federal Government can increase taxes to pay the debt. However, there are some problems that continue as a result of a large net national debt. The first burden of the debt is that a larger portion of the taxes paid by future generations of Americans will be used to pay interest on the debt. These tax dollars could be put to a much better use, such as investments in infrastructure and education.

A second burden of the huge net national debt is its effect on private investment. This is defined by economists as the crowding-out effect. According to this theory, a growing net national debt will decrease private investment and reduce the growth rate of private capital stock. As the growth rate of worker productivity declines because of a decrease in the growth rate of capital, the growth rate per capita GDP (gross domestic product divided by the labor force), will decline. Therefore, a growing net national debt has the potential to retard the growth rate of a nation's future standard of living.

**The Social Security Trust Fund**

Also, a political hot button is the Social Security Trust Fund. The major portion of the $4,756 billion in the intra-governmental holdings or about $2,757 billion belongs to the Social Security Trust Fund. However, the trust fund is only an accounting entry backed by non-marketable bonds issued by the Federal Government. The actual cash is used by the Federal Government for general expenditures or paying down the net national debt. For example in fiscal year 2013 the budget results released by the Treasury Department showed a federal government deficit of $706 billion. In addition there was a decrease in the intra-government accounts of $33 billion. Therefore, when the change in Social Security and other government trust funds are added to the Federal Government's deficit of $706 billion the combined deficit is $673 billion. The increase in the Federal Government Debt from $16,059 billion in 2012 to $16,732 billion in 2013 and the reasons for the increase is demonstrated in Table 18-6.[1]

## Table 18-6

### Change in Federal Debt

Federal Government Debt ($ in Billions)

| Year | Held by Public | Held by Government | Total Debt |
|---|---|---|---|
| 2013 | $11,976 | $4,756 | $16,732 |
| 2012 | $11,270 | $4,789 | $16,059 |
| | ------------ | ------------ | ------------ |
| Change | $ 706 | $ -33 | $ 673 |

Changes in Gross Federal Debt 2013 v. 2012

| Description | Increase in Debt |
|---|---|
| Federal Government Deficit | $ 706 |
| Social Security Trust Fund | $ 37 |
| Civil Service Retirement Fund | $ -106 |
| Military Retirement Fund | $ 13 |
| Medicare Trust Funds | $ -24 |
| Other Federal Trust funds | $ 47 |
| | --------- |
| Total Changes in Gross National Debt | $ 673 |

Source: GAO United States Government Accountability Office Report to the Secretary of the Treasury, Nov. 2013 Page 26.

The problem with the Social Security Trust Fund is that if sometime in the future Social Security revenues are less than expenses, (estimated by the Social Security Administration to occur in 2017) the only source of paying the difference between receipts and benefits is to exchange non-marketable debt with marketable debt or in other words to increase the net national debt. Also, Congress lowered the FICA tax in 2012 to stimulate the economy. The reduction in payroll taxes resulted in a deficit in the Social Security Trust Fund in 2012. The FICA payroll tax rate was restored to its 2011 level for 2013.

## The Burden of the Twin Deficits

The international current account deficit and the net federal deficit taken together are linked to the international financial markets. The current account deficit must be offset by capital inflows from foreign citizens and foreigners finance a large part of the net national debt. A simple sources and uses of fund's statement can be used to show the relationship of these twin deficits to the financial markets.

### International Financial Markets - Sources and Uses of Funds

| **Sources of Funds** | **Uses of Funds** |
| --- | --- |
| Domestic Savings | Investments |
| Foreign Capital Inflow | Government Budget Deficit |

A nation's economy can compensate for an increase in government budget deficits by reducing private investment, increasing the rate of savings, and increasing net capital inflows. Net capital inflows are created by net imports. Critics of the federal government's fiscal policy during the last 20 years, charge that the mismanagement of the budgeting process has left the nation burdened with debts owed to foreign lenders. This has caused export industries to lose market share in an increasingly competitive global economy and has reduced aggregate business investment as a result of the crowding-out effect.

## EFFORTS TO REDUCE THE FEDERAL DEFICIT

By 1984, the federal budgetary process was in such bad shape that Herbert Stein, President Nixon's Chairman of the Council of Economic Advisors, wrote an article that was published in the December issue of the Economists. In that article Stein states that, "We have no long-run budget policy." In response to this and many other criticisms, Congress has passed three bills designed to reduce or eliminate the deficit.

### The Gramm-Rudman-Hollings Act of 1985

This law established a declining set of deficit targets, beginning with a deficit target of $144 billion for fiscal year 1987 and to eliminate the deficit by fiscal 1991. An exception was written into the law allowing the deficit ceiling to be waived in the event that real gross national product grew at an annual rate of 1 percent or less, for two consecutive quarters. The deficit targets were revised in 1987, which delayed balancing of the budget until 1993. The feature that was supposed to give this law some real ability to control expenditures was a provision for making mandatory spending cuts if Congress failed to provide a budget that would be within $10 billion of the Act's target. However, the targets developed by the Gramm-Rudman-Hollings Act were not met as the federal deficit was $221 billion in fiscal year 1990, compared to a target of $100 billion.

One of the major reasons that this act failed to meet its deficit reduction targets was that entitlements such as social security, Medicare, and aid to dependent families, were exempted from its cost reduction provisions. Alice Rivlin, who was President Clinton's budget director, wrote in the October 3, 1989, issue of the Wall Street Journal, that the Gramm-Rudman-Hollins Act was a "well intentioned experiment that failed."

### The Budget Deficit Reduction Act of 1990

The growth of the deficit in fiscal year 1990 resulted in a new reform effort. This was the Budget Deficit Reduction Act of November, 1990. The act consisted of a negotiated package of spending cuts (primarily defense) and tax increases that were to total $500 billion for the five years from fiscal 1991 through fiscal 1995. In addition, this act included a new approach to automatic enforcement, a "pay-as-you-go" mechanism. Under this provision, spending was divided into three broad categories: defense, domestic, and international. In theory, if any new legislation pushed spending above a set ceiling for any category, all the programs in the category would be cut proportionately to bring the category back into balance.

On September 30, 1990, President Bush explained the new law to the public by stating that: "The bipartisan leaders and I have reached agreement on the federal budget. Over a period of five years, the deficit would be reduced by $500 million." However, the budget deficit continued to increase as spending increased faster than revenue, even with the new taxes that were enacted under the law. In fiscal year 1991, the federal deficit rose to $270 billion, in fiscal 1992 to $290 billion and was over $255 billion in fiscal 1993.

## The Omnibus Budget Reconciliation Act of 1993

In August of 1993, Congress passed, by a one vote margin, a new deficit reduction law. The new law called for some spending cuts as a result of a proposed reduction in the federal civilian work force. The federal work force was reduced from an average of 2.989 million in fiscal year 1992 to 2.858 million in June of 1994, a decrease of over 130 thousand workers. However, the bulk of the savings from this staff reduction was used to fund the Clinton administration's 1994 crime bill. The revenue raising provisions of the bill called for marginal tax increases on the "wealthy" by raising the top rates, from 31 percent of adjusted gross income to 36 percent, for all married couples earning more than $140,000 per year. The 1990 bill increased the top rates from 28 percent to 31 percent. Also, the gasoline tax was raised by 4.3 cents per gallon following a raise of 5 cents per gallon in 1990.

The tax increase provisions of this bill were sold to the public as a way to make the rich pay their "fair share." However, the wealthy did not become rich because they are stupid. Rich people usually employ tax lawyers and accountants who advise them on how to pay a minimum of taxes legally. For example, the total income-tax receipts in 1991, the first year after the 1990 budget act was signed, actually fell. U.S. Treasury figures on income-tax receipts in 1991 show that the wealthy (defined here as people who earn $200,000 a year or more) paid $106.1 billion in income taxes in 1990, but in 1991, after the tax increase, paid $99.6 billion. The tax revenues received in 1991 from this group amounted to a reduction of $7.1 billion over the taxes received in 1990. This is because the wealthy found tax shelters in Municipal Bonds, stopped investing in business expansion and curtailed other activities that would increase their tax burden.

Therefore, the only addition to federal tax revenues that resulted from the Budget Reduction Act of 1993 were from the 4.3 percent increase in the tax on gasoline and additional taxes on social security payments from our so called wealthy senior citizens that earn over $34,000 per year.

The debate over the gross national debt will continue well into the twenty-first century. Some debt is necessary for it provides an investment instrument for millions of Americans. Therefore, The question is not whether the debt should exist, but how much should be outstanding at any period of time, and also, how much of a burden should be placed on future taxpayers?

**NOTES:**

**Chapter 18**
**National Debt and International Trade Deficits**

1.  GAO United States Government Accountability Office, <u>Report to the Secretary of the Treasury</u>, November 2013 pg. 1-26.
2.  Hyman, David, <u>Economics, Third Edition</u>, Irwin Business Publications, Burr Ridge, IL, 1994, p. 809.

# CHAPTER 19

---

# EMPLOYMENT AND UNEMPLOYMENT

*"In a Global Economy a worker has two things to offer; skills or the willingness to work for low wages." --Lester Thurow*

## THE EMPLOYMENT ACT OF 1946

The Full Employment Act of 1946 sought to strengthen the economic gains to the U.S. economy that had resulted from massive government spending during World War II (1939—1945). Applying the theory of John Maynard Keynes, who argued that intensive government spending was necessary to end economic depression, President Harry S. Truman (1945–1953) proposed a 21-point program in 1945 to boost the U.S. economy. The plan called for full employment legislation, an increased minimum wage, and better unemployment and social security benefits as well as housing assistance. Truman believed the bill would ensure that the country would not slip back into depression because it allowed the initiation of remedial action, such as tax cuts and spending programs if economic indicators shifted downward. In January of 1945 four senators, Robert F. Wagner of New York, James E. Murray of Montana, Elbert Thomas of Utah and Joseph O'Mahoney of Wyoming, sponsored a bill that was designed to guarantee full employment. However, because of strong reaction by business interest, the bill as originally written could not be passed.

Full employment was therefore reduced to a goal of high employment. The Employment Act was finally passed by congress and signed by President Truman in 1946. The bill stated that it now was the recognized responsibility of the federal government to provide an environment where those able, willing, and seeking to work, could find employment. In addition, the Employment Act of 1946 created the

Council of Economic Advisors to consult with the president on measures to enhance employment and economic policy. The passage of the Employment Act of 1946, with its provision for a council of economic advisors, was very important to the history of economics. It established economics firmly in the center of modern American political theory.

## MEASURING EMPLOYMENT

To understand the goals of the Full Employment Act of 1946 it is necessary to analyze what the terms employment and unemployment mean and how they are measured. Data on employment and unemployment is calculated and released monthly by the U.S. Bureau of Labor Statistics in the Employment Situation Summary. The release contains data from two separate surveys: The Household Survey and the Establishment Survey. The Household Survey is a monthly sample survey of approximately 60,000 households. The most publicized data from the Household Survey is each month's unemployment rate. The unemployment rate is the percentage of the U.S. labor force that is unemployed. It is calculated by dividing the number of unemployed individuals by the total civilian work force. An individual is counted as unemployed if they are over the age of 16 and are actively looking for a job, but cannot find one. Students, those individuals who choose to not work, and retirees are not in the labor force, and therefore are not counted in the unemployment rate. Table 15-1 details the employment and unemployment statistics for March 2013.

### Who is Unemployed?

Unemployment varies significantly among groups of individuals and geographic sectors of the economy. Table 19-2 shows the unemployment rates for December 2013 for a number of groups of individuals, with unemployment ranging from 6.0 percent for adult women to 20.2 percent for teenagers.

**Table 19-1: Calculation of the Unemployment Rate – December 2013: Numbers in Thousands.**

| +Population | Thousands | Description |
|---|---|---|
| Total civilian members of population | 246,745 | Including those under 16, the military and persons in institutions |
| Those not in the Labor force , | 91,808 | Retired, students, individuals choosing not to work |
| = Labor force | 154,937 | Total population minus those not in the labor force |
| Minus Persons Employed | 144,586 | Individuals with jobs |
| Equals Unemployed | 10,351 | Individuals without a job and actively seeking employment |
| Unemployment Rate = | Unemployed ----------------- Labor Force | $\dfrac{10,351}{154,937} = 6.7\%$ |
| | | |

**Source: Table A. Major Indicators of labor market activity, seasonally adjusted data BLS Household Survey January 2014.**

Table 19-2 shows changes in the unemployment rate in each of the reported groups from December 2013 compared to December 2012. For December 2013, the largest number of unemployed was in teenagers 20.2 percent and African Americans 11.9 percent. There are also large differences between the level of education obtained and the rate of unemployment. For the month of December 2013 the unemployment rate among those with less than a high school diploma was 9.8 percent and only 3.3 percent for those with a Bachelor's degree or higher.

# Table 19-2: Unemployment Rates by Group

| Description of Group | Unemployment Dec. 2012 | Rate Dec. 2013 | % Change |
|---|---|---|---|
| Adult Men | 7.2 | 6.3 | -0.9 |
| Adult Women | 7.3 | 6.0 | -1.3 |
| Teenagers | 24.0 | 20.2 | -3.8 |
| White Workers | 6.9 | 5.9 | -1.0 |
| African American (Black) | 14.0 | 11.9 | -2.1 |
| Hispanics | 9.5 | 8.3 | -1.2 |
| All Workers | 7.9 | 6.7 | -1.2 |

| Total 25 Years or Older Description of Group | Participation Rate % | Unemployment Rate % Dec. 11 |
|---|---|---|
| Less than a high school diploma | 43.7 | 9.8 |
| High School graduate no college | 58.0 | 7.1 |
| Some college or Associate Degree | 67.6 | 6.1 |
| Bachelor's degree or higher | 75.3 | 3.3 |
| Total Civilian Work Force | 62.8 | 6.7 |

**Source: Household Survey Table A-4 Employment status of the civilian population 25 years and over by educational attainment, January 2014, seasonally adjusted**.

The participation rate shown in Table 19-2 is calculated by dividing the civilian labor force for each category by the total population in that group. It is an indication of the percent of the total civilians in that category that are participating in the labor force. For example, for the total civilian work force the participation rate for December 2013 (62.8 percent) was calculated by dividing the civilian work force (154,937) by the total civilian population (246,745). The above table indicates that there is a wide disparity between the level of education in both the participation rate and the unemployment rate of these groups. For example, for those civilians with a bachelor's degree or above there is a moderate rate of unemployment at 3.3 percent while over 9.8 percent of those who have less than a high school diploma are not employed and to make matters worse only 43.7 percent of this population actually participates in the job market. In addition, the civilian work force that is under 20 years of age (teenagers) had the highest unemployment rate mainly because they have not yet obtained the necessary skills to meet employer demands.

This would indicate that there is a strong correlation between those that are employed and the education and skills that they bring to the job market. Another way to explain the high unemployment rate in a growing economy is that there is a mismatch between the skills required in the labor market (the demand for labor) and the skills that are available in the labor market (supply of labor). This is an indication that our schools, especially in the K-12 grades are not turning out students with the skills needed to participate in the labor market. This is a long-term problem that can not be solved by short-term fiscal or monetary policy changes. What is needed is a plan to increase the educational obtainment of America's workers now and in the future.

## Unemployment Rate Change, Dec. 2013 vs. Dec. 2012

The unemployment rate for December 2012 was 7.9 percent compared to 6.7 percent for December 2013. Although the unemployment rate decreased by 1.2 percent there were some important differences in the number as shown below:

| Description | Dec. 2012 | Dec. 2013 | Change |
|---|---|---|---|
| Civilian Labor Force | 155,485 | 154,937 | -548 |
| Participation Rate | 63.6 | 62.8 | -0.8 |
| Employed | 143,212 | 144,586 | 1,374 |
| Unemployed | 12,273 | 10,351 | -1,922 |
| Not in Labor Force | 88,865 | 91,808 | 2.943 |
| Unemployment Rate | 7.9 | 6.7 | -1.2 |

The unemployment rate for December 2013 was 1.2 percent lower than December 2012. The civilian labor force decreased by 548 thousand and the number of persons employed increased by 1,374 thousand. This is an indication that employment situation improved from the previous year. However, while the unemployment was reduced to 6.7 percent the number of persons who gave up looking for work (those not in the labor force) increased by 2,943 thousand from December 2012 to December 2013. If the change in the number of those persons not looking for work were added to both sides of the equation, the unemployment rate would have been 8.4 percent for December 2013. This is an indication that the employment situation has not improved much since December 2012.

| Description | Dec. 2012 | Dec. 2013 | Change |
|---|---|---|---|
| Labor Force | 155,485 | 154,937 | -548 |
| Persons Not Looking | 88,865 | 91,808 | 2,943 |
| Unemployed | 12,273 | 10,351 | -1,922 |

Adjustments

$$\frac{Unemployment \quad (2,943 + 10.351) \quad 13,294}{Labor\ Force \quad (2,943 + 154,937)\ 157,874} = 8.4\ \%$$

## The Establishment Survey - Employment by Industry

Table 19-3 shows the employment and data for the month of December 2007, the month of December 2013, the change from December 2007 through December 2013 and the increase in jobs from November 2013 through December 2013. The data is from the Establishment Survey.

The Establishment Survey is derived from a monthly sample survey of about 160,000 businesses and government agencies. The Establishment Survey breaks down employment and unemployment numbers by major industry classifications. The industry breakdown helps the Bureau of Labor Standard to better understand where the bulk of unemployment comes from. For example Table 19-3 shows that the gain of jobs for the Month of December 2013 was 74 thousand over November 2013. Employment in the private sector increased by 87 thousand and employment in government fell by 13 thousand jobs.

Table 19-3 also contains employment data for December 2007 which the National Bureau of Economic Research determined was the start of the last recession. From the start of the recession through

December of 2013 the economy experienced a loss of, 1,275 thousand jobs. The largest job losses were concentrated in three industries, Construction, Manufacturing, and Trade, Transportation and Utilities. Only four industries Mining and Logging, Professional and Business Services, Education and Health Services and Leasing and Hospitality showed employment gains.

**Table 19-3**
**Industry Payroll Employment (in Thousands)**

| Industry | Dec. 2007 | Dec. 2013 | Dec. 2007 To Dec. 2013 | Dec. 2013 vs. Nov.. 2013 |
|---|---|---|---|---|
| Mining and Logging | 743 | 891 | 148 | 4 |
| Construction | 7,523 | 5,833 | -1,690 | -16 |
| Manufacturing | 13,777 | 12,028 | -1,749 | 9 |
| Trade, Transportation and Utilities | 26,725 | 26,286 | -439 | 69 |
| Information | 3,025 | 2,672 | -353 | -12 |
| Financial Activities | 8,243 | 7,915 | -328 | 4 |
| Professional and Business Services | 18,109 | 18,789 | 680 | 19 |
| Education and Health Services | 18,570 | 20,823 | 2,253 | 0 |
| Leasing and Hospitality | 13,551 | 14,291 | 740 | 9 |
| Other Services | 5,517 | 5,500 | -17 | 1 |
| Government Services | 22,369 | 21,849 | -520 | -13 |
| Total Employed | 138,152 | 136,877 | -1,275 | 74 |

**Source: Table B1. Employment, Hours and Earnings: From the Current Employment Statistics Survey, January, 2014**

## The Costs of Unemployment

Unemployed workers often do not have the income to support themselves or their families. The stress of being unemployed is reflected through increases in alcohol and drug abuse, marital problems, and criminal activity among those who are unemployed. State and federal governments reduce the personal financial cost of being unemployed through the unemployment compensation provided to many unemployed workers. Government spending is funded mostly from tax revenues. Therefore, unemployment compensation spreads out the cost of being unemployed among taxpayers, instead of having the entire burden fall on the unemployed worker. Also, the availability of unemployment compensation reduces the pressure on an unemployed worker to accept any job offer and may actually tend to slightly raise the jobless rate in the short-term.

## Types of Unemployment

Economists use the term the Natural Rate of Unemployment to explain why the unemployment rate is always greater than zero. The natural rate of unemployment is an equilibrium in which the volumes of job-seeking by workers and worker-seeking by employers reach a balance controlled by fundamental determinants of the relative prices of the two activities. In addition policymakers have adopted the view that the natural rate of unemployment varies over time. For example, during the period from 1960 through 1989, the natural rate of unemployment was considered to be between 5 and 6 percent. However, during the 1990's when unemployment fell to rates as low as 3.9 percent, many economists revised their estimates at between 4 and 5 percent. In the twenty-first century many economists consider the historical natural rate of unemployment to again be between 5 and 6 percent or even higher.

There are three types of unemployment; each describes the particular circumstances of the individual who is not employed. Frictional unemployment is temporary unemployment arising from the normal job search process. Frictional unemployment refers to those people who are seeking better or more convenient jobs. Frictional unemployment always exists in any economy and prevents the unemployment rate from being zero.

Structural unemployment is the result of changes in the economy caused by technological progress and shifts in the demand for goods and services. Structural changes eliminate some jobs in certain industries, such as the apparels industry in the U.S. which has lost many jobs to China, and create new jobs in faster growing areas such as professional and business services. Persons who are structurally unemployed do not have marketable job skills and may face prolonged periods of unemployment, as they must often be retrained or relocate in order to find employment.

Cyclical unemployment is caused by a drop in economic activity such as an inventory reduction by U.S. auto manufacturers due to a reduction in sales. If this kind of unemployment hits many industries at the same time it causes an overall inventory reduction which leads to an economic downturn. Once the economy recovers, many of these companies seek to rehire the employees that were laid off. At the level of unemployment that economists consider to be the lowest possible, the normal rate of unemployment, the only unemployment that exists is due to friction in the labor market and structural changes in the economy.[1]

## Controversy – Which measure of employment is more accurate

There has been much political discussion about the failure of the number of employed to increase as real GDP increased by over 3 percent in 2006 and by 2.6 percent in 2007. Part of the explanation could be the increase in productivity that the economy experienced in both 2006 and 2007. The recession of 2008 changed the argument of job growth to one of job losses as the number of unemployed increased steadily throughout the year. For December 2013, the household survey showed total employment of 144,586 thousand while the payroll survey showed 136,877 thousand a difference of 7,709 thousand. Also, the household survey showed a gain in jobs from November 2013 of 143 thousand while the payroll survey showed a gain of employment of only 74 thousand jobs. This difference is an indication that there may be another variable which is the data itself. The major reason for the difference results of the two surveys is that the household and payroll surveys use different definitions of employment and distinct survey and estimation methods. Some of the major differences between the two surveys are shown in Table 19-4.[2]

**Table 19-4: Trends in Payroll and Household Survey Employment Survey Methods**

| Comparison By: | Household Survey (CPS | Payroll Survey (CES) |
|---|---|---|
| Universe | Civilian non-institutional population age 16 and over | Non-farm wage and salary jobs |
| Type of Survey | Monthly sample survey of approximately 60,000 households | Monthly sample survey of about 160,000 businesses and government agencies |
| Major Outputs | Labor force, employment, unemployment, and associated rates with significant demographic detail | Employment hours, and earnings with significant industry and geographic detail |
| Reference period | Calendar week that includes the 12th of the month | Employer pay period that includes the 12th of the month |
| Employment concept | Estimate of employed persons (multiple job holders are included once | Estimate of Jobs (multiple job holders counted for each job) |

The Bureau of Labor Statistics is hard at work trying to reconcile the two surveys and both surveys are needed for a complete picture of the labor market. In the meantime, the two political parties will probably use the survey that best supports their position. For the month of December 2013, the Democrats might use the household survey to show job gains of 143 thousand and that employment has stabilized as a result of their policy changes. Meanwhile the Republicans might use the establishment survey showing a gain of 74 thousand jobs for the same month to argue that the administration's policies are not leading to any significant job growth. Interestingly enough, the surveys from the Bureau of Labor Statistics often support both positions.

**NOTES:**

**Chapter 15**
**Employment and Unemployment**

1.  National Council of Economic Education, <u>A Case Study: The Unemployment Rate</u>, February 6, 2004, p. 6.
2.  U.S. Department of Labor, Bureau of Labor Statistics, <u>Labor Statistics From the Current Population Survey</u>, November, 2011.

# CHAPTER 20

---

## ECONOMICS AND
## PUBLIC CHOICE

*"In order to get better government policy, we'd better look not to electing better people, but to changing the structure of the rules which constrain them." —James Buchanan*

### THE NATION-STATE TO THE FISCAL STATE

By the late nineteenth century, the nation-state that had been in existence since the sixteenth century, was being made over into an economic agency. This trend has been referred to by economists, including Joseph Schumpeter, as the evolution from the nation-state to the "fiscal state." The job of the leaders of the nation-state was seen as maintaining the climate for economic growth, keeping taxes low and encouraging savings. The great depression gave rise to the belief that the national government should control its country's economic environment.

Since World War II, most developed countries have come to believe that there are no economic limits to what government can tax or borrow and, therefore, no economic limit to what government can spend. Schumpeter pointed out that as long as governments have been around, the budget process has begun with an assessment of revenues. Expenditures would be allocated to causes based on available resources. Since the supply of "good causes" was inexhaustible, and the demand for spending was therefore infinite, the budget process consisted of deciding where to say no. As long as revenues were considered as a constraint, it was difficult for a government to act as either a social or an economic agent.[1]

Following World War II, most developed countries had adopted the financial theories of John Maynard Keynes. However, what was lacking from Keynes's theory was the role that would be played by government. Keynes assumed that a wise and efficient government, would faithfully apply sound fiscal policy. However, fiscal policy must be applied by people, in this case politicians and government bureaucrats. Economic theory can often become dangerous in the hands of politicians, who quite often assume that there are no limits to the revenues that government can obtain. In the hands of modern day politicians, government has become the master of the individual in society. By using taxes and expenditures, government can redistribute society's income. However, there is a serious question as to whether modern governments have succeeded in bringing about a meaningful redistribution of income. Vilfredo Pareto (1848-1923) the Swiss sociologist developed a law concerning income distribution. Pareto's Law stated that income distribution between major classes in society is determined by two factors: the culture of the society, and the level of productivity within the economy. According to Pareto, the more productive an economy was, the greater would be the equality of income. Taxes, Pareto argues, cannot change the inequality of income.[2]

## THE PUBLIC CHOICE SCHOOL OF ECONOMICS

Keynesian economics assumes an efficient and benevolent government to carry out fiscal policy. However, governments in most developed countries, have become such heavy spenders that they can no longer use fiscal policy to counteract the effects of recession. In the United States, the federal government reached the limit of its ability to tax and borrow in the 1980's. This made fiscal policy practically useless during the recession of the early 1990's. Worst of all, the fiscal state has become a "pork-barrel state." If the budget process starts with the determination of expenditures rather than a realistic forecast of revenues, there is no fiscal discipline; government spending becomes the means for politicians to obtain votes. Politicians, therefore, run on platforms designed to convince local voters that they will extract a larger part of the federal budget for spending projects in their districts, then their opponents. In the fiscal state, the looting of the federal treasury is done by politicians to ensure their own election.

The pork-barrel state thus increasingly undermines the foundations of a free society. The elected representatives use the taxes of their constituents to enrich special-interest groups, who in turn, are heavy contributors to the elected official's campaign fund. Joseph Schumpeter warned in 1918 that the fiscal state would in the end undermine government's ability to govern. Eighteen years later, Keynes hailed the fiscal state as the great liberator of a depressed economy. Keynes argued, that government, no longer limited by restraints on expenditures, could govern effectively by manipulating government spending and taxation. However, in the 1990's, it is becoming quite clear that Schumpeter might have been right.

## Economic Rent Seeking

One of the key elements of the Public Choice theory is economic rent seeking. Economists define economic rent, as any payment to a factor of production in excess of its opportunity cost. An example is the huge salaries that sport figures earn. Major league athletes usually earn much more than they could earn using the same time in, for example, teaching a course in economics.

Entrepreneurs are constantly attempting to earn such profits by lowering unit costs, introducing new products or creating brand images in the minds of consumers. When they are successful the income that they earn may be substantially higher than their competitors. However, economic profit that is earned as a result of private market activity is not the only category of economic rents. Many business managers and workers, through labor unions, often turn to government in search of economic rents rather than trying to gain a competitive advantage through the marketplace. An additional profit earned, because of a government program that raises prices or serves to reduce unit costs, is worth just as much as profit earned through the marketplace. Often profit earned from developing a competitive advantage in the marketplace is short term. This is because the competition may develop a new process or a new product that reduces unit cost or better satisfies customer needs. Government regulations, on the other hand, cannot only create opportunities to earn economic rents, but often shield those opportunities from competitors.

Political rent seeking is often referred to by economists as the act of obtaining and defending economic rent through government action. Government restrictions on market activity are often found in the areas of price controls and restrictions on competition. An example of price controls is the case of milk price supports. This occurs when the government places a floor on the market price of milk. If the price of milk falls below the floor price, the federal government purchases the excess milk in order to maintain the targeted price. Public choice economists see this policy as a classic case of political rent seeking. This is because a large portion of the benefits of price supports goes to farmers who are not in need of the supports. However, politicians who are in search of votes, would rather support a bill that has the backing from a large group of farmers instead of only the farmers that actually need assistance.

Government restrictions on competition are another way of generating rents. For example, tariffs and import quotas shield domestic firms from foreign competition. By eliminating foreign competition, firms are able to raise prices above the competitive market level. There are also examples of rent seeking within the domestic economy. For instance, licensing fees and professional examinations restrict the number of competitors who can enter such fields as public accountants, medicine and law.

The theory that government policies do not always promote efficiency and fairness is not a new one. Economists have long been aware of the law of unintended consequences. However, political choice theorists go beyond the tendency of government policies to have effects that are vastly different from their original intentions. Political choice economists argue that the element of rent seeking in the formulation of government policy suggests that there is a systematic tendency for government programs to cause rather than cure economic efficiencies.[3]

## James Buchanan, Fiscal Responsibility and Public Choice

As early as the 1970's, it had become apparent that the use of fiscal policy to counteract recession and inflation, did not always work.

Fiscal policy to stimulate an economy and avoid a recession was used by President Johnson in the mid 1960's. However, fiscal policy was not effective in fighting the inflation of the 1970's. Also, as a result of the huge budget deficits of the 1980's, fiscal policy lost its ability to combat a recession. A new school of economic theory was needed to explain why fiscal policy, the main tool of Keynesian economics, no longer worked. This new theory was developed by James M. Buchanan, who currently is a professor with George Mason University. In 1986, Buchanan won the Nobel Memorial Prize in Economics, for his work in what became known as "The Public Choice Theory." The public choice theory is a study of how people use the institutions of government to promote private ends. The public choice school attempts to explain some of the modern day economic and political problems, for example:

- Why does the United States suffer from continuing budget deficits?

- Why do special interest groups proliferate?

- Why do bureaucracies continue to expand despite presidential promises to trim them?

A basic principle of public choice theory is that people act in the same way in both public and private roles. In analyzing people's private choices, economists have long assumed that people act in rational pursuit of self-interest. As consumers, they maximize their utility; as entrepreneurs, they maximize profit. Therefore, public choice theorists assume that the actions of people, in public roles, are guided by self-interest as well.

**The Problem of Budget Deficits**

Buchanan, does not show politicians simply as economic villains. He searches for the reasons that encourage them to act hypocritically. Buchanan argues that it is the budgeting system that leads to government deficits. Buchanan uses the theories of Jeremy Bentham to explain the spending programs initiated by Congress. Politicians want to please their constituents. People, according to Bentham, would prefer pleasure to pain. Government spending programs bring visible pleasure to some groups of people, and taxes are painful. Therefore, politicians assume that constituents would prefer pleasure to pain or high spending and low taxes to balanced budgets. It does not take a financial wizard to conclude that this will translate into budget deficits.

Critics of the public choice school argue that if persistent budget deficits hurt the economy, people will begin to feel the pain and demand a balanced budget. Buchanan answers these critics by explaining that budget deficits do hurt, but the pain is not direct. Reductions in spending programs have an immediate effect. However, even though the result of reduced spending is a more healthy economy, the benefits of fiscal responsibility, are long-term. Budget deficits are created by lowering taxes and raising government spending. Both of these actions by government tend to please taxpayers and beneficiaries. Deficits may reduce the economy's ability to grow, but the effects are indirect. Deficits require people to imagine the future and to determine how they will be affected in the long run.

Buchanan argues that deficit spending ignores the future, and it harms future generations. He even raises a moral question; are deficits a form of taxation without representation? Congressmen today enhance their constituents' present welfare, as well as their own re-election probability, by jeopardizing the welfare of their grandchildren. The unborn cannot vote. Yet congress, by creating large deficits, is presenting each of them with a future financial liability.[4]

## The Power of Special Interest Groups

Elected representatives often have interests of their own that do not match those of the voters that elected them. For a politician, re-election is the highest priority. However, getting elected costs money. Therefore, a representative must become proficient at raising campaign funds. Lobbyists for favor-seeking special-interest groups offer the richest sources of contributions for political candidates. Campaign contributions do not buy votes directly, but they buy time on representatives' crowded schedules. Often the side that receives the most time to present its viewpoint, is the side that wins the legislative battle.

In order to present their views to congress, special-interest groups hire people or firms to lobby for them. Lobbying, by definition, is any method used to communicate with elected officials for the purpose of educating or persuading them toward the views of a special-interest group. In order for an individual voter to communicate with their elected officials, they must send them letters or telegrams, take out newspaper ads or telephone their office directly. Few voters feel that they have enough at stake in any one issue to justify the effort of any of these means of communication. However, groups of people with common interest can share the costs of making their views known to their representatives. They can hire full-time lobbyists to present their views to state and federal legislatures. As a result, their influence may be much greater than would be possible if each member acted individually.[5]

## The Expansion of Government Bureaucracies

The actual work of government, at all levels, is accomplished in the multitude of departments, agencies and bureaus that are collectively known as "The Bureaucracy." Government bureaus bear some resemblance to private firms. Both bureaus and firms use the hierarchical principle of management. However, despite the many similarities, bureaus are different from private companies. One of the major differences is the self-interest of the bureaucrats. Government managers are not judged on the basis of their contribution to profit or the building of market share for the firms' products. Bureaucrats are judged, and paid, on the basis of the size of their organization. Therefore, the major interest of the heads of government bureaus is the expansion of their organizations.

In a government bureau, the value of a job to the organization is determined by a staff of personnel specialists. As of June, 1994, the federal government had almost 2.9 million workers. The basic pay scale for government workers is broken down into 15 different pay categories with 10 different pay steps in each category. This pay scale does not even include the executive service of the federal government, which has its own pay scale. This type of organization, by its very size and complexity alone, makes it impossible to accurately evaluate each job. Therefore, job grades in the federal government are, for the most part, determined by the size of the organization or the size of the staff, not on the complexity of the job.

Salary, perquisites such as office size, type of furniture, travel budgets, prestige and most promotions, all tend to increase as the bureau or staff that a manager is in charge of, increases. Thus, agency directors actively lobby congress and the administration for increases in their budgets and responsibilities. It is rare to see an agency argue that some function it now performs is not required. It is virtually unknown for an agency to return unspent funds to the treasury. Most agencies feel that if they do not spend all of the funds that are allocated to them, their next year's budget will be reduced. Therefore, there is no incentive to spend less than the budget allotment and every incentive to constantly lobby congress for additional funds. A consequence of the way agencies are managed is that they often grow larger than congress originally intended. Congress originally sets up an agency in response to lobbying pressure from an interested group of voters. However, after the agency has been set up, pressure for expansion comes from both interested voters and the agency itself.[6]

## Economics and Public Choice

Many economists regard the public choice school with some skepticism. However, most economists admit that this theory offers at least one important lesson. The lesson is that the public should not assume that government takes economically prudent steps in the face of political opposition. Modern economic textbooks point out that market imperfections such as monopolies and the uneven distribution of income, may be cured by government action. Public choice theorists ask the question: will the government actually do its theoretical duty? Just as the market may have imperfections, government is not perfect. Adam Smith told us that people act in their own self-interest. Government employees are people too. Why then should we expect a government employee to be any different than the rest of us?

NOTES:

## Chapter 20
## Economics and Public Choice

1.   Drucker, Peter, <u>Post Capitalist Society</u>, Harper Business, New York, N.Y., 1993, p. 126.
2.   Drucker, p. 131.
3.   Dolan, Edwin G. & Lindsey, David E., <u>Economics, Seventh Edition,</u> The Dryden Press, Orlando, FL, 1994, p. 460.
4.   Buchholz, Todd G., <u>New Ideas From Dead Economists</u>, Penguin Books, New York, N.Y. 1989, p. 252.
5.   Dolan & Lindsey, p. 710
6.   Dolan & Lindsey, p. 715.

# CHAPTER 21

---

# MONEY, BANKING AND THE FEDERAL RESERVE SYSTEM

*No matter who you are, making informed decisions about what to do with your money, will help build a more stable financial future for you and your family -- Alan Greenspan*

## WHAT IS MONEY?

Money according to Adam Smith is a commodity or token that everyone will accept in exchange for the things they have to sell. In any society, money is the asset, commodity or token that serves as a medium of exchange. Different societies throughout history have quite different money systems. The major historical types of money were Commodity moneys, Fiat money, and Fiduciary money.

Commodity moneys have value in non-monetary uses equivalent to the monetary value of the commodity. Historically, copper, gold and silver coins have been the most used in European and East Asian societies. An example is the gold and silver coins that have values roughly equal to the price the metal would command if it were used to create jewelry. Fiat money is a monetary standard that people are required by law to accept as a medium of exchange or a standard of deferred payment. It is money because the government that issued the money (usually paper money) says that it is and guarantees its use for payment of goods and services. Bank money is also called fiduciary money because it is based on the trust people have that the bank will honor its obligation and pay as promised. Fiduciary money may be based on promises to pay in commodity money such as gold coins or in fiat money such as U.S. dollars. Modern monetary systems are largely based on fiduciary money. The two major kinds of fiduciary money are bank notes and checking accounts. Bank notes were widely used in the in Europe and America during the nineteenth century. Bank notes in The United States were replaced by Treasury notes after the Civil War. Today in most modern societies checks are used as money. Therefore, the Federal Reserve includes checking accounts and travelers checks in its M1 definition of money.

## The Functions of Money

Money has three functions in the economy: It is a medium of exchange, a unit of account, and a store of value. These three functions distinguish money from other assets. A medium of exchange is an item that buyers give to sellers when they purchase goods and services. When you buy a football at a sporting goods store, the store gives you the brand new football, and you give the store money in the form of fiat money, U.S. bills and coins or fiduciary money, bank checks or bank debit cards. The transfer of money from buyer to seller allows the transaction to take place. When you walk into a store you are confident they will accept your money for the football because money is commonly accepted as a medium of exchange.

A unit of account is the yardstick people use to post prices and record debts. When you go shopping you observe that a Wilson NFL football costs $25 and a hamburger at McDonald's costs $2. Similarly, if you take out a loan from a bank, the size of your future loan repayments will be measured in dollars, not in a quantity of other goods. When we want to measure and record economic value, we use money as a unit of account.

A store of value is an item that people can use to transfer purchasing power from the present to the future. When a seller accepts money today in exchange for a good or service, that seller can hold the money and become a buyer of another good or service at another time. A person can also transfer purchasing power from the present to the future by buying and holding stocks, bonds and real estate. The term wealth is used to refer to the total of all stores of value, including both money and non-monetary assets. Economists use the term liquidity to describe the ease with which an asset can be converted into the economy's medium of exchange. Because money, either coin paper or checking deposits, is the economy's medium of exchange, it is the most liquid asset available. When people decide in what form to hold their wealth, they have to balance the liquidity of each possible asset against the asset's usefulness as a store of value. Money is the most liquid asset, but it is far from perfect as a store of value. When prices rise, the value of money falls, for example, when goods and services become more expensive, each dollar can buy less. This link between the price level and the value of money is important for understanding how money affects the economy and why interest is paid to investors for the use of their money.[1]

Interest is the price that borrowers pay for the use of someone else's money. Interest on a loan of money such as a bank loan or a sale of a corporate or government bond is based on three conditions: Liquidity, market risk and default risk. Liquidity is the price that the lender demands for temporarily giving up the current opportunity to buy a good or service with money. Market risk is the probability that interest rates in the market for a comparable security will increase due to an increase in inflation. Increased rates of inflation will lead to higher prices for goods and service resulting in a reduction in the value (price) of the security. If the owner of the security needs to redeem it prior to maturity they may have to accept a reduction in the face value of that security. Default risk is based on the probability that the borrower will not repay the loan or bond when it matures. Interest is therefore determined by adding together the liquidity value, the market risk and the lender's default risk of a bank loan on a particular security. This is why a U.S. government issued security with a short-term maturity such as a 90 day Treasury Bill has a lower rate of interest than a 10 Year Government Bond.

## The Federal Reserve Definitions of Money

The quantity of money circulating in the economy is referred to by the Federal Reserve as the money supply. There is more than one definition of the money supply; the most obvious is currency, the paper bills and coins in the hands of the public and the vaults of banks. However, currency is not the only asset that can be used to buy goods and services. Almost all stores accept personal checks and bank debit cards which act as electronic checks. Wealth held in a checking account is almost as convenient for buying things as wealth held in a consumer's wallet. Therefore, checking account deposits and travelers checks are included in the definition of money. Also, savings accounts can easily be converted into cash without loss of principle along with deposits in money market accounts such as negotiable orders of withdrawal (NOW) accounts.[2]

In a complex economy such as that of the United States, it is not easy to distinguish between what is called money and assets that cannot. The coins in an individuals pocket are clearly part of the money supply and the Golden Gate Bridge in San Francisco clearly is not, but there are many alternatives between these extremes for which the choice is less clear. Therefore, the Federal Reserve has developed definitions of money and the money stock based on the liquidity of the assets considered. Table 21-1 shows the items included in the money supply developed by the Federal Reserve.

From December 2007 to December 2008 the M1 money supply increased by 17.0 percent. The largest increase was in demand deposits at commercial banks. This trend has continued through 2011. In 2012 M1 increased by \$303.2 billion and M2 increased by 432.7 over 2011. In 2013 M1 increased by \$114.4 billion or 8.5 percent over 2012. M2 increased by \$348 or 4.4 percent over 2012. The largest increase was in demand deposits and savings deposits at commercial banks. This large increase is an indication that the Federal Reserve System continues to make large deposits at commercial banks to purchase government securities

**The Federal Reserve Defines the M1 and M2 Money Supply as follows:**

**M1:** The sum of currency held outside of depository institutions, Federal Reserve Banks, and the U.S. Treasury; travelers checks; and demand and other checkable deposits issued by financial institutions (except demand deposits due to the Treasury and depository institutions), minus cash items in the process of collections and Federal Reserve float.

**M2:** M1 plus savings deposits (including money market deposit accounts) and small denomination (under $100,000) time deposits issued by financial institutions, and shares in retail money market mutual funds (funds with initial investment of under $50,000), net of retirement accounts.

### Table 21-1

### Money Stock Measures – December 2013 vs. 2012

| Money Market Measure | Dec 2012 $ in billions | Dec 2013 $ in billions | Change 2013 vs. 2012 |
|---|---|---|---|
| **M1** | $ | $ | $ |
| Currency in Circulation | 1,090.9 | 1,159.8 | 68.9 |
| Travelers Checks | 3.8 | 3.5 | -.3 |
| Demand Deposits at Commercial Banks | 901.7 | 1016.1 | 114.4 |
| Other Checkable Deposits | 443.7 | 468.9 | 25.2 |
| Total M1 | **2,440.1** | **2,648.3** | **208.2** |
| **M2 = M1 Plus** | | | |
| Savings Deposits | 6694.5 | 7,133.2 | 438.7 |
| Small Denominations Time Deposits | 632.6 | 545.0 | -87.6 |
| Money Market Funds | 635.1 | 632.4 | -2.7 |
| Total M2 Additions | **7,962.2** | **8,310.6** | **348.4** |
| **Total M2** | **10,402.3** | **10,958.9** | **556.6** |

## HOW BANKS CREATE MONEY

Based on the above information you can see that the Federal Reserve has several definitions of money which include bank demand, savings and time deposits. Changes in the quantity of money originate with actions of the Federal Reserve System, depository institutions, or the public. The actual process of money creation takes place primarily in commercial banks. Checkable liabilities of banks are considered to be money. These bank liabilities are customers' accounts. They increase when customers deposit currency and checks and when the proceeds of loans made by the banks are credited to borrower's accounts. Many years ago bankers discovered that they could make loans merely by giving their promises to pay, a bank note, in some acceptable commodity such as gold, to borrowers. In this way, banks began to create money. More notes could be issued than the gold that they held in their vaults because only a portion of the notes outstanding would be presented for payment at any one time.

Transaction deposits are the modern counterpart of bank notes. It was a small step from printing notes to making book entries crediting deposits of borrowers, which the borrowers in turn could spend by writing checks, thereby effectively printing their own money. The modern bank must be prepared to convert deposit money into currency for those depositors who request currency. In addition the bank must make remittance on checks written by depositors and presented for payment by other banks. Finally, it must maintain legally required reserves, in the form of vault cash and/or balances at its Federal Reserve Bank. This is called the reserve requirement and is explained in a previous chapter. The Federal Reserve, through its ability to vary both the total volume of reserves and the required ratio of reserves to deposit liabilities, influences banks' decisions with respect to their assets and deposits. One of the major responsibilities of the Federal Reserve System is to provide the total amount of reserves consistent with the monetary needs of the economy at reasonably stable prices.

As an example of how banks create money, let's assume that expansion of the money stock M1 is desired by the Federal Reserve System. One way the central bank can initiate such an expansion is through purchases of securities in the open market for $10,000. Payment for the securities adds to bank reserves. The purchase is made from a government securities dealer and is deposited in the dealer's bank account, for example, at NY Bank A. At the same time, Bank A's reserve account at the Federal Reserve is credited for the amount of the securities purchase. The Federal Reserve System has added $10,000 of securities to its assets, which it has paid for, in effect, by creating a liability on itself in the form of bank reserve balances.

Commercial Banks are required to hold reserves equal to only a fraction of their deposits. Reserves in excess of this amount may be used to increase earning assets; loans and investments. Under current regulations, banks are required to keep 10 percent in reserves against their transaction accounts. If NY Bank A receives a $10,000 deposit and the reserve requirement is 10%, they need to retain only $1,000. The remaining $9,000 is excess reserves. This amount can be loaned or invested. What banks do when they make loans is to accept promissory notes in exchange for credits to the borrowers' transaction accounts. Loans (assets) and deposits (liabilities) both rise by $9,000. Reserves are unchanged by the loan transaction. But the deposit credits constitute new additions to the total deposits of the banking system. If the bank holding the $9,000 of deposits just created, in turn make loans equal to their excess reserves, then loans and deposits will rise by a further $8,100 ($9,000 x .90) in the second stage of expansion. This process can continue until deposits have risen to the point where all the reserves provided by the initial purchase of government securities by the Federal Reserve System are just sufficient to satisfy reserve requirements against the newly created deposits.

Carried through to theoretical limits, the initial $10,000 of reserves distributed within the banking system can give rise to an expansion of $90,000 in bank credit and supports a total of $100,000 in new deposits under a 10 percent reserve requirement. The deposit expansion multiplier for a given amount of new reserves is thus the reciprocal of the required reserve percentage (1/.10 = 10). The multiple expansions is possible because the banks as a group are like one large bank in which checks drawn against borrowers' deposits result in credits to accounts of other depositors, with no net change in the total reserves.[3]

However, a given increase in bank reserves is not necessarily accompanied by an expansion equal to the theoretical potential based on the required ratio of reserves to deposits. What happens to the quantity of money will vary, depending upon the reactions of banks and the public. A number of leakages may occur such as the public might choose to hold more money as currency and banks might not be able to turn all excess deposits into loans. For example, the relationship between currency in circulation and demand and savings deposits can be used as a proxy for the cash drain ratio. An estimate of the cash drain can be developed using the data in Table 21-1 and dividing currency in circulation by the total of demand and savings deposits ($1,159.8/$8,149.3 billion). This equation results in a cash drain ratio of about 14 percent. The deposit expansion multiplier formula then can be restated as follows:

$$DEM = \frac{1}{RR + Cash\ Drain} \qquad \frac{1}{.10 + .14} = 4.2$$

This reduces the deposit expansion multiplier from 10 to 4.2 percent. If the banking system's holdings of excess reserves is considered the multiplier would be reduced even further.

## BALANCE SHEET OF THE FEDERAL RESERVE SYSTEM

Each week, the Federal Reserve posts its current release H.4.1. This release is titled Factors Affecting Reserve Balances and shows the current numbers from what is commonly called the Federal Reserve Balance Sheet. The one power that the Fed unquestionably possesses is the ability to create money. It traditionally did so by buying Treasury securities from the public, crediting the sellers' banks with newly created Federal Reserve deposits (a "liability" from the Fed's point of view), and adding the securities purchased to the Fed's asset holdings. Those newly created Federal Reserve deposits are essentially electronic credits that the banks could use to receive delivery of cash from the Federal Reserve.

Table 21-2 details the Federal Reserve Balance Sheets for 2012 and 2013. The assets of the Federal Reserve have increased by $1,124 billion for 2013 over 2012. There was a large increase in treasury securities held during the period as the Fed increased its holdings by $551 billion. There was also a large increase in Mortgage Backed Securities of $570 Billion. Total Securities Held by the Federal Reserve increased by $1,103 billion which accounted for 98 percent of the increase in the total assets held by the Fed.

## Table 21-2
## Federal Reserve Balance Dec. 2012, vs. Dec. 2013

| Federal Reserve Assets ($ Millions) | Dec. 26 2012 | Dec. 25 2013 | Change 2013 vs. 2012 |
|---|---|---|---|
| Treasury Securities | $1,656,930 | 2,208,829 | 551,899 |
| Federal Agency Debt | 76,783 | 57,221 | (19,562) |
| Mortgage Backed Securities | 926,558 | 1,496,943 | 570,385 |
| Securities Held | 2,660,271 | 3,762,993 | 1,102,722 |
| Repurchase Agreements | 0 | 0 | 0 |
| Loans | | | |
| Discount Window | 26 | 25 | (1) |
| Term Asset-Backed Securities Loan Facility | 558 | 97 | (461) |
| Other Credit | 29 | 70 | 41 |
| Total Loans | 613 | 192 | (421) |
| Maiden Lane LLC | 1,495 | 1,626 | 131 |
| Other Federal Reserve Assets | 218,201 | 28,503 | (189,698) |
| Miscellaneous Assets | 70,108 | 281,602 | 211,494 |
| Total Assets | 2,950,688 | 4,074,916 | 1,124,228 |
| Currency in Circulation | 1,167,122 | 1,238,524 | 71,402 |
| Reverse Repurchase Agree. | 99,853 | 151,257 | 51,404 |
| None Reserve Deps. with Fed | 84,570 | 169,603 | 85,033 |
| Other Liabilities and Capital | 66,491 | 64,802 | (1,689) |
| Reserve Balances | 1,532,651 | 2,450,730 | 918,079 |
| Total Liabilities and Capital | 2,950,688 | 4,074,916 | 1,124,229 |

In 2008 The Fed extended credit to the Maiden Lane LLC that was created as a device for handling the $30 billion loan that was part of the Bear Stearns deal. All of these operations by themselves would have increased the money supply and the Fed's total assets. To prevent that from happening, the Fed sold off a comparable volume of its holdings of Treasury securities. By the end of December 2008, the Fed had replaced more than $258 billion of its holdings of Treasury securities with assorted riskier loans. The largest increase in the Fed's assets in 2009 and 2010 was their holdings of Mortgage Backed Securities which totaled $908 billion in 2009 and $1,010 billion in 2010. In 2011 the Fed reduced its holdings of Mortgage Backed Securities by $164 billion and increased its purchases of Treasury Securities by $662 billion. The Fed was buying treasury securities to help fund the federal budget deficit.

Another measure that the Fed employed to allow this ballooning of its assets was to start paying banks an interest rate on reserves equal to its target for the fed funds rate itself, essentially eliminating any incentive for the banks to lend fed funds and encouraging banks instead to simply let excess reserves accumulate. As of December 26, 2013, banks were sitting on about $170 billion in excess reserves with the Fed, doing absolutely nothing with them. The Fed was in effect lending those funds in place of the banks. The Fed also increased its year end Reserve Balances by $918 billion over 2012.

## Description of the Federal Reserve Balance Sheet Loan Assets

The key loan asset items on the Federal Reserve Balance Sheet, with descriptions provided by the Federal Reserve Release H-4, are listed below:
1. Repurchase and Reverse Repurchase Agreements: The Fed uses repurchase agreements, also called "RPs" or "repos", to make collateralized loans to primary dealers. In a reverse repo or "RRP", the Fed borrows money from primary dealers. The Fed uses these two types of transactions to offset temporary swings in bank reserves; a repo temporarily adds reserve balances to the banking system, while reverse repos temporarily drains balances from the system. Repos and

reverse repos are conducted with primary dealers via auction. In a repo, dealers bid on borrowing money versus various types of general collateral. In a reverse repo, dealers offer interest rates at which they would lend money to the Fed versus the Fed's Treasury general collateral, typically Treasury bills.

2. The Asset-Backed Commercial Paper Money Market Mutual Fund Liquidity Facility: is a lending facility that provides funding to U.S. depository institutions and bank holding companies to finance their purchases of high-quality asset-backed commercial paper (ABCP) from money market mutual funds under certain conditions. The program is intended to assist money funds that hold such paper in meeting demands for redemptions by investors and to foster liquidity in the ABCP market and money markets more generally.

3. Commercial Paper Funding Facility: The Federal Reserve created the Commercial Paper Funding Facility (CPFF) to provide a liquidity backstop to U.S. issuers of commercial paper. The CPFF is intended to improve liquidity in short-term funding markets and thereby contribute to greater availability of credit for businesses and households. Under the CPFF, the Federal Reserve Bank of New York will finance the purchase of highly rated unsecured and asset-backed commercial paper from eligible issuers via eligible primary dealers.

4. Maiden Lane LLC: On June 26, 2008, the Federal Reserve Bank of New York (FRBNY) extended credit to Maiden Lane LLC under the authority of section 13(3) of the Federal Reserve Act. This limited liability company was formed to acquire certain assets of Bear Stearns and to manage those assets through time to maximize repayment of the credit extended and to minimize disruption to financial markets. Payments by Maiden Lane LLC from the proceeds of the net portfolio holdings will be made in the following order: operating expenses of the LLC, principal due to the FRBNY, interest due to the FRBNY, principal due to JPMorgan Chase & Co., and interest due to JPMorgan Chase & Co. Any remaining funds will be paid to the FRBNY.8

## Quantitative Easing I, II and III

This is a government monetary policy recently used by The Federal Reserve Banks to increase the money supply by buying government securities or other securities from the market.

Quantitative easing increases the money supply by flooding financial Institutions (Brokerage firms and Commercial Banks) with capital in an effort to promote increased lending and liquidity.

The Federal Reserve increased its holdings of Securities by $769 billion from December 2009 through December 2011. Federal Reserve Chairman Ben Bernanke Stated in November 3, 2010 that the Fed planned to again increase its holdings of securities and increasing the money supply by about $600 billion during the first half of 2010. The Federal Reserve continued to expand the money supply by purchasing about 85 billion in government securities each month through 2013. For 2014 Janet Yellen, the new Federal Reserve Chairman, plans to reduce the buying of Fed securities to about 65 billion per month and slowly phase out the purchasing of Fed securities sometime in 2015.

## The Feds Explanation on the Purchases of Treasury Securities

On November 3, 2010, the Federal Open Market Committee (FOMC) decided to expand the Federal Reserve's holdings of securities in the System Open Market Account (SOMA) to promote a stronger pace of economic recovery and to help ensure that inflation, over time, is at levels consistent with its mandate. In particular, the FOMC directed the Open Market Trading Desk (the Desk) at the Federal Reserve Bank of New York to purchase an additional $600 billion of longer term Treasury securities by the end of the second quarter of 2011.

The FOMC also directed the Desk to continue to reinvest principal payments from agency debt and agency mortgage-backed securities into longer-term Treasury securities. Based on current estimates, the Desk expects to reinvest $250 to $300 billion over the same period, though the realized amount of reinvestment will depend on the evolution of actual principal payments. Taken together, the Desk anticipated conducting $850 to $900 billion of purchases of longer-term Treasury securities through the end of the second quarter. This would result in an average purchase pace of roughly $110 billion per month.[8]  For 2012 The Fed continued to purchase securities and expanding the money supply by about $735 billion over 2011.

### An Opposing View of QE II and III From Larry Kudlow

Fed head Ben Bernanke and the FOMC dropped a new policy bomb at their meeting this week. Now they say inflation is too low. That's the real problem. And the solution, punch up the money supply and punch down the dollar.

The Fed actually has opened the door even wider for more money-creating, balance-sheet expanding, Treasury-bond-buying actions at its next scheduled meeting, which will come the day after the midterm elections on November 3. That's when QE2 may sail. "Quantitative easing" is what they call it. I call it dollar whack-a-mole.

One of the cornerstones of economic growth in a free-market model is domestic price stability and a stable, reliable dollar. This is crucial for confidence and capital formation. In fact, Nobelist Robert Mundell always argued for low tax rates to spur growth and a steady dollar linked to gold to ensure price stability.

But now we are moving deeper into monetary Keynesian fine-tuning to control the economy. That, plus an overspending Keynesian fiscal policy, may be combined with higher tax rates and an ever-weakening dollar. It's totally wrong. It's exactly the reverse of Mundell's thesis. Sinking the greenback and pumping more money into the system while raising tax rates and overspending is, over time, a prescription for stagflation: too much money chasing too few goods.

Now think of this: With all the Fed's pump-priming since late 2008, there is still $1 trillion of excess bank reserves sitting on deposit at the central bank. This massive cash hoard suggests that liquidity is not the problem for the financial system or the economy. And putting another $1 trillion into excess reserves only doubles the problem.

A much better idea would be a fiscal freeze on spending, tax rates, and regulations. This is apparently what the tea-party driven Republican congressional leaders intend for their election platform. Such a freeze would go a long way toward reducing the massive overhang of uncertainty that has plagued the economy and stifled the animal spirits. The Fed can print money, but it can't print new jobs or growth. On the other hand, a rollback of the big-government obstacles to growth would get folks to put money to work. Not only the $1 trillion in excess bank reserves, but the massive corporate cash hoard, estimated at roughly $2 trillion.[9]

**NOTES:**

**Chapter 21**
**Money, Banking and the Federal Reserve System**

1.  Mankiw, Gregory, N., <u>Principles of Economics,</u> The Dryden Press, Orlando, FL, 1998, p. 593.
2.  Mankiw, p. 595.
3.  Federal Reserve of Chicago, <u>Modern Money Mechanics,</u> Chicago, IL, P. 1-6.
4.  Colander, David, C., <u>Macroeconomics,</u> Irwin Business Publications, Burr Ridge, IL, 1994. p. 471.
5.  Colander, p. 478.
6.  Heilbroner, Robert, <u>Making of Economic Society, 9th Edition,</u> Englewood Cliffs, N.J., Prentice Hall, 1993, p. 229.
7.  Federal Reserve Release H-4. December 30, 2009.
8.  Federal Reserve Bank of New York, Statement Regarding the Purchase of Treasury Securities, November 3, 2010.
9.  Kudlow, Larry, <u>Destroying King Dollar Is Not the Solution</u> Townhall, September 24, 2010.

# CHAPTER 22

---

# ECONOMIC GROWTH AND THE
# INTERNATIONAL MONETARY SYSTEM

*Socialism is a philosophy of failure, the creed of ignorance, and the gospel of envy, its inherent virtue is the equal sharing of misery. - Winston Churchill*

## MEASURING ECONOMIC GROWTH

In a global economy, the basic goals of consumers are often similar. These goals are, survival, growth, and prosperity. What makes countries different, from an economic point of view, is the probability of the attainment of each of these basic goals. In many of the world's developed countries, the goals of growth and prosperity are obtainable and measurable. In almost all of the undeveloped countries, the goal is often only survival, and often that goal is not achieved.

Economists use two measures of growth, real national income and per capita real national income. The term real means that gross national income has been adjusted for the effects of inflation using the country's gross domestic product deflator. As more goods and services are produced, the real income of a nation increases, and people are usually able to consume more. Per capita real national income is a term used by economists to describe the ratio between a country's real national income and its population. The ratio is calculated as follows:

$$\text{Per capita real national income} = \frac{\text{Real national income}}{\text{Total population}}$$

On the basis of this formula, a country could experience growth in its real gross domestic product, but if the population is growing at an even faster rate, output per person actually will fall. If economic growth is defined as a rising real per capita national income, then a nation's output of goods and services must increase faster than its population.

Governments can facilitate economic growth in many different ways. If a country is undeveloped, its government must first establish a set of laws that provide basic stability. In order to increase a country's total output, it must increase its productive capability. To increase the productivity of its assets a country must increase its capital investment either through its internal savings or foreign investment. Therefore, a stable government is the first requirement for increasing a country's national income.

Governments can also facilitate the growth in real per capita national income through the use of macroeconomic policy. However, to increase a country's real per capita income, in the long-run, macroeconomic policy must be directed at increasing production, i.e., increasing aggregate supply. In order to increase the supply of goods and services, government investment must be directed toward improving the performance of the factors of production, i.e., labor, land, capital, and technology.

## Labor

Economic growth depends on the size and quality of the labor force. Education and training are the key success factors in the quality of a nation's labor force. Therefore, government programs directed at improving education and training will result in increased productivity and, in turn, increased per capital output.

## Capital

To produce goods efficiently, capital must be combined with labor. The ability of a country to invest in capital goods is tied to its ability to generate domestic savings. A lack of current savings can be offset by borrowing, but the availability of borrowing is limited by the prospects of a country's future potential to save. However, the lower the standard of living in a country, the harder it is for its people to forgo current consumption in order to save. Governments can facilitate capital investment with a tax system that rewards personal savings and by direct investment in their county's infrastructure, i.e., roads, bridges, and telecommunication systems.

## Land

Capital and labor can be combined with land to produce goods and services. Abundant natural resources can contribute to economic growth, but natural resources alone do not generate growth. Government can help manage natural resources so that there is a maximum amount of value that is added to the resources through the production process. A country is usually better off if it can increase the value of its natural resources rather than selling the resource to other countries in its natural state. For example, government could prevent the sale of raw timber to foreigners and only permit the export of finished wood products.

## Technology

Advances in technology allow the production of more output from a given amount of resources. This means that technological progress accelerates economic growth for any given rate of increase in the labor force and the stock of capital. However, technological change depends on the scientific community. The more educated a population, the greater its potential for technological advances. Education gives industrial countries a substantial advantage over developing countries in creating new products and in improving the manufacturing process. Government can assist in technological development by directly investing in research and development. The greater the investment made for research and development, by a country, the better its chances for technological advancement.

The above analysis of the factors of production provides a foundation for the next step in the examination of world growth and prosperity. Therefore, this model will be used to determine the probability of growth in real per capita national income in the undeveloped countries, the ex-communist countries, and the industrialized countries of the world.

## PROSPECTS FOR GROWTH IN THE UNDEVELOPED COUNTRIES

As a group, developing countries have performed poorly compared to developed countries. Over the last half century, only two groups of countries have moved from the category of developing country to middle-income countries. These two groups are the Oil-Producing Countries and the Asian Tigers (Taiwan, South Korea, Singapore and Hong Kong). From 1950, the developing countries' growth rates were about equal to those of developed countries, but their per capita national income rate of growth was much lower. What makes it so difficult for developing countries to create a successful program for per capita growth is that social, political, and economic problems blend into one another and cannot be considered separately. The institutional structure that is taken for granted in the United States often doesn't exist in these countries.[1]

Economists have identified several general obstacles to real per capita national income growth in undeveloped countries. These problems include, political instability, excessive foreign debt, poor or inappropriate education, and overpopulation.

### Political Instability

In order to perform properly an economy needs a set of consistent rules and regulations. Any plan for economic development requires financial investment, either internally through savings or externally through investment of borrowing. Foreign lenders will not invest in a country that is subject to political instability. Political instability also restricts internal investment. There are usually only a small percentage of people who have any money to save. However, these people often channel their investments out of their own country as a hedge against a revolution. Well-off people in developing countries often provide major inflows of capital to developed countries.

## Excessive Foreign Debt

In the 1970's, developing countries borrowed from foreign banks to finance development projects by private domestic firms. However, as a result of political corruption and economic mismanagement, the investments were often unproductive. The governments that had guaranteed these loans eventually were put in a position of having to repay them without the financial resources to do so. In many of these countries annual interest payments exceeded their export earnings. Meanwhile no payments were made on the principle. Accordingly, the 1980's were a period of intense negotiation designed to prevent developing countries from defaulting on their loans. The United States government, along with most of the developed countries and the International Monetary Fund were active in these negotiations. The result was that loans were restructured to prevent default, but the undeveloped countries, for the most part, had exhausted their borrowing capability.

## Poor or Inappropriate Education

In less developed countries, workers are often illiterate and they have little training. Low productivity is a result of poorly educated human capital as well as physical capital. Also, developing countries tend to empathize the wrong type of education. In developing countries only the well-off are usually educated. The best students qualify for scholarships in western countries. The training that they receive is often based on business techniques that are practiced in developed countries. Often their education is not relevant to the problems facing their own countries. This often causes a "Brain Drain," where the best and brightest students from the undeveloped countries move to developed countries to obtain jobs that are relevant to their education.

## Overpopulation

There are two ways that a country can increase per capita real national income. These two methods are:

- Decrease the number of people in the country without decreasing total income.

- Increase national income without increasing the population.

Thomas Carlyle gave economics its nickname, "The Dismal Science." Carlyle was commenting on the population growth theories of Thomas Malthus. Remember, from chapter number 4, Malthus predicted that society's prospects are dismal because population tends to outrun the means of subsistence. This view was cemented into economic thinking in the law of marginal productivity. According to this law, as more and more people are added to a fixed amount of land, the output per worker gets smaller.

Through technological progress, most western economies have avoided the fate predicted by Malthus because growth in output has exceeded growth in population. In contrast, many developing economies have not avoided the fate that Malthus predicted. This is because diminishing marginal productivity has exceeded technological change, and the economic growth that developing countries' experience isn't sufficient to offset the increased growth in population. The result is a constant or falling rate of growth in real per capital national income.[2]

On the basis of the history of per capita real national income growth in the world's richest countries, an iron law of economic development can be stated. No country can become rich without an extended period of good economic performance and an equally long period of very slow population growth. Therefore, when it comes to the prospect of getting rich, in most of the undeveloped countries, the dismal science provides a most dismal forecast.

## THE INTERNATIONAL MONETARY SYSTEM

The fall of communism in Eastern Europe has had far reaching affects on the economic development of Western Europe. In addition the evolution of the current international monetary system should have equally profound affects on tomorrow's world economy. The fuel that drives international economic growth is obviously money and the fuel injector that keeps the economic engine burning is the international exchange mechanism. Governments have three basic choices in determining a foreign exchange policy. They can develop a system of flexible exchange rates, partially flexible exchange rates or a fixed exchange rate. When governments do not enter into foreign exchange markets at all, but leave the determination of exchange rate up to the international money market, the country has a flexible exchange rate. When governments sometimes buy or sell currencies to influence the exchange rate, while at other times they let international currency market forces operate, they have partially flexible exchange rate. If government chooses a particular exchange rate and offers to buy and sell currencies at that price, it has a fixed exchange rate.[3]

An effective way to explain how the various foreign systems work is to present a brief history of the international exchange rate system. Beginning with the Paris Conference of 1867 and lasting until 1933, most of the world economies had a system of relatively fixed exchange rates under what was called a gold standard. Under a gold standard, the amount of money a country issued had to be directly tied to gold. Each country participating in a gold standard agreed to fix the price of its currency relative to gold. That meant a country would agree to pay a specified amount of gold upon demand to anyone who wanted to exchange that country's currency for gold. To do so, each country had to maintain a stockpile of gold. When a country fixed the price of its currency relative to gold, it fixed its currency's price in relation to other currencies. Under the gold standard, a country made up a difference between the quantity supplied and the quantity demanded of its currency by buying or selling gold to hold the price of its currency fixed in terms of gold. How much a country would need to buy and sell depended upon its balance of payments deficit or surplus. If a country ran a deficit in the balance of payments, it was required to buy its currency and to sell gold to stop the value of its currency from falling.

Since gold served as reserves to a country's currency, a balance of payments deficit would result in a flow of gold out of the country. This resulted in a reduction in a country's money supply often at times when an increase in the money supply was needed to fight a recession. It was in this way that the gold standard determined a country's monetary policy and forced it to adjust to any international balance of payments disequilibrium. Adjustments to a balance of payments deficit were often politically unpopular for they led to recessions and prevented the Federal Reserve System from counteracting the recession with monetary policy. For all practical purposes, President Roosevelt ended the gold standard in the United States, when he abandoned the gold standard in 1933.

As World War II was coming to an end, the United States and its allies met to establish a new international economic order. After a considerable amount of debate, they agreed upon a system named after the resort in New Hampshire where the meeting was held, i.e., the Bretton Woods system. The Bretton Woods system established the International Monetary Fund to oversee the international economic order. The IMF was empowered to arrange short-term loans between countries. The Bretton Woods system also established the World Bank, which was empowered to make longer-term loans to developed countries. Today the World Bank and the IMF continue their central roles in international financial affairs. The Bretton Woods system was based upon mutual agreements about what countries would do when experiencing balance of payments surpluses or deficits. It was essentially a fixed exchange rate system.[4]

The Bretton Woods system reflected the underlying political and economic realities that were present after World War II. The European economies were in a state of almost total destruction and the United States was the only one of the allies whose economy was almost untouched by the war. In order to rebuild their economies, Europe would have to import large amounts of equipment and borrow large amounts from the United States to finance these purchases. The establishment of fixed exchange rates helped to provide the financial stability that was necessary to rebuild Europe. In addition, the Bretton Woods system provided a mechanism for long-term loans from the United States to Europe that could help sustain the fixed exchange rates that were established. However, one of the major difficulties of the Bretton Woods system was the shortage of a currency in which countries could hold their liquid financial assets, i.e., a reserve currency. To offset that shortage, the IMF was empowered to create a basket of international currencies called "Special Drawing Rights."

However, SDR's never became established as an international currency and the United States dollar soon began serving as a reserve currency. To get dollars into the hands of foreigners, the United States had to run a deficit in its international balance of payments current account. Remember that a current account deficit or net imports results in a reduction of the gross domestic product of a country.

By the early 1970's the number of dollars held by foreigners was far greater than the amount of gold the United States held in its vaults at the Fed. This meant that the United States could not redeem in gold all of the dollars that were held by foreigners. This situation came to a head when France in 1971 demanded a redemption in gold for the dollars held by the French central bank. As a result of this demand, the United States ended its policy of exchanging gold for dollars at the predetermined price of $35 per ounce and with that change, the Bretton Woods system effectively came to an end.[5]

The present international monetary exchange rate system is a partially flexible one. Most western country's exchange rates are allowed to fluctuate although, at various times, governments buy and sell their own currencies in order to affect short-term fluctuations. While most Western countries exchange rates are partially flexible, certain countries have agreed to fixed exchange rates of their currencies in relation to the rates of a group of certain other currencies.

## The European Monetary System

The European Common Market countries allow their currencies' value to fluctuate only within a narrow range while other currencies are fixed relative to the dollar. Also, in 1991 the European Common Market countries have all signed the Maastricht Treaty which is a document designed to establish the basic rules of trade between these countries. One of the goals of this treaty is to establish a European single currency by the year 2000. To obtain the goal of a uniform currency, the European Community governments set up the European Monetary Institute and a national European central bank. This they believe is a necessary step towards developing a truly common market for the fifteen nations that make up the European Community.

The European Monetary System is an arrangement by which most nations of the European Union (EU) linked their currencies to prevent large fluctuations relative to one another. The EMS was organized in 1979 to stabilize foreign exchange and counter inflation among its members. In 1994 the European Monetary Institute was created as a transitional step in establishing the European Central Bank and a common currency. The European Central Bank was established in 1998 and is responsible for setting a single monetary policy and interest rate for those countries that would participate in the single rate currency. On January 1, 1999 eleven countries in the European Economic and Monetary Union, Austria, Belgium, Finland, France, Germany, Ireland, Italy, Luxembourg, the Netherlands, Portugal and Spain, gave up their own currencies and adopted the new "Euro" for foreign and electronic payments. The introduction of the euro was widely regarded as a major step toward European political unity. At its introduction the euro had an exchange rate slightly greater than the U.S. Dollar (worth about $1.17); however, by the end 1999, its value was reduced to $1.00. The rate of inflation is a major reason why currencies trade at different exchange rates. For example, from 1996 through 2000 the U.S. gross domestic product deflator increased by only 7 percent or an average of 1.75 percent per year. The low rate of inflation in the U.S. relative to the rate in Europe is the major reason that the euro initially traded below the value of the U.S. dollar.

In January of 2001, Greece adopted the euro bringing its members up to twelve. Of the European Union members not adopting the euro (Denmark, Great Britain, and Sweden), the most notable is Britain, which continues to regard itself as more or less separate from Europe. Nonetheless, British Prime Minister Tony Blair announced plans to consider adopting the euro somewhere between 2002-2005. In all three nations there was strong public anxiety that dropping their respective national currencies would give up too much independence. Finally, euro coins and notes will be introduced into circulation in January 2002, and the local currencies of the euro members are to be removed from circulation. Participating countries will retain their existing currency tokens until that time. However, the values of participating currency units have been irrevocably fixed against the new euro currency by the European Monetary Union. Currently the EMU has expanded to 16 members. In 2004 Slovenia adopted the euro in 2007, Cyprus and Malta followed in 2008 and Slovakia joined in 2009. Countries that have adopted of the euro as their sole currency are referred to as members of the Eurozone.

Since it was set up, the markets have been cautious about the Euro. The currency had performed well until a global economic downturn began in 2008. In general, countries worldwide suffered badly. In particular, Eurozone members with weaker economies (e.g. Portugal, Ireland, Italy and Spain) struggled to repay their debts, which damaged confidence in the euro. The situation in the Eurozone worsened in 2010 when Greece suffered a financial crisis. Despite initial reluctance, Eurozone countries gave €80bn worth of loans to Greece. In return Greece had to cut its public spending and allow EU auditors to assess its finances. After concern that other weak eurozone economies would face similar crises, a European Financial Stability Facility (EFSF) was created to provide up to €440bn worth of loans to struggling eurozone states. The EFSF will be based in Luxembourg.

**NOTES:**

**Chapter 22**
**Economic Growth and the International Monetary System**

1. Colander, David, C., <u>Macroeconomics,</u> Irwin Business Publications, Burr Ridge, IL, 1994. p. 471.
2. Colander, p. 478.
3. Heilbroner, Robert, <u>Making of Economic Society,9th Edition,</u> Englewood Cliffs, N.J., Prentice Hall, 1993, p. 229.
4. Heilbroner, p. 229.
5. Colander, p. 456.

# CHAPTER 23

---

# THE BATTLE OF THE TITANS

*"Most managers are nearsighted. Even though today's competitive landscape often stretches to a global horizon, they see best what they know best: the customers geographically closest to home." –Kenichi Ohmae*

## THE BATTLE OF THE TITANS

After World War II, America served as the major stimulus for the world economy. Whenever the world sank into recession, the United States would use its fiscal and monetary policies to invigorate demand. Foreign exports to America would rise, pulling the exporting countries out of their economic slump. American macroeconomic stimulus, starting in the fall of 1982, pulled the industrial world out of its sharpest post-world War II recession. In 1983 and 1984 most of the growth in both Europe and Japan could be traced to exports to the American market. However, for the first time the United States found itself burdened with a large trade deficit. America's effortless exports became a thing of the past. In the 1990's, the total production of America's industries is no longer large enough to pull the entire world out of a recession.

In response to this new environment, governments are increasingly managing international trade. Non-tariff import barriers are rising everywhere. The trend is clear. America signs a free trade arrangement with Canada and Mexico. Europe talks about associate memberships in the European Community. In the twenty-first century the rules of the game will be written by that group of businesses or countries that control the largest markets.[1]

## THE CASE FOR EUROPE

If the Europeans are going to write the rules for international trade in the twenty-first century, it will be for a system of "Managed Trade" and "Quasi Trading Blocks." Free trade is great in theory, but in actual practice it interferes with what Adam Smith labeled as "Self-interest." If countries act in their own self-interest, only managed trade agreements are possible in the real world. In other words, countries will negotiate with other potential trading partners to develop contracts that define the rules of international trade. Both countries and trading blocks will negotiate the terms of the contracts based on their own interests not on the mutual interest of the entire world.

### The European Union

Two events make Europe the focal point of attention in the 1990's. First, in Western Europe on December 31, 1992, the European Community integrated, and instantly became the world's largest economic market. The countries that make up the European Community have almost 337 million citizens. In 1995, Sweden, Austria, and Finland all joined the European Community, bringing its number of countries to 15 and its members to more than 360 million people. Secondly, in Middle and Eastern Europe communism has dissolved and is being replaced by capitalism. The ex-communist economies have low wages, well-educated populations, and are located conveniently next to the world's largest market.

Some Middle and Eastern Europe countries will probably be offered associate memberships in the newly integrated European Community. Their special access could close Europe's markets for mid and low-income countries elsewhere in the world

Throughout history, those who control access to the world's largest market, wrote the rules of international trade. Britain wrote the rules of world trade in the nineteenth century. The United States did it in the twentieth century. As the world's largest market, Europe could write the rules of world trade in the twenty-first century. The combination of Western and Eastern Europe has 850 million well-educated people. Imagine what could occur if they paired the high-tech science capabilities of the former Soviet Union with the world-class production capabilities of the Germans, the financial capabilities of the British, and the design abilities of the French and Italians.

## Germany: Europe's Largest Industrial Base

Although the wheels of European integration have been set in motion, the timing of the unification is still far from certain. For example, Germany with the largest industrial base of any European country, has many internal problems that must be addressed before unification can fully take place.

In the October, 1994, elections, German Chancellor Helmut Kohl won his fourth term in office. However, the coalition of Chancellor Kohl's Christian Democratic Union and the smaller Free Democratic Party together won only 49 percent of the vote. Mr. Kohl's greatly reduced majority made it difficult for him to make any radical changes in the German government. Many Germans, including Chancellor Kohl, were troubled by the long-term prospects for economic growth, social restructuring, and the unification of East Germany. They believe that an overbearing bureaucracy and exorbitant labor, tax and welfare costs are stifling initiative and encouraging many businesses to leave the country. Financially, German unity has drained the country's strength and will continue to be a burden well into the twenty-first century.

On September 27, 1998, Social Democrat Gerhard Schroeder defeated Helmet Kohl after 16 years in office. Once considered a maverick and political outsider, Schroeder promised economic stability, domestic security and continuity in foreign affairs. The results, both political and economical, of Schroeder's first year in office was mixed. As early as October of 1999, the German business community had written him off as an ineffective populist with a soft spot for government meddling. And after losing half-dozen state elections in 1999 and control of the upper house of Parliament, his government was in danger of collapse. Recently, Schroeder has begun to earn the respect of German business as he is pushing through the broadest tax cuts since World War II and scraping obstacles to corporate restructuring sparking an increase in mergers and acquisitions among German companies.[2]

As a result of his reforms, the German economy started to boom in 2000. The percent increase in the gross domestic product more than doubled in 2000 over 1999, foreign investment also doubled and venture capital investment was plentiful. Still plenty could happen in Germany to check Schroeder's reformist ambitions. The world was on the verge of a recession in 2001, which will slow down the growth of most of the economies of Europe. Yet if Schroeder stays the course, he may not only spur the remaking of Germany, but also bring pressure on France into moderating its left wing political philosophy.

Still there are reforms that Schroeder is not willing to tackle. He isn't willing to undertake bold labor reforms. He hasn't touched regulations that make it tough to lay off workers, a key business concern that is politically sensitive. Also, Schroeder is only starting to deal with the touchy issue of pensions. Within 20 years, more than half of Germany's adult population will be over 60, creating an unbearable strain on the government budget. And the political waters will get increasingly treacherous as Schroeder presses on with his reforms. The opposition Christian Democrats have recovered from a campaign finance scandal and have a new leader in Angela Merkel and he will be looking for a political opening that will appeal to both workers and businesses.

Even though some improvements have been made under Schroeder inefficiency and red tape continue to clog the German production engine. For example, it can often take as much as three months just to change a telephone number in Germany. German's work fewer hours and take longer holidays than most other European workers. However, German labor unions continue to advocate a shorter workweek.

As a result, of high labor costs in Germany many German companies are moving some of their production facilities out of the country. Germany's many internal problems such as an overbearing bureaucracy and exorbitant labor, tax and welfare costs, will tend to slow their economic growth. This, in turn, will serve to reduce the speed of the unification of all of Western Europe. In addition to the problems in Germany, all of the countries in the European Community have internal problems and many of these problems will have to be resolved before a truly unified Europe can emerge.[3]

**The Third Way**

In 1994 Tony Blair was chosen as the new leader of the British Labour Party. By 1996 the "New Labour Party" as Blair called it, was gaining in popularity while at the same time a long recession reduced support for the Conservatives. The rise in popularity culminated in a landslide victory for Blair and the Labour Party in the Elections of May 1997.After taking office, Blair pledged to abide by federal spending limits and programs established by the Conservative Party. At the same time, he launched ambitious new programs calling for better relations with the European Union (EU), separate parliaments for Scotland and Wales, and reforms in welfare and health.

Tony Blair and German Chancellor Schroeder together attempted to develop a new political philosophy somewhere between European conservative and socialist philosophy. Together they created what was to be called "The Blair/Schroeder Manifesto" to explain their new political theory. The Manifesto was titled: " Europe: The Third Way/Die Neue Mitte." The Third Way document talks of flexibility, adaptation to world competition and encouragement to entrepreneurship in away familiar to those accustomed to a British politics. German's though are not as enamored of Third Way assaults on welfare as the British are. German's still prefer their familiar social-minded economic model which has brought them wealth and comfort. Outdated as the German system may be, it's still theirs and telling them to trade it for a new theory will be a hard sell for Schroeder.

The Third Way was not designed as a document simply to outline British and German political philosophy, an additional purpose was to present the new theory to the other 13 countries in the European Union. The introduction to the Manifesto attempts to place modern Europe in an economic and social perspective as it argues that: " Social democrats are in government in almost all the countries of the (European) Union. Social democracy has found new acceptance-but only because, while retaining its traditional values, it has begun in a credible way to renew its ideas and modernize its programmes. It has also found new acceptance because it stands not only for social justice but also for economic dynamism and the unleashing of creativity and innovation. According to the Manifesto, "The trademark of this approach is the New Centre in Germany and the Third Way in the United Kingdom. Other social democrats choose other terms that suit their own national cultures. " The essential function of markets must be complemented and improved by political action, not hampered by it. The introduction concludes by saying, "With this appeal (manifesto), we invite other European social democratic governments who share our modernizing aims to join in this enterprise."[4]

While the Third Way political theory has gained some inroads in countries such as The Netherlands and Spain, there are still many skeptics in Europe. For example, Lionel Jospin, the French prime minister, asked to explain the differences between his position and the Third Way, said, "Since society cannot be reduced to an exchange of goods, the market cannot be its sole motive force. So we are not liberals of the left, we are socialists." He also, claimed he did not know what the Third Way was, but if it were "something inserted between social democracy and liberalism," then he wasn't interested. And in Italy, prime minister Massimo D'Alema, a former communist, continues to grapple with and overloaded and over-manned state and with a welfare system that pays such generous pensions that, within a decade, will account for an unsupportable 20 percent of the countries budget. In summary, a united Europe that is capable of becoming the market leader of the twenty-first century is not yet united enough to accomplish this feat.

## European and World Trade

Another question that will require some strategy development is how will Europe deal with Japan? To protect their international trade position against the Japanese, Europe will probably be forced to develop an exclusionary and projectionist trading block. As for the United States, this is one circumstance in which being the only military superpower will be beneficial. Europe cannot put up trade barriers against the United States and at the same time continue a military partnership.

As the Europeans continue their economic integration, some of the ex-communistic economies will succeed in moving to a market economy and will rapidly raise the living standards of their citizens. The number of ex-communistic countries that do succeed will depend upon the degree of outside help. Western Europe will have no choice but to help Eastern Europe to improve their economies. Preventing Western migration, reducing border tensions and lowering ethnic hatreds all demand economic success in Middle and Eastern Europe.

## THE NEW LEADERS IN EUROPE

### Changes in Germany

During the first decade of the twenty first century there were many changes in the leadership in Europe. In Germany the Christian Democratic Union (CDU) leader Angela Merkel became Germany's first woman chancellor. In foreign policy Angela Merkel has struck a markedly different tone from Chancellor Gerhard Schroeder.

Among the changes foreseen are:

- An end to anti-Americanism; the agreement says Germany will not see itself as a counterweight to the US, but as a partner

- A firmer commitment to the NATO alliance as well as the EU; the Schroeder government backed controversial plans with France, which some saw as a challenge to NATO

- A stricter line on Russian backsliding from democracy; Germany will give high priority to Russia's progress on the rule of law and a political settlement in Chechnya

- Fair and open dealings in Europe; Germany will be more mindful of the concerns of Poland and other EU states; the old Franco-German partnership will cease to be exclusive

## Changes in France

In France, on May 6<sup>th</sup> 2007 voters choose Nicolas Sarkozy as their new President. The conservative standard-bearer Sarkozy handily beat Socialist candidate Ségolène Royal to succeed Jacques Chirac as President of France. The win also gives Sarkozy's ruling Union for a Popular Majority party (UMP) a considerable boost which resulted in a victory in the parliamentary elections on June 10 and 17 2007. The parliamentary victory gave France's conservative party the power necessary to push through the vast modernization and liberalization program promised by Sarkozy.

While his campaign had focused almost exclusively on domestic issues, Sarkozy emphasized international affairs in his victory speech, including an "appeal to our American friends to tell them that they can count on our friendship," but also insisting that Washington "accept that friends can think differently." He called for greater European cooperation, and for a new trans-Mediterranean partnership to speed economic development in Africa countries, which he saw as important to help curb immigration into Europe.

## Changes in Great Britain

James Gordon Brown assumed office as the Prime Minister of the United Kingdom in June 2007, after the resignation of Tony Blair and three days after becoming leader of the governing Labour Party. Before this, he served as Chancellor of the Exchequer in the Labour government from 1997 to 2007 under Blair. Brown has a PhD in history from the University of Edinburgh and spent his early career working as a TV journalist. He has been a Member of Parliament since 1983.

Gordon Brown might have wondered what he had gotten himself into, as his popularity sank along with the economy. But in October 2008 Mr. Brown rebounded, after he pulled together a bailout plan for Britain's teetering banks that became a model followed by the United States and most of Europe. As Washington and the European Union groped for a way to quickly address the mounting dangers, Mr. Brown offered banks like Royal Bank of Scotland, Barclays and HSBC

Holdings up to £50 billion ($88 billion) to shore up their capital in exchange for preferred shares. His plan also provided a guarantee of about £250 billion ($438 billion) to help banks refinance debt. The Bank of England will double the amount it lends to banks under its special liquidity plan to £200 billion. Mr. Brown also took a tougher line with the banks, removing the management of the companies that received government funding.

The United Kingdom general election of 2010 was held on May 6, 2010 to elect members to the House of Commons. None of the parties achieved the 326 seats needed for an overall majority. The conservative party, led by David Cameron, won the largest number of votes and seats but was still twenty seats short. This resulted in a hung parliament where no party would be able to command a majority in the House of Commons.

Coalition talks began immediately between the conservatives and the liberal democrats and lasted for five days. There was an aborted attempt to put together a labour/liberal democrat coalition but on May 11, 2010 Gordon Brown suddenly announced his resignation as Prime Minister, marking the end of 13 years of labour party control. This coalition was accepted by Queen Elizabeth II, who then invited David Cameron to form a government and become Prime Minister. Just after midnight on May 12, the liberal democrats emerged from a meeting of their Parliamentary party and Federal Executive to announce that the coalition deal had been "approved overwhelmingly", sealing a stable coalition government of Conservatives and Liberal Democrats. The election of conservative David Cameron as the Prime Minister highlighted a shift in European politics as its three largest economies, Germany, France and now Great Britain had elected conservative governments.

## THE CASE FOR JAPAN

The ideas central to Japanese economic thought derive extensively from American and British tradition but with a stronger Marxian component than is thought reputable in the English speaking countries. The Marxian influence relieves Japanese economic and political thought of the notion of a social dichotomy, even conflict, between the private market economy and the state. In Japan the state is the executive committee of the capitalist class. The result is an accepted cooperation between industry and government that is unthinkable in the American and British tradition. Japan also, has a commitment to educate and train its people at all levels, not just its college educated people. The result of this commitment to education is the highly competent Japanese labor force with its ample engineering and management talent.

Central also to the Japanese success is the avoidance of relatively sterile, unproductive investment in military operations. The use of a generous flow of savings for civilian capital formation as opposed to military purposes and the availability of engineering, scientific and business talent for civilian industry goes far to explain the industrial success and eminence of Japan. We have seen that, in the classical view, a worker was added when his contribution at the margin exceeds his cost. The Japanese worker is added as an integral part of the enterprise, and for life. Not surprisingly, this induces a loyalty not likely in the Western tradition.

## The Japanese Business Strategy

Kenichi Ohmae, in his classic book "The Mind of a Strategist," explains the basic Japanese business strategy. The Japanese secret is that they have tapped a universal human desire to build, to belong to an empire, to conquer neighboring empires, and to become the world's leading economic power. Their goal is market-share maximization and value-added maximization not simple profit maximization. The Japanese business strategy, on bringing new products to market, is to enter the market on the low end. Their initial strategic emphasis is to improve their production technology and to test the market in Southeast Asia. The next step is to expand their products to the medium and high end of the market through economies of scale, improving the image of the products, and marketing the product worldwide. The final step in the Japanese business strategy is to "Win the World." They develop this final strategy through global brands, non-price competition and overseas production of products. The Japanese business strategy is not just to become a player in the world market. The Japanese business strategy is to dominate the world market.[5]

Two basic Japanese business goals are to lengthen time horizons and to accept a lower rate of return. To accomplish these goals, impatient consumption oriented stockholders must be kept under control. The Japanese have organized their business groups to do just that. Japanese business group members own 78 percent of the shares listed on the Tokyo Stock Exchange. With interlocking ownership, Japanese business firms hold impatient consumption oriented shareholders at bay. Members of the business group do not gain by being paid high dividends. They improve their profits because they receive preferential treatment as preferred suppliers and customers.

In developing national strategies, the Japanese goal is to focus on those industries with high income elasticity of demand. This is an economic term meaning that there is a high rate of response to changes in demand caused by a change in price. In addition, the Japanese strategy concentrates on industries that have high rates of growth in productivity, and high value added to products per employee. High value added means that high wages can be paid to employees. With falling prices due to reduced unit costs of production and high income elasticity of demand, markets will be expanding rapidly as consumer incomes grow, and there will be no need to reduce the labor force.

In the 1990's there are seven industries that the Japanese Minister of International Trade believes meets the high value added criteria. These industries are microelectronics, the new materials science industries, biotechnology, telecommunications, civilian aircraft manufacturing, robots plus machine tools, and computers plus software. The Japanese believe that their government has an important role to play in accelerating economic growth. This means raising investments in plant and equipment, skills, infrastructure, and research and development above the levels that would occur in unhindered markets. They believe that market participants have too much interest in the present. In Japan, the government essentially represents the interest of the future in the present.[6]

However, not all Japanese citizens are in love with their government. The Japanese worker faces a marginal federal tax rate of 20 percent that is about the same as the U.S. worker. Japan continues to have a large trade surplus with both Europe and the United States. The United States has continued to negotiate trade agreements with Japan in an ongoing attempt to open Japanese domestic markets to American products and services. For example, in December of 1996, the United States and Japan reached an agreement, that would open Japan's $341 billion insurance markets, to foreign competition. The deal will give U.S. insurance companies a chance to compete for a bigger share of Japan's market that is now dominated by a Japanese cartel.

Japan and the United States have a history of bitter disagreement on several trade fronts, most notably autos, alcoholic beverages, semiconductors and photography equipment and film products. The successful insurance agreement settles one of the biggest trade barriers between the two nations. Japanese policy holders under the agreement will have freedom of choice and new products will become available as a result of worldwide competition. If this becomes a standard for other agreements between the United States and Japan, for opening the Japanese domestic markets to international products and services, it could result in a severely reduced Japanese export surplus position with both the United States and Europe.

**Japan in the Twenty-First Century**

The current Japanese economy is in a state of recession and the political environment is still a bit shaky. Recently Japan has experienced unemployment rates they have not seen since the government began compiling statistics in 1953 as the rate in July of 2001 hit 5 percent. The global downturn in demand for electronics and other technology products has prompted job cuts in Japan as production stalls and exports shrink. Rising bankruptcies and weakness in the construction industry have also hurt. For decades, Japan had boasted relatively low unemployment rates. In 2001 even the top companies that have historically offered lifetime employment are trimming their work force.

The global electronics downturn is crimping exports and dealing a blow to Japanese electronics companies as the following companies have recently announced layoffs: Toshiba Corp. (18,800), Fujitsu Ltd.

(16,400), NEC (4,000) Hitachi Ltd. (14,700) and Mitsubishi Electronic Corp. (1,000). Prime Minister Junichiro Koizumi is attempting to carry out economic reforms that may even increase the short term pain. Past Japanese administrations have relied on public-works spending (a Keynesian remedy) to jump-start the economy. But Koizumi is backing more basic changes such as privatizing the public sector and encouraging new, more profitable businesses.

Koizumi was promising to clean up the massive bad debts at the nation's banks, estimated to total at least $359 billion. This effort is expected to send the unemployment rate even higher. Japan's leading business daily the Nihon Keizai Shimbun reported in August of 2001 that the nation's woes weren't caused by a merely temporary downturn but rooted in deep changes in manufacturing that are sending jobs overseas where there is cheaper labor. " The wave of globalization can't be stopped," the paper reported. "The unraveling of the lifetime employment system (in Japan) can't be turned back."

**The Recession in Japan**

Liberal Democratic Party leader Taro Aso became Japan's 59th Prime Minister after sweeping a Sept. 24, 2008 vote in Parliament. His chief order of business will be to restore public confidence in the LDP as the party that can lead the nation out of recession and restore economic growth. But his first job will be to stay in office long enough to make a difference. His two predecessors, Shinzo Abe and Yasuo Fukuda, resigned after about a year amid abysmal public approval ratings.

On Nov. 17, 2008 Japan's government declared that the second largest economy in the world had slipped into recession for the first time since 2001. The Cabinet office of Prime Minister Taro Aso said that gross domestic product had contracted at an annual rate of 0.4% in the three months up to September, its second consecutive quarter of negative growth. The unwelcome news comes as little surprise. For months, newspapers have been awash with ways consumers can "return to the home" to protect themselves against the economic downturn. But the frugality that has gripped Japan in recent months might be part of the problem. Analysts see it as symbolic of a deep-rooted pessimism held by the Japanese public, evidenced by abysmally low consumer confidence and the subsequent shuttering of thousands of small- and medium-sized businesses this year. Even if the recession Japan now faces ends up less severe than those in the U.S. and Europe, the grim consumer outlook has the potential to put off a full recovery.[8]

On June 4, 2010 Japan's parliament installed Naoto Kan as Japan's new prime minister, handing the outspoken populist the task of quickly reclaiming public support squandered by his predecessor ahead of July elections. "My task is to rebuild this nation," Kan said after he was chosen ruling party chief. Pledging to confront problems linking "money and politics," he also stressed the need to spur economic growth.

Kan, 63, was finance minister under the unpopular Yukio Hatoyama, who stepped down on June 4 amid plunging approval ratings over broken campaign promises and a political funding scandal. As prime minister, Kan faces daunting choices in how to lead the world's second-largest economy, (based on exchange rate comparisons) which is burdened with massive public debt, sluggish growth and an aging, shrinking population. He must also rally voter support ahead of upper house elections next month. Kan, known for standing up to Japan's powerful bureaucrats, is the country's sixth prime minister in four years.

## THE CASE FOR THE UNITED STATES

Economically, in the years after World War II, the United States had five overwhelming economic advantages over Europe and Japan.

- In 1950 the American market was more than nine times as large as the next largest market, the United Kingdom. Mass manufacturing was effectively an American monopoly, where unit cost levels were beyond the dreams of the largest foreign producers.

- Americans were superior in technology to the rest of the world. World War II had destroyed the scientific establishments in most of Europe and Japan.

- American workers were more skilled than those found abroad. Americans had invented mass compulsory public elementary and secondary education. With the passage of the GI bill, America was the first nation to give its veterans the opportunity for mass college education.

- America was the richest country in the world. Because Americans had more discretionary income, the first mass market for most consumer products began in the United States.

- American managers were the best educated and trained in the world.

However, in the 1980's, the rest of the world began to catch up with the income levels in the United States. As a consequence, the relative size of the American market got smaller. In addition, modern telecommunications, and transportation technologies have created a world where the size of one's internal market is less important than it used to be. Global market economies of scale and scope are open to everyone, even if they live in relatively small countries.

The Reagan Administration in the 1980's changed the emphasis of antitrust policy by returning to the "Rule of Reason" criteria for judging if an individual firm's action would substantially lessen competition. Also, the Justice Department now considers how a merger or acquisition would effect the total market for a firm's products not just the company's domestic market. This has led to the recognition that big business is not necessarily bad, but actually may be required to compete in international markets.

## American Industry in the 1990's

The strong stock market during the 90's provided companies with increased value, at least on paper, that enables them to fund merger deals with stock swaps. However, many companies view this as a short term window of opportunity. The trend toward global markets is creating a "Musical Chairs" environment where companies believe that they have to merge so that they are not left without a chair. This is creating a perceived urgency to grow, to be able to compete in the global marketplace. So far, the Justice Department is showing little desire to challenge this wave of mergers. The result is that America, which already has more large corporations than any other country, is being allowed to increase the size of many of its companies in order to compete in the global economy of the twenty-first century.

American commercial banks are also got into the growth mode in order to compete with the large foreign banks. The Federal Reserve has approved a large number of mergers among commercial banks in the 1990's. While some of these mergers and acquisitions were approved to improve the safety of the banking system, other mergers were allowed to give large banks the ability to compete on a global basis. For example, in the 90's the Fed allowed Chemical Bank to merge with Chase Bank and Nation's Bank to merge with Bank of America to form a banks that were equal in size to Citibank. In 2001 Chase was again allowed to merge with J.P. Morgan. Also, Congress changed the Glass-Steagall Act of 1933 to allow banks to compete in the brokerage business. These events continued to set the stage for the evolution of super large financial services conglomerates. Even the American farmer, who was already the most productive in the world, is joining the trend toward large size and increased mechanization by using computer modeling techniques to improve their productivity.

**America's Problems and Competitive Advantages**

While America has many competitive advantages, there are also reoccurring problems that have to be addressed. For example, the rest of the world noticed the payoff from America's system of mass education, copied it, and in many cases improved the system. Comparative international examinations given to elementary and secondary school students reveal that Americans at all age levels know less than citizens in other advanced countries. Those Americans who graduate from college catch up with their foreign counterparts, since most of the rest of the industrial world has not made the human and physical investments necessary to shift from elite education to mass education, and America's graduate schools are the best in the world. However, to be a success, an economy requires more than just a college educated labor force. To operate the manufacturing firms of America, factory workers are also needed. The new technologies that are coming into the office and factory are going to require everyone to have levels of math competence that are far above those needed in the past.[7]

For those that do not go on to college, a poor education starting position is compounded by less on the job investment in skills. Ordinary American workers receive little training beyond what is required to perform their assigned jobs. At the same time technology has moved in directions that require a much better educated and more skilled work force. Today's factories require workers to use linear programming, and statistical quality control. To use statistical quality control, every production worker must master it. To master statistical quality control requires learning some simple operations research, but to learn what must be taught, workers must know algebra.

Our politicians often tell their constituents that they will spend more tax dollars to retrain displaced factory workers. We should ask these politicians one simple question about this proposed training. Training in "What?" During the 1990's, the United States has experienced large job losses in its manufacturing concerns. Often these job losses result in structural unemployment. This is a type of unemployment where the job skills do not match the available jobs. For example, if a worker in a large steel mill loses his job, can he be retrained to work in a computerized mini-steel mill? The answer to this question, for all practical purposes, is no. This is because the worker in the large steel mill must be re-educated before they are retrained. Therefore, retraining in this circumstances, means going back to school to learn the mathematical skills that were not acquired in the first place.

In the 1990's education attainment and increases or decreases in earnings will be highly correlated. American society is now divided into two different earnings groups; a skilled group with rising real wages and an unskilled group with declining real wages (the less educated, the bigger the income reduction; the more educated, the bigger the income gains). What is needed in the United States is a program that is directly related to the problem of structural unemployment not just more political rhetoric.

## THE PEOPLES REPUBLIC OF CHINA:

China's economy during the past 30 years has changed from a centrally planned system that was largely closed to international trade to a more market-oriented economy that has a rapidly growing private sector and is a major player in the global economy. Reforms started in the late 1970s with the phasing out of collectivized agriculture, and expanded to include the gradual liberalization of prices, fiscal decentralization, increased autonomy for state enterprises, the foundation of a diversified banking system, the development of stock markets, the rapid growth of the non-state sector, and the opening to foreign trade and investment. Annual inflows of foreign direct investment rose to nearly $108 billion in 2008. China has generally implemented reforms in a gradualist or piecemeal fashion. In recent years, China has re-invigorated its support for leading state-owned enterprises in sectors it considers important to "economic security," explicitly looking to foster globally competitive national champions.

The restructuring of the economy and resulting efficiency gains have contributed to a more than tenfold increase in GDP since 1978. Measured on a purchasing power parity (PPP) basis that adjusts for price differences, China in 2009 stood as the second-largest economy in the world after the US, and the third largest economy if the European Union is treated as an individual country. However, in per capita terms the country is still lower middle-income country. The Chinese government faces numerous economic development challenges, including: (a) reducing its high domestic savings rate and correspondingly low domestic demand through increased corporate transfers and a strengthened social safety net; (b) sustaining adequate job growth for tens of millions of migrants and new entrants to the work force; (c) reducing corruption and other economic crimes; and (d) containing environmental damage and social strife related to the economy's rapid transformation. Economic development has been more rapid in coastal provinces than in the interior, and approximately 200 million rural laborers and their dependents have relocated to urban areas to find work. One demographic consequence of the "one child" policy is that China is now one of the most rapidly aging countries in the world. Deterioration in the environment, notably air pollution, soil erosion, and the steady fall of the water table, especially in the north, is another long-term problem. China continues to lose arable land because of erosion and economic development. In 2006, China announced that by 2010 it would decrease energy intensity 20% from 2005 levels. In 2009, China announced that by 2020 it would reduce carbon intensity 40% from 2005 levels. The Chinese government seeks to add energy production capacity from sources other than coal and oil, and is focusing on nuclear and other alternative energy development. In 2009, the global economic downturn reduced foreign demand for Chinese exports for the first time in many years. The government vowed to continue reforming the economy and emphasized the need to increase domestic consumption in order to make China less dependent on foreign exports for GDP growth in the future.

Below is a list of the GDP of the top tem economies of the world. The data is from the CIA World Fact Book.[10]

Gross Domestic Product by Country          2010 ($ in Billions)

| 1. United States | $14,660 |
| 2. Peoples Republic of China | $ 5,878 |
| 3. Japan | $ 5,459 |
| 4. Germany | $ 3,316 |
| 5. France | $ 2,583 |
| 6. United Kingdom | $ 2,247 |
| 7. Brazil | $ 2,090 |
| 8. Italy | $ 2,055 |
| 9. Canada | $ 1,574 |
| 10. India | $ 1,538 |

**THE G 20**

The G20 was formed in 1999 as a response to the financial crises of the 1990's. The G-20 is a forum for emerging economies and the world's richest nations to talk about global economic stability. Usually, G-20 finance ministers and central bankers gather. On November 15,

2009 the heads of state of all G20 countries met for the first time in Washington to discuss world economic policies.

The G-20 is comprised of 20 of the world's largest economies: Argentina, Australia, Brazil, Canada, China, France, Germany, India, Indonesia, Italy, Japan, Mexico, Russia, Saudi Arabia, South Africa, South Korea, Turkey, the United Kingdom, the United States and the European Union, The leaders of the world's 20 biggest rich and emerging economies, who had gathered in Washington, DC, did not remake global finance as some of them had promised. Nor, as others had hoped, did they come up with a detailed set of coordinated fiscal measures to counter the deepening global downturn. Nonetheless, the five-page communiqué contained more than just diplomatic blather.

The most significant fact about the G20 meeting was the guest list. This was the first time that the leaders of all these rich and emerging economies—which between them represent almost 90% of global GDP—had gathered for an economic summit

The G20's leaders laid out a detailed plan for financial reform. The G20 leaders made a collective pledge not to raise any barriers to trade and investment over the coming year. The success of this gathering has permanently changed the machinery of international economic co-operation. The centre of global economic summitry has shifted from the G7 (the rich countries' club) to a broader group. A follow-up meeting was held on April 30th 2009. Even in areas that primarily affect them alone, such as the regulation of the most sophisticated financial instruments, rich countries will no longer set the agenda on their own.

## TWENTY FIRST CENTURY ECONOMIC LEADERS

America starts the twenty-first century with a position second to none. America has the world's largest gross domestic product, the most manufacturing companies and the largest homogeneous market. Also, the 90's was a decade where American companies discovered how to increase their productivity through the use of new information technologies. The factories of the previous decades are being retooled and robots not humans perform the repetitive production tasks. In addition, the invention of the Internet has changed the way most

American companies get and analyze information. E-commerce has become a major ingredient in the marketing strategy of large and small companies alike. Companies now distribute information and manuals via their Web Sites. The paperless society that was talked about in the 70's could actually become a reality in the twenty-first century. During the 90's America's steady increase in productivity, about 2.5 per cent per year, was greater than the rate achieved in Japan or Germany. If productivity continues to increase in the twenty-first century at a rate close to that of the previous decade, America will easily retain its current position as the economic leader of the free world.

## NOTES:

### Chapter 23
### The Battle of the Titans

1.  Thurow, Lester, Head To Head, New York, N.Y., William Morrow and Company, Inc., 1992, p. 20.
2.  Gumbel, Peter, Kohl Wins Narrowly In German Elections, The Wall Street Journal, October 17, 1994, p. A 11
3.  Ewing, Jack, Karnitschnig, Matt, and Fairlamb, David, Gerhard Schroeder: The Accidental Reformer, Business week, International, London, England, , May 1, 2000, p. 5-6.
4.  Blair, Tony, Schroeder, Gerhard, Europe: The Third Way/Die Neue Mitte, Amsterdam, Holland, The Amsterdam Post, June 1999.
5.  Ohmae, Kenichi, The Mind of the Strategist, New York, NY, Penguin Books, 1988, p. 113.
6.  Thurow, p. 118.
7.  Thurow, p. 145.
8.  Masters, Coco, Clock Starts Running for Japan's Aso, Time Magazine, Sep. 24, 2008
9.  Economists.com, Not a Bad Weekend's Work, Washington, DC November 16th, 2008
10. CIA World Fact book, May, 2011

# CHAPTER 24

---

# ECONOMICS AND POLITICS
# IN THE 1990's

*"The Taxpayer - that's someone who works for the Government but doesn't have to take a Civil Service Examination." —Ronald Reagan*

## THE CONGRESSIONAL CAMPAIGN OF 1994

In the summer of 1994, the majority of the Republican members of the House of Representatives gathered on the steps of the Capital to start the fall election campaign. By this time it was clear that a majority of the middle class voters were fed up with the entire political process. Many voters had begun to question the goals and promises made to them by their representatives. More and more, the conservative middle class voters were questioning whether the small amount of "Pork" that was brought back into their states was worth the price they had to pay in additional taxes to fund the national debt. There was a growing feeling among voters that Congress is not held accountable for its actions and does not follow the rules that it imposes on the rest of the American people. To take advantage of this sentiment, 367 of the Republican candidates for seats in the House of Representatives, led by House Minority Leader Newt Gingrich of Georgia, responded with a new set of written promises, a "Contract with America."

## THE CONTRACT WITH AMERICA

The purpose of the Republican contract was to draw a distinction between a campaign promise and a signed contract. The

House document was designed to address the key concerns of the American People. The Contract stated that, within the first one hundred days of the 104th Congress, they would bring to the House Floor the following bills:

**1.     The Fiscal Responsibility Act:** A balanced budget/tax limitation amendment and a legislative line-item veto to restore fiscal responsibility to an out-of-control Congress, requiring them to live under the same budget constraints as families and businesses.

**2.     The Taking Back Our Streets Act:** An anti-crime package including stronger truth in sentencing, "good faith" exclusionary rule exemptions, effective death penalty provisions, and cuts in social spending from the 1994 crime bill to fund prison construction and additional law enforcement to keep people secure in their neighborhoods and kids safe in their schools.

**3.     The Personal Responsibility Act:** Discourage illegitimacy and teen pregnancy by prohibiting welfare to minor mothers and denying increased AFDC (Aid to Families with Dependent Children) for additional children while on welfare, cut spending for welfare programs, and enact a tough two-years-and-out provision with work requirements to promote individual responsibility.

**4.     The Family Reinforcement Act:** Child support enforcement, tax incentives for adoption, strengthening rights of parents in their children's education, stronger child pornography laws, and an elderly dependent care tax credit to reinforce the central role of families in American society.

**5.     The American Dream Restoration Act:** A $500-per-child tax credit, begin repeal of the marriage tax penalty, and creation of American Dream Savings Accounts to provide middle-class tax relief.

**6.     The National Security Restoration Act:** No U.S. troops under UN command and restoration of essential parts of our national security funding to strengthen our national defense and maintain our credibility around the world.

7.    **The Senior Citizens Fairness Act.** Raise the Social Security earnings limit, which currently forces seniors out of the work force, repeal the 1993 tax hikes on Social Security benefits, and provide tax incentives for private long-term care insurance to let older Americans keep more of what they have earned over the years.

8.    **The Job Creation and Wage Enhancement Act:** Small business incentives, capital gains cut and indexation, neutral cost recovery, risk assessment/cost-benefit analysis, strengthening of the Regulatory Flexibility Act and unfunded mandate reform to create jobs and raise worker wages.

9.    **The Common Sense Legal Reform Act.** "Loser pays" laws, reasonable limits on punitive damages, and reform of product liability laws to stem the endless tide of litigation.

10.    **The Citizen Legislature Act.** A first-ever vote on term limits to replace career politicians with citizen legislators.

The Contract with America was an attempt by the Republicans to personalize the congressional elections by asking voters:

- How much of your taxes does Congress waste?

- Why doesn't Washington listen to your concerns?

- Can social programs be increased in the long-run through borrowing and running huge deficits?

The contract promised specific actions on what the voters perceived to be the country's greatest problems. The contract ended by stating: "Respecting the judgment of our fellow citizens as we seek their mandate for reform, we hereby pledge our names to the Contract With America."[1]

# THE MIDDLE CLASS REVOLT

On November 8, 1994, the "Contract with America," was put to the test of the American voters. The results of the election were beyond even the most optimistic of the Republican pollsters. When the 104th Congress convened, in 1995, conservative Republicans were in charge of both houses of Congress. The Republicans won a majority in the Senate, by seizing 9 new seats bringing their total to 53 versus 47 for the Democrats. In the House, Republicans gained an almost unprecedented 52 seats. The races for Governor throughout the country reported an equally devastating blow for Democrats as 11 state houses were lost to the Republicans. In addition, every incumbent Republican Representative and Senator won reelection.

# ACCOMPLISHMENTS OF THE 104th CONGRESS

Following is the record of the legislation that was passed by 104th Congress and signed by President Clinton:

• Telecommunications: Congress rewrote the nation's telecommunications laws, to promote competition and remove some of the regulations on telephone, cable and broadcast companies.

• Welfare: Congress ended the federal guarantee of cash assistance to all low-income mothers and children, gave states broad authority to run welfare programs, and also gave the states block grants to offset the additional costs.

• Health: This law made it easier for workers to keep health insurance coverage if they lose or leave their jobs. Also, they enacted a pilot program for Medical Savings Accounts.

• Farm Bill: This bill replaced the decades old commodity subsidy programs with fixed, but declining subsidy payments that aren't linked to market prices or farmers' planting decisions.

- Minimum Wage: This bill raised the minimum wage by 50 cents, to $4.75 an hour, to take effect on October 1, 1996, and then to $5.15 on September 1, 1997. Also the bill included $10 billion in small business tax breaks over a five year period. This legislation was initiated by the Democrats and approved by a majority of both houses.

- Line-Item Veto: This gave the President power to rescind individual items in spending bills unless Congress passes a "disapproval bill," which is subject to a veto.

- Immigration: Cracked down on illegal immigration by authorizing a large increase in the U.S./Mexico boarder patrol officers.

- Shareholder Lawsuits: Limited lawsuits initiated by disgruntled investors against companies who had a large drop in the market value of their stock holdings in those firms.

- Terrorism: The legislation expanded the federal power to prosecute and punish certain crimes related to terrorism.

However, the 104th Congress had several initiatives that either failed to pass or were vetoed by the President, as follows:

- Budget Reconciliation: The Republican sponsored bill to balance the federal budget was vetoed by President Clinton. This resulted in a shutting down of the federal government during two separate occasions. The bill included $245 billion in tax cuts over seven years, and spending restrictions on the growth in Medicare and some other entitlement programs.

- Balanced-Budget Amendment: A constitutional amendment requiring the federal budget to be balanced was defeated in the Senate by two votes.

- Term Limits: A constitutional amendment to limit the terms of members of Congress, was defeated by the House of Representatives.

- Regulatory Overhaul: This legislation would have required the federal government to document costs and benefits of proposed regulations.

- Product Liability: This bill would have capped punitive damages in product liability suits. The bill was vetoed by the president.

The spending agreement for fiscal year 1997 reached between the President and the Republican-led Congress marked a major retreat from the promises, in the Contract with America, on the issue of a balanced budget. After two years in power, Republicans can boast of cutting spending on general government programs, below the levels approved by the Democratic-led Congress, in the fiscal year 1995 budget. However, it was not until fiscal year 1998 that the Federal budget was balanced. Also, the major reason for the budget surplus that was achieved in fiscal year 1998 was a 7.1 percent increase in revenue versus a 3.8 percent increase in government spending. While Congress did hold the line on spending during 1998, the major credit for balancing the federal budget should go to the American people whose hard work and increased productivity led to increased federal tax revenues.

## THE ELECTIONS OF 1996

Borrowing from the theme of Ronald Reagan's "Morning in America" campaign, in 1984, President Clinton presented a positive message to the voters, in the elections of 1996. The president cast himself as a moderate centrist, a defender of core government services and a provider of modest new "tools" to help families with the twin constraints of time and money management. Even as Republican challenger Robert Dole began to attack the President's alleged ethical lapses, Mr. Clinton simply kept smiling, stayed on a positive course, and offered nothing in rebuttal.

The strategy worked and William Clinton became only the third Democrat, beside Woodrow Wilson and Franklin D. Roosevelt to be re-elected to the presidency in the twentieth century. As Karl Rove, a top Republican strategist for than Governor George W. Bush of Texas, noted in the Wall Street Journal; "Its awfully hard to knock off an incumbent Democratic who's willing to run as a Republican." The President had engineered a great comeback after the Republicans gained control of both the House and Senate in the 1994 elections. The key to the President's re-election was the perception that the Republicans had gotten on the wrong side of popular issues such as Medicare, education, and the environment. In addition, the economy was expanding and consumer confidence was building. However, the voters decided to hedge their bets on the newly positioned, more moderate President Clinton, by electing Republicans to a continued majority in both Houses of Congress.

While the campaign was a success, it provided virtually no road map for the re-elected President to follow over the next four years. There remained a question in the minds of many political analysts as to whether America will have a liberal, conservative or middle-of-the-road President. Big government proposals had little chance of passage in a Republican Congress. Therefore, the President agenda was to work with Congress on specific programs such as a balancing the budget, improving education, helping people who loose their jobs to continue their health insurance, to expand NAFDA to include Chile, and some middle class targeted tax cuts.

In summary, the verdict of the electorate in 1996, was a divided government balanced between liberal and conservative philosophy. A sort of American version of "The Third Way." Corporate America, as witnessed by the week long increase in stock prices after the election, was pleased with the outcome. This is probably the best that the voter could expect in an America of diminished expectations for government and a reduced faith in politicians.[2]

## CLINTON'S SECOND TERM

President Clinton's second term showed mixed results. The economy continued to grow as real GDP increased by $1.411 trillion from 1996 through 2000 or an average growth of 3.6 percent. Also, the unemployment rate dropped below 4.5 percent a historically low rate. However, Clinton's second term was rocked by several scandals. For example, on March 16, 1998 a Democratic fund-raiser pleaded guilty to funneling $20,000 in illegal donations to the 1996 Clinton presidential campaign. On May 15 of that year, the same Democratic fund-raiser told federal investigators that he arranged for Chinese government money to be funneled to the Democratic Party in 1996. Accepting campaign funds from foreign countries is a violation of United States federal law.

Clinton's biggest problem during these years was a result of a sexual relationship he had with a young intern and ultimately lying about it to the American people. On September 11, 1998, the U.S. House of Representatives released a report from special prosecutor Ken Star (The Star Report), revealing in great detail the sexual encounters between Clinton and the young intern. The report also listed possible grounds for impeachment including allegations of perjury, witness tampering, obstruction of justice and abuse of power.

On December 19, 1998, the House of Representatives approved two articles of impeachment against President Clinton. The first article charged that the president had given "perjurious, and false testimony to a federal grand jury." The second article charged that the president had committed "obstruction of justice" in the sexual harassment lawsuit filed earlier against him by another female. Clinton thus became the first elected president in history to be impeached by Congress. A two-thirds majority vote in the Senate on either article of impeachment is required to remove the president from office. On February 12, 1999, the U.S. Senate voted not to remove President Clinton from office as neither article of impeachment received even a simple majority vote. However, the Clinton scandal consumed the better part of a year of American public life.[3]

## THE PAST AND THE PRESENT

On April 27, 1994, Richard Nixon, the thirty-seventh President of the United States, was laid to rest. Speaking for his country President Clinton said, "On behalf of former Presidents Gerald Ford,

Jimmy Carter, Ronald Reagan and George Bush, and on behalf of a grateful nation, we bid farewell to Richard Nixon." It was an extraordinary day of reconciliation. Strongmen expressed humility. Partisan men laid aside their differences. Henry A. Kissinger, who was President Nixon's Secretary of State, in his speech noticeably fought to hold back his tears as he led the audience of 2,800 invited friends, family and foreign dignitaries in saying good-by to his friend. Kissinger spoke fondly of Nixon as he said; "He stood on pinnacles that dissolved into precipice. He achieved greatly and he suffered deeply, but he never gave up."

Henry Kissinger's fond farewell to Richard Nixon can be used as a lesson of how Americans respond to a challenge. When the Soviet Union first sent a man into space, we responded by making not one but two trips to the moon. When a nation that was one of our close friends and ally was invaded by a dictator, we responded in the Gulf War, with the greatest military might the world has ever witnessed. When our entire automobile industry was threatened by an economic invasion of well-made Japanese products, we responded with a whole new line of well-made American automotive products.

The June 19, 1995, issue of The Wall Street Journal, Stephen K. Yoder presented an article entitled, "Back In The Running: U.S. companies are once again competing for a big piece of the consumer electronics market." According to the article, during 1994, Americans for the first time spent more on personal computers and software than on color televisions. The result of this trend in spending habits is that the consumer electronics market has changed in a way that puts U.S. companies in the running again. This is because households are increasingly purchasing computers, printers, phone equipment and other electronic gadgets that use computer chips as their electronic brains. U.S. companies are once again becoming key players in this industry because consumer electronics is moving from analog technology toward digital technology. U.S. companies are strong in digital electronics because of their lead in computers and their experience selling advanced electronic devices to industry and the military.

Macroeconomic policy still has the same three basic goals: full employment, long-run price stability, and economic growth. So in the

1990's we are left with two basic but less than perfect theories about how to achieve these goals. A conservative government that does nothing to improve the standard of living of its people is not acceptable. On the other hand, a liberal government that spends unwisely and one that creates burdensome regulations is no improvement. Perhaps what is needed is a new theory, one that incorporates the better of the two existing ones.

The old saying that, "A rising tide lifts all boats", is a god starting point for developing future economic policy. Businesses need to invest in improving the productivity of the factors of production. Government programs that assist this process are good for the economy and should be continued and even strengthened. In a January 21, 1997, article in The Wall Street Journal, author Bernard Wysocki Jr. describes a new approach to long-term prosperity. The theory was developed by Paul M. Romer, an economist at Stamford University. His ideas go by the name of "New Growth Theory." According to Dr. Romer, ideas and technology discoveries are the driving engines of economic growth, especially ideas that are codified in a chemical formula, or embodied in a peace of computer software or, in some way, improve the efficiency of the factors of production.

However, is this really a new theory or a modern version of Joseph Schumpeter's circular flow of funds model? In other words, is this a new approach to economic policy or just, as Todd Buchholz once wrote, "New Ideas From Dead Economist."

**NOTES:**

**Chapter 24**
**Economics and Politics in the 1990s**

1.  Gingrich, Newt, & Armey, Dick, <u>The Contract With America,</u> New York, NY, Times Books, 1994, Pgs. 9-11.
2.  Cable News Network, <u>The Clinton Years</u>, Timelines, October 2001.
3.  Rozell, Mark J., <u>The Clinton Scandal in Retrospect</u>, Political Science & Politics, Find Articles.com, September, 1999

# CHAPTER 25

---

# THE TWENTY FIRST CENTURY – THE GEORGE W. BUSH ADMINISTRATION

*A government big enough to give you everything you want, is strong enough to take everything you have. -* ***Thomas Jefferson***

## THE ELECTION OF 2000

On November 7, 2000 American voters went to the poles to elect a new president. The contest was between Al Gore, Vice President for eight years under Bill Clinton and George W. Bush the Governor of Texas and eldest son of former president George H.W. Bush. Stripped of many normally winning Republican issue (the cold war, crime, the economy), Bush took a lesson from the 1996 election, and proceeded to run on historically Democratic issues (education, health care, and social security). Bush did continue to pursue one Republican strategy with a proposal to lower individual tax rates. Bush's background was different than the typical candidate for national office as he had an extensive business background, and a Masters Degree In Business Administration from Harvard University. Bush started his campaign with less experience in public life than just about anyone in a century and proceeded to attract more money in the first four months of his campaign than anyone had ever raised in just two years.

The certified results of the election on November 7 was that George W. Bush won the presidency with the closest vote in the history of America elections. However, the actions of the next 35 days resembled more a soap opera than an orderly transition of power. Shortly before 8 p.m. all of the major television networks estimated that Vice President Gore had beaten Governor Bush in the key state of Florida. But as the night went on and results came in from the state's heavily republican Panhandle region, the networks were forced to retract that estimate.

As the night wore on it became clear that the victor in Florida would win the electoral votes necessary to claim the presidency. In the morning of November 8th a series of early-morning events set the stage for a protracted presidential battle. First, at about 2:15 a.m., the major networks called Florida and the election for Bush. Al Gore, hearing that he probably will lose Florida by about 50,000 votes called Texas Governor Bush and conceded the election. But 45 minutes later, while Gore was en route to a rally in Nashville to give a concession address, aides reach him and tell him that Bush's lead in Florida has shrunk dramatically. Gore than called Bush to rescind his concession. "Let me make sure I understand," Bush said, "You're calling me back to retract your concession."

By 4:15, the major networks are forced to pull their forecast that Bush was the president-elect and the nation's focus immediately turned to Florida. Bush and Gore's campaigns respond by sending teams of lawyers to Florida. The close race triggered an automatic recount of ballots under Florida state law. As the legal proceedings continue, many Americans hear the word "Chad", a reference to the small piece of paper punched out of punch card ballots for the first time

On November 17th, the Florida Supreme Court blocked Florida's Secretary of State from any vote certification until it can rule on the Democrats' motion to allow hand recounts to be counted. On November 21st, the Florida Supreme Court ordered hand counts to continue, and gave counties five days to complete them. On November 26th The Florida Secretary of State certified the results of the Florida vote after the state Supreme Court deadline expired, giving Bush a 537-vote lead over Gore. On November 27th Gore's lawyers moved to contest the Florida result in a circuit court in Tallahassee. Circuit court judge N. Sanders Sauls rejected Gore's contest to Florida results, finding the vice president failed to show that hand recounts would have affected the results. Meanwhile the U.S. Supreme Court asks the Florida Supreme Court to explain it's reasoning in extending the hand recounts.

On December 8th, divided 4 to 3, the Florida Supreme Court ordered manual recounts in all counties with significant numbers of presidential under votes (ballots where no selection for president was made). The Bush lawyers reacted by appealing the decision to the U.S. Supreme Court and sought an injunction to stop the hand counts. Bush's lawyers argued that the Florida Supreme Court overstepped its bounds by ordering a manual recount.

On December 12th the U.S. Supreme Court ended the debacle handing down a 5 to 4 decision that settled the matter and effectively declared George W. Bush to be the 43rd president of the United States. On December 14th the Florida Supreme dismissed the case "Albert Gore, Jr. vs. Katherine Harris (Florida Secretary of State)" based on the U.S. Supreme Court ruling as it stated, "The per curiam opinion of the Supreme Court Majority specified that in order for a manual recount to continue it would require not only the adoption of adequate statewide standards for determining what is a legal vote, and practicable procedures to implement them, but also orderly judicial review of any disputed matters that might arise. "Because it is evident that any recount seeking to meet the December 12 date (a date determined by Florida State Election Law) will be unconstitutional for the reasons we have discussed, we reverse the judgment of the Supreme Court of Florida ordering a recount to proceed."

So on December 12, 2000 George W. Bush was officially declared to be the new president of the United States. The election of 2000 was one of the closest in the history of the United States. George W. Bush won the election with an electoral college vote of 271 to Al Gore's 266 but lost the popular vote by 541 thousand. However, Bush was not the only president to lose the popular vote and win the election, two other presidents were elected by receiving a majority of the electoral votes and losing the popular vote. The other two presidents were Rutherford Hayes in 1876 and Benjamin Harrison in 1888.

On December 13, 2000, President-Elect George W. Bush delivered his acceptance speech from the chamber of the Texas House of Representatives by saying:

The spirit of cooperation I have seen in this hall is what is needed in Washington, D.C. It is the challenge of our moment.

After a difficult election, we must put politics behind us and work together to make the promise of America available for every one of our citizens.

Bush than outlined his major programs as follows:

Together, we will work to make all our public schools excellent, teaching every student of every background and every accent, so that no child is left behind. Together we will save Social Security and renew its promise of a secure retirement for generations to come. Together we will strengthen Medicare and offer prescription drug coverage to all of our seniors. Together we will give Americans the broad, fair and fiscally responsible tax relief they deserve. Together we'll have a bipartisan foreign policy true to our values and true to our friends, and we will have a military equal to every challenge and superior to every adversary.

Bush continued with an attempt to reconcile the two parties after the election:

I was not elected to serve one party, but to serve one nation. The president of the United States is the president of every single American, of every race and every background. Whether you voted for me or not, I will do my best to serve your interests and I will work to earn your respect.

## THE FIRST YEAR OF THE NEW CENTURY

During his first six months in office President Bush concentrated in three areas: Tax reduction, an energy policy and education reform legislation. The progress during 2001 was as follows:

### Tax Reform

The Tax Reform and Rebate Act of 2001 was signed into law on June 6, 2001. The new tax law cut individual income taxes by $1.35 trillion over ten years. "Across-the board tax relief does not happen very much in Washington, D.C., in fact it has happened only twice: President Kennedy's tax cut in the 60s and President Reagan's tax cut in the 80's," Bush said. "And now it's happened for a third time. And it's about time."

The new law reduces the lowest rate from 15 to 10 percent, and the highest rate from 39.6 percent to 35 percent. Some of the law's provisions are delayed several years, but eventually will double the child tax credit from $500 to $1,000, reduce the tax penalty on married couples and fully repeal the tax on estates.

## Education Reform

On January 8, 2002, President Bush signed into law the "No Child Left Behind Law of 2001. The Act, which embodies the administration's education reform plan sent to Congress on January 23, 2001, was the most sweeping reform of the Elementary and Secondary Education Act since ESEA was enacted in 1965. It redefines the federal role in kindergarten through grade 12 education and will help close the achievement gap between disadvantaged and minority students and their peers. The new law is based on four basic principles: increased accountability for results, more choices for parents and students, greater flexibility for states, school districts and schools and putting reading first. However, the real value of the Act will be in the implementation by the States and Local School Districts.

## The Energy Plan

On May 16th President Bush released an energy strategy with an eye toward the long term. The new plan, according to Bush, would encourage new, environmentally friendly exploration for new sources of oil and natural gas, while encouraging conservation efforts and developing other sources of energy as well. The major parts of the plan are as follows:

Executive orders and agency reviews aimed at easing regulations the industry says slow the siting and licensing of power plants and gas refineries

The energy bill created the most controversy in Congress of the three bills. The Democrats arguing over conserving energy as the best way to handle energy shortages and Republicans arguing that increased energy supply is equally important in solving the countries long-term energy problems.

## AMERICA'S NEW WAR

The front cover of Newsweek's September 24th 2001 issue showed three firemen raising the American flag over "ground zero." Ground zero is usually a term used to describe a war zone, however, in this case it was the location of the World Trade Center in New York City. The caption on the front page read "God Bless America." The picture, taken by Thomas E. Franklin, simultaneously showed the tragedy that had just occurred in New York City and the heroics displayed by its government workers and average citizens. On September 11, 2001 two large jet airplanes crashed into the twin towers of the world trade center and one jet crashed into the Pentagon in Washington DC and instantaneously changed the lives of the people of and entire country and perhaps the entire free world.

While the final toll of the victims in the World Trade Center will possible never be known it is estimated by the City of New York that just fewer than 3,000 people were either dead or missing including over 300 city firefighters and 40 policemen. In total, this was the worst act of aggression ever committed on American soil.

## AMERICA STRIKES BACK

On September 20, 2001 President Bush delivered an Address to a Joint Session of Congress and the American People which set the tone for the prosecution of the war against terrorists.

In the normal course of events, Presidents come to this chamber to report on the state of the Union. Tonight, no such report is needed. It has already been delivered by the American people.

Tonight we are a country awakened to danger and called to defend freedom. Our grief has turned to anger, and anger to resolution, whether we bring our enemies to justice, or bring justice to our enemies, justice will be done.

And on behalf of the American people, I thank the world for its outpouring of support. America will never forget the sounds of our National Anthem playing at Buckingham Palace, on the streets of Paris, and at Berlin's Brandenburg Gate.

President Bush continued by outlining the events of September 11th and America's resolution to eliminate the terrorists that committed these acts.

Americans have known surprise attacks, but never before on thousands of civilians. Americans are asking who attacked our country? The evidence we have gathered all points to a collection of loosely affiliated terrorists organizations known as al Qaeda. They are the same murderers indicted for bombing American embassies in Tanzania and Kenya, and responsible for bombing the USS Coll.

The terrorist practice a fringe form of extremism that has been rejected by Muslim scholars and the vast majority of Muslim clerics. The terrorists' directive commands them to kill Christians and Jews, to kill all Americans, and make no distinction among military and civilians including women and children.

The leadership of al Qaeda has great influence in Afghanistan and supports the Taliban regime in controlling most of that country. The United States respects the people of Afghanistan – but we condemn the Taliban regime. It is not only repressing its own people, it is threatening people everywhere by sponsoring and sheltering and supplying terrorists. By aiding and abetting murder, the Taliban regime is committing murder.

Our war on terror begins with al Qaeda, but it does not end there. It will not end until every terrorist group of global reach has been found, stopped and defeated.

We are not deceived by their pretense of piety. We have seen their kind before. They are the heirs of all the murderous ideologies of the 20th century. By sacrificing human life to serve their radical visions – by abandoning every value except the will to power – they follow in the path of fascism, and Nazism, and totalitarianism. And they will follow that path all the way, to where it ends: in history's unmarked grave of discarded lies.[3]

On October 7, 2001 President Bush again addressed the nation from the Treaty Room of the White House. Bush outlined in this speech the beginning of air strikes on Afghanistan.

On my orders, the United States military has begun strikes against al Qaeda terrorists training camps and military installations of the Taliban regime in Afghanistan. We are joined in this operation by our staunch friend, Great Britain. Other close friends, including Canada, Australia, Germany and France, have pledged forces as the operation unfolds. More than 40 countries in the Middle East, Africa, and across Asia have granted air transit or landing rights. Many more have shared intelligence. We are supported by the collective will of the world.

Bush goes on to describe the immediate focus of the war on terrorism, which became know as "The Bush Doctrine".

Today we focus on Afghanistan, but the battle is broader. Every nation has a choice to make. In this conflict, there is no neutral ground. If any government sponsors the outlaws and killers of innocents, they have become outlaws and murders themselves. And they will take that lonely path at their own peril.

Bush concluded his speech by outlining strategy for the coming battle.

In the months ahead, our patience will be one of our strengths – patience with the long waits that will result from tighter security; patience and understanding that it will take time to achieve our goals; patience in all the sacrifices that may come. Today, those sacrifices are being made by members of our Armed Forces who now defend us so far from home, and by their proud and worried families. A commander-in-chief sends America's sons and daughters into battle in a foreign land only after the greatest care and a lot of prayer. We ask a lot of those who wear our uniform. We ask them to leave their loved ones, to travel great distances, to risk injury, even to be prepared to make the ultimate sacrifice of their lives. They are dedicated, they are honorable; they represent the best of our country. And we are grateful.[4]

## THE RECESSION OF 2001

The American economy and especially the stock market do not like surprises. Consequently, on September 12, 2001 the stock market showed an across the board decline with the Dow Jones Index dropping over 600 points. The shock of the attack on September 11 sent the airline travel and vacation industry into a tailspin. On December 21, the Bureau of Economic Analysis in a news release indicated that a recession was at hand as it reported real gross domestic product decreased at an annual rate of 1.3 percent in the third quarter of 2001. In November of 2001 the National Bureau of Economic Research's Business Cycle Dating Committee said the U.S. economy had entered a recession in March of 2001 after a 10-year expansion. According to their Web site the NBER defines a recession as "A significant decline in activity spread across the economy, lasting more than a few months, visible in industrial production, employment, real income and wholesale-retail trade."

The President, Congress, and the Federal Reserve were working to avoid a recession or at least to lessen its effect. Since the beginning 2001 the Federal Reserve had lowered the target rate on fed funds twelve times with the rate by year-end 2002 standing at 1.25 percent.

But many analysts are worried that the rate cuts won't do enough to encourage American consumers to pick up their spending again now that their confidence has been hurt by the September 11 attacks. One of the major problems with the economy is that companies simply spent too much money on new technologies and equipment in the 1990s. When demand for new products dried up in 2000, manufacturers stopped making new goods until their backlog could be sold off. With many manufacturers experiencing what the Fed calls "low capacity utilization" no amount of cheap credit is going to persuade companies to borrow to buy more equipment until they know somebody is going to buy what they produce

In August of 2002, The Bureau of Economic Analysis released its revised estimates of GDP for 2001. The revised data showed a reduction in Real Gross Domestic Product for each of the first three quarters of 2001. Also, the annual growth in Real GDP was revised downward from 1.3 percent to 0.3 percent. According to the revised estimates, GDP reached a peak in the fourth quarter of 2000 and decreased 0.6 percent in the first quarter of 2001, 1.6 percent in the second quarter, and 0.3 percent in the third quarter. The revised data indicates that by all economic definitions, there was a mild recession in 2001. The major reason for the recession was a reduction in gross private domestic investment of 10.7 percent versus 2000. The entire reduction was due to a decrease in business spending on new factories, business equipment and software during 2001.

For 2002, the economy showed modest growth as real GDP increased at an annual rate of 5.0 percent in the first quarter, 1.3 in the second quarter, and 4.0 for the third quarter and 1.4 percent for the fourth quarter. For the entire year real GDP grow at a rate of 2.4 percent. The Federal Reserve, at its August meeting, was still predicting growth rates for GDP in the 3 percent range for 2003, but to hedge their bets the Fed decreased the federal funds rate by 50 basis points to 1.25 percent at their November 2002 meeting.

## THE NOVEMBER 2002 ELECTIONS

On November 5th, 2002 Americans went to the polls and voted in record numbers. The results of the election was that Republicans maintained control of the House of Representatives and gained control of the Senate. Not since 1902 has a first-time Republican president seen his party win both the House and the Senate in a midterm election. Senator Trent Lott, the new Senate majority leader, commented on the election results by saying Republicans had been "fired up about the campaign, particularly with President Bush on the trail to provide support." But even Senator Lott acknowledged that the scope of the victory "did exceed our hopes and expectations."

For at least 2 more years, Republicans will control all three branches of government allowing them to shape the political battles to come. Already, President Bush's advisors have been at work on a possible set of new tax cuts whose centerpiece would be the permanent extension of his 10-year reduction of income taxes, including reducing or eliminating both the marriage tax and the inheritance tax. In addition, in November of 2002, President Bush signed a new law creating the Department of Homeland Security.

## MAJOR LEGISLATION ENACTED IN 2003

### Medicare Prescription Drug, Improvement and Modernization Act

President Bush signed this Act in December of 2003, which he referred to as "the greatest advance in health care coverage for America's seniors since the founding of Medicare." The Act provided a prescription drug plan for seniors starting in 2006. Other provisions of this Act increased payments to Medicare providers, provided new preventive health care benefits to seniors, established health care savings accounts, and curtailed the number of employers expected to drop retire health care coverage by providing a subsidy to firms with a retirement health plan certified to be at least the equivalent of the standard Medicare drug plan. The plan was criticized by conservatives for being too expensive and by liberals by not providing enough benefits. However, the American Association of Retired People (AARP) advocated passage of the plan as a good start in providing at least some prescription drug benefits to seniors.

## Jobs and Growth Tax Relief Reconciliation Act of 2003

This Act was signed into law on May 28th 2003. The major purpose of the act was to stimulate economic activity especially business investment. The major provisions of the Act were to decrease temporarily the tax rates on stock dividends and capital gains, to increase temporarily incentives to speed up investment in capital equipment by allowing faster depreciation write-offs and to accelerate many of the individual income tax reductions provided in the 2001 tax cuts.

While it is difficult to determine the exact effect of the tax cuts on business investment in 2003 the direction of change is predictable. The third quarter of 2003 showed an increase in GDP of 8.2 percent, followed by a 4.1 percent in the fourth quarter. The largest percent increase, 12.8 percent in the third quarter and 15.1 percent in the fourth quarter, was in nonresidential investment in business equipment and software. For all of 2003, GDP increased by 3.1 percent with consumer expenditures increasing by 3.1 percent and gross private domestic investment by 4.3 percent. With the better than expected growth rates for 2003, GDP grew in the 4 to 5 percent range for 2004 and many economists are forecasting a growth of over 3 percent for 2007.

## GULF WAR II

After taking power in 1979, Iraq's president Saddam Hussein launched his country into 2 disastrous conflicts, the Iran-Iraq War in the 1980's and the invasion of Kuwait in 1990. After their defeat at the hands of a United States led force in 1991, Iraq signed a peace treaty with the United Nations requiring them to eliminate all chemical, biological and nuclear weapons. The U.N. Monitoring, Verification, and Inspection Commission (UNMOVIC) and the International Atomic Energy Agency (IAEA) were selected to supervise the elimination of these "Weapons of Mass Destruction". The inspections continued until December of 1998 when the inspectors left Iraq at the request of that country's government.

After the War in Afghanistan, the attention of the U.S. government turned to Iraq and the violations of the U.N. peace agreement with that country. In his address to the United Nations on September 12, 2002, President Bush said: "The history, the logic, and the facts lead to only one conclusion: Saddam Hussein's regime is a grave danger. To suggest otherwise is to hope against the evidence. To assume his regime's good faith is to bet the lives of millions and the peace of the world in a reckless gamble. And this is a risk we must not take." President Bush then challenged the U. N. to enforce its previous resolutions, against the Iraq.

On November 8, 2002 the 15 member United Nations Security Council voted to approve resolution 1441 which unanimously adopted strengthening the weapons inspection for Iraq and gave Baghdad "a final opportunity to comply with its disarmament obligations." The resolution stated that Iraq remains in material breach of the U.N. Security Council resolutions relating to Iraq's 1990 invasion of Kuwait and requires that Baghdad give UNMOVIC and IAEA a complete and accurate declaration of all aspects of its chemical, biological and nuclear weapons programs, ballistic missiles systems, as well as information on other chemical biological, and nuclear programs which are supposed to be for civilian purposes within 30 days. Finally resolution 1441 warns Iraq that "it will face serious consequences" if it continues to violate its obligations as spelled out in the resolution.

Iraq did provide the U.N. with a description of its current chemical and biological weapons, but declared that they no longer had any of these weapons. The report was basically a rehash of old documents and did not satisfy even the most lenient members of the Security Council. The question then became what is the real role of the U.N. inspectors, to search for Iraq's weapons of mass destruction or to supervise their destruction? This question and the one of how long the inspectors should continue the search for WMD became the subject for debate among the members of the U.N. Security Council with France threatening to veto any further resolution to disarm Iraq by force. In the meantime the United States and Britain had assembled an armed force of about 250 thousand troops in Kuwait and Qatar.

Finally, the patience of President Bush and Britain's Prime Minister Tony Blair had worn out. On March 17, 2003, the United

States declared that the "diplomatic window has closed" for a peaceful resolution to the Iraq showdown and that President Bush would warn Saddam Hussein latter that day that the only way to avoid war was to leave the country. In a State Department news conference, Secretary of State Colin Powell said the crisis on Iraq was a "test the United Nations did not meet."

On Thursday March 20, 2003 Gulf War II started with the bombing of an Iraq building where the U.S. believed Iraq's president and some high-ranking officers were staying. After that attack Saddam Hussein was not seen in public again and although there were some videotape messages seen on Iraqi television, it was never certain if he had survived the attack. By Friday a bombing attack from a coalition lead by the United States and Britain started and a ground force headed from Kuwait towards Iraq. After just three weeks of war, U.S. tanks rolled unmolested into the center of Iraq's capital city to a tumultuous welcome from jubilant residents. U.S. military leaders proclaimed an end to Saddam Hussein's control of Baghdad, stopping just short of declaring victory in the campaign to oust the Iraqi president and to destroy the Baath Party Regime.

Television cameras showed stunning images of American troops walking on the streets of Baghdad among residents celebrating the downfall of the Baath Party after more than two decades of police-state control. Just 24 hours earlier, it appeared that U.S. forces might be in for a prolonged bout, but most Iraqi resistance melted away after another night of relentless pounding by U.S. warplanes and artillery. The people of Baghdad poured into the streets in celebration, waiving at U.S. troops and tearing down posters and busts of the Iraqi president. In one scene Iraqis attacked a giant statue of Saddam Hussein with sledgehammers. With the help of U.S. Marines who ran a cable from their tank to the 20-foot tall statue, they pulled it down literally yanking the image of the fallen leader out of his boots.[5]

On May 1, 2003, President Bush from the deck of the aircraft carrier USS Abraham Lincoln declared a formal end to the major combat operations in Iraq. The U.S. lead coalition had again defeated the forces of Iraqi and this time had freed the people of Iraq. However, restoring the peace and creating a democratic government in a county that has no recent experience in such a government will be at best a most difficult task.

On September 13, 2003 U.S. and coalition forces operating in the dark of night found Saddam Hussein in a hole beneath the courtyard of a hut near Dawr, a village 10 miles from his hometown of Tikrit. Saddam stayed inside this chamber whenever he perceived a threat. Soldiers were seconds from firing into the hole, or tossing a grenade, when Saddam's upraised hands signaled that he was prepared to surrender. "I am Saddam Hussein. I am the president of Iraq and I am willing to negotiate." One of the solders with an American sense of humor called down to the man in the whole "President Bush sends his regards." President Bush later warned that the danger to Americans in Iraq from the Baath party dead-enders or renewed attacks by foreign fighters will continue. However, the capture of Saddam moves Iraq into a decidedly new phase of the war. Saddam Hussein was consequently tried in an Iraqi court and convicted of crimes against humanity. He was executed by hanging in early January of 2007.

The United States and Britain have the necessary industry but will need the cooperation of many other industrialized countries to complete this monumental task of creating a democracy in the heart of the Middle East. According to President Bush, almost 300,000 Iraqi soldiers and police officers are trained and ready to take over an ever increasing amount of the task to secure the country. The future will tell the world if they are ready for the task of governing their own country, but the balance of political power in both Great Britain and The United States may rest on the outcome.

## THE 2004 PRESIDENTIAL ELECTION

President Bush took the oath of office for his second term as president on January 20, 2005. In his inaugural speech he defined his second term as a fight for freedom in every nation. "The best hope for peace in our world is the expansion of freedom in the entire world." Bush continued by saying, "Across the generations we have proclaimed the imperative of self-government, because no one is fit to be a master, and no one deserves to be a slave. Advancing these ideals is the mission that created our Nation. It is the honorable achievement of our fathers. Now it is the urgent requirement of our nation's security and the calling of our time. Bush continued this theme with a bold new policy statement. "It is the policy of the United States to seek and support the growth of democratic movements and institutions in every nation and culture, with the ultimate goal of ending tyranny in our world."

Bush concluded his address by saying: "When the Declaration of Independence was first read in public and the Liberty Bell was sounded in celebration, a witness said, "it rang as if it meant something." "In our time it means something still. America, in this young century, proclaims liberty throughout the entire world, and to all the inhabitants thereof. Renewed in our strength, tested but not weary, we are ready for the greatest achievements in the history of freedom."[4] However, the good feelings did not last long as the war in Iraq dragged on with no end in sight, the President and the Republican Congress was gradually loosing the support of many American voters.

## THE ELECTIONS OF 2006

On November 6, 2006 voters went to the polls to show their approval or disapproval of the Republican controlled Congress. In a rout Democrats won a 51st seat in the Senate and regained total control of Congress after 12 years of near-domination by the Republican Party. One of the key points of voter displeasure was the perceived lack of progress in the war in Iraq. The shift dramatically altered the government's balance of power, leaving President George W. Bush without Republican congressional control to drive his legislative agenda. Democrats hailed the results and issued calls for bipartisanship even as they vowed to investigate administration policies and decisions.

As watershed elections go, this one rivaled the Republican takeover in 1994, which made Newt Gingrich speaker of the House, the first Republican to run the House since the 1950's under President Dwight Eisenhower's administration. This time the shift comes in the midst of an unpopular war, with a Congress scarred by scandal and just two years from a wide-open presidential contest.

Democrats will have nine new senators on their side of the aisle as a result of Tuesday's balloting. Six of them defeated sitting Republican senators from Pennsylvania, Ohio, Missouri, Rhode Island, Montana and Virginia. The other three replaced retiring senators from Maryland, Minnesota and Vermont.

In the House, Rep. Nancy Pelosi Democrat from California became the first female Speaker of the House of Representatives. She called for harmony and said Democrats would not abuse their new status. She said she would be "the speaker of the House, not the speaker of the Democrats." She said Democrats would aggressively conduct oversight of the administration, but said any talk of impeachment of Bush "is off the table."

Positioning for the 2008 Presidential and Congressional elections had already begun. In Congress, Democrats were now the party in power and the American voters expect some positive results. The issue of social security running out of money by 2018 was still not resolved. The democrats will most likely try to increase taxes on social security by increasing the taxable income level to about $200,000 per year. Also, the minimum wage will most likely be increased; however, the remaining question will be the outcome of the war in Iraq.

## IT'S THE ECONOMY STUPID

In the first quarter of 2008 many economists including Federal Reserve Chairman Ben Bernanke were worried that a recession was eminent in 2008 and perhaps had already started. To avoid a recession or to at least reduce the severity of one, Congress passed and President Bush signed a bill to provide over 100 million in tax rebates to American consumers and tax breaks amounting to about $ 50 million to American businesses. This was in addition to the economic stimulus that was being provided by the war in Iraq. The stimulus package has a political element as well as an economic rational. The new Democratic led Congress did not want to see a recession during their first term and President Bush did not want to leave office with the country in a recession.

## NOTES:

# Chapter 25
## The Twenty-First Century – The George W. Bush Administration

1. Department of Education, <u>No Child Left Behind Reauthorization of the Elementary and Secondary Education Act,</u> Washington, DC, January 8, 2002.
2. CNN.com, <u>September 11: Chronology of Terror,</u> September 12, 2001.
3. White House News Release, <u>Address to a Joint Session of Congress and the American People,</u> Washington, DC, September 20, 2001.
4. White House News Release, <u>Presidential Address to The Nation,</u> Washington, DC, October 7, 2001.

# CHAPTER 26

---

# THE TWENTY FIRST CENTURY – THE BARACK OBAMA ADMINISTRATION

*" The definition of insanity is doing the same thing over and over again and expecting different result." - Albert Einstein*

## THE ELECTIONS OF 2008

The 2008 presidential elections were held on November 4th. After a long primary campaign, Republican's choose John McCain a long time Senator from Arizona and a Viet Nam War Hero and Democrats choose Barack Obama a young senator from Illinois. Young and charismatic but with little experience on the national level, Obama smashed through racial barriers and easily defeated John McCain to become the first African-American destined to sit in the Oval Office as America's 44th president. He was the first Democrat to receive more than 50 percent of the popular vote since Jimmy Carter in 1976.

The son of a Kenyan father and a white mother from Kansas, the 47-year-old Obama has had a startlingly rapid rise, from lawyer and community organizer to state legislator and U.S. senator, now just four years into his first term. He is the first senator elected to the White House since John F. Kennedy in 1960. After the longest and costliest campaign in U.S. history, Obama was propelled to victory by voters dismayed by eight years of George W. Bush's presidency and deeply anxious about rising unemployment and home foreclosures and a battered stock market that has erased trillions of dollars of savings for Americans. In the Congressional elections Democrats fell short of the 60 votes they need to stop filibusters in the Senate and made more modest gains in the House than the leading prognosticators expected.

As president, Obama faces daunting problems. How to fix a financial system no one seems to fully understand. How to defeat terrorist enemies sheltered in the territory of our putative ally Pakistan. How to live up to the high expectations so visible in the cheering and tearful faces of his followers. Do President Obama and the Democrats have a mandate? Obama got a larger percentage than any other Democrat since 1964, and Democrats have congressional majorities comparable to those in Bill Clinton's first two years. But a Democratic policy of increased taxes on high earners seem ill-suited to a country facing a recession.

## THE RECESSION OF 2008 AND 2009

The Business Cycle Dating Committee of the National Bureau of Economic Research met by conference call on Friday, November 28, 2008. The committee maintains a chronology of the beginning and ending dates (months and quarters) of U.S. recessions. The committee determined that a peak in economic activity occurred in the U.S. economy in December 2007. The peak marks the end of the expansion that began in November 2001 and the beginning of a recession. The expansion lasted 73 months; the previous expansion of the 1990s lasted 120 months.

A recession is a significant decline in economic activity spread across the economy, lasting more than a few months, normally visible in production, employment, real income, and other indicators. A recession begins when the economy reaches a peak of activity and ends when the economy reaches its trough. Between trough and peak, the economy is in an expansion. The committee viewed the payroll employment measure, which is based on a large survey of employers, as the most reliable comprehensive estimate of employment. This series reached a peak in December 2007 and has declined every month since then. Another common measure of a Recession is two consecutive quarters of negative growth in real GDP. This occurred in the third and fourth quarters of 2008.

### The Troubled Asset Relief Program:

On October 2008, President Bush signed into law the Emergency Economic Stabilization Act of 2008. That legislation created the Troubled Asset Relief Program (TARP), which authorizes the Department of the Treasury to purchase or insure up to $700 billion of troubled assets. The term "troubled asset" is defined as:

(A) Residential or commercial mortgages and any securities, obligations, or other instruments that are based on or related to such mortgages, that in each case was originated or issued on or before March 14, 2008, the purchase of which the Secretary determines promotes financial market stability and;

(B) Any other financial instrument that the Secretary, after consultation with the Chairman of the Board of Governors of the Federal Reserve System, determines the purchase of which is necessary to promote financial market stability.

The legislation also requires the Congressional Budget Office (CBO) to prepare an assessment of each of those reports within 45 days of its issuance.

For the remainder of 2008, the Secretary of the Treasury had the authority to purchase $350 billion in assets. The Obama Administration has submitted a plan indicating its intent to use the remaining $350 billion; that funding will become available unless a joint resolution disapproving it is enacted. As of the end of December, 2008 the Treasury had spent $247 billion of the first $350 billion and had plans in place for most of the rest of that half of the funds. Currently the Treasury has had to borrow the full amount disbursed, thereby increasing debt held by the public by $247 billion. Disbursements and commitments so far fall into three categories: capital purchases, loans, and other actions.

1. **Capital Purchases**: Through June 30, 2009, the Treasury had purchased $203.19 billion in shares of preferred stock and warrants from about 214 U.S. financial institutions through its Capital Purchase Program (CPP). The largest such transactions involve Citigroup, JP Morgan Chase, and Wells Fargo, at $25 billion each; Bank of America, at $15 billion; and Morgan Stanley and Goldman Sachs, at $10 billion each. Each financial institution that received such funds is required to

pay a dividend equal to 5 percent of the government's investment in that institution for the first five years, and 9 percent thereafter. In addition, the Treasury has purchased $40 billion in preferred stock from the American International Group (AIG). That company is required to pay a dividend of 10 percent a year; the shares are redeemable by the company but have no set maturity date.

**2. Automotive Industry Financing Program:** As of June 30, 2009 $54.15 billion has been disbursed to this program. The Treasury has agreed to lend $18.4 billion to General Motors (GM) and Chrysler. The first loan disbursement of $4 billion was made to GM on December 31; another $4 billion was conveyed to Chrysler on January 2. The Treasury has also committed to disburse another $5.4 billion to GM on January 16 and an additional $4 billion at a later date contingent on the release of the second $350 billion of TARP funding. Finally, the Treasury is set to lend another $1 billion to GM to be used by the company to purchase equity in GMAC. The GM loans are accompanied by warrants, and the Chrysler loan is accompanied by an additional promissory note.

**3. Other Actions:** The Treasury, the Federal Reserve, and the Federal Deposit Insurance Corporation (FDIC) have, in combination, agreed to guarantee a $306 billion portfolio of assets owned by Citigroup. Through the TARP, the Treasury is responsible for up to $5 billion of potential losses on those securities. Furthermore, the Treasury is responsible for $20 billion in credit protection (against debtors that do not pay because of insolvency or protracted default) for the Federal Reserve's Term Asset-Backed Securities Loan Facility.

The Financial Stability Oversight Board is responsible for reporting the results of the Troubled Asset Relief Program to Congress each quarter. Since TARP was authorized, Treasury has implemented a range of programs aimed at stabilizing the financial system and preserving homeownership. As of June 30, 2010, it had disbursed $385 billion for TARP loans and equity investments, and Treasury has already recouped some of these disbursements. As of June 30, 2010, Treasury had received almost $25 billion in dividend and interest payments and warrant repurchases and more than $198 billion in repayments.

Table 26-1 shows the TARP activity from inception through June 30, 2010. Additional proceeds includes dividends from equity securities, interest income from loans and securities, proceeds from repurchases of warrants and warrant preferred stock, and proceeds from warrant auctions. Treasury has sold 2.6 billion shares of Citigroup common stock for $10.5 billion, of which $8.5 billion is included in "Repayments," and $2.0 billion, which represents gains on the sales, is included in "Additional Proceeds." As of June 30, 2010, Treasury still owned 5.1 billion shares of Citigroup common stock.

**Table 26-1**
**TARP Program Disbursements, Repayments, and Additional Proceeds, as of June 30, 2010 (dollars in billions)**

| Program | Total Cash Disbursed | Repayments | Additional Proceeds |
|---|---|---|---|
| Capital Purchase Program (CPP) | $204.9 | $146.9 | $17.3 |
| Targeted Investment Program | 40.0 | 40.0 | 4.3 |
| Automotive Industry Financing Program | 79.7 | 11.2 | 2.4 |
| American International Group Investments | 47.5 | 0.0 | 0.0 |
| Home Affordable Modification Program | 0.3 | N/A | N/A |
| SBA 7(a) Securities Purchase Program | 0.1 | <0.1 | <0.1 |
| Term Asset-Backed Securities Loan Facility | 0.1 | 0.0 | 0.0 |
| Public Private Investment Program | 12.4 | 0.4 | 0.1 |
| Asset Guarantee Program (AGP)2 | 0.0 | 0.0 | 0.6 |
| Totals | $385.0 | $198.5 | $24.7 |

The Department of the Treasury reports that as of February 28, 2014 that 98 percent of the total TARP disbursements have been repaid.

Source: Department of the Treasury Web Site: www.treasury.gov

## The American Recovery and Reinvestment Act of 2009

This Act was passed by the 111th Congress and signed into law by President Obama on February 17, 2009. The Act is intended to provide a stimulus to the U.S. economy in the wake of the economic downturn that began in December of 2007. The Act includes federal tax cuts, expansion of unemployment benefits and other social welfare provisions, domestic spending in education, health care, and infrastructure including the energy sector. The major categories and amounts of the Stimulus plan are listed in Table 26-2 below:

The American Recovery and Reinvestment Act of 2009 passed Congress with no Republican votes in the House and only 3 in the Senate. Many Republicans criticized the bill for not providing enough tax relief. Only 36 percent of the stimulus was for tax reductions. Some Democrats argued that the amount of stimulus was not large enough to end the recession. The Congressional Budget is often used by Congress as an authority on budget matters. A February 4, 2009, report by the (CBO) said that while the stimulus would increase economic output and employment in the short run, the gross domestic product would, by 2019, have an estimated net decrease between 0.1% and 0.3% (as compared to the CBO estimated baseline budget) The CBO estimates that enacting the bill would increase federal budget deficits by $185 billion over the remaining months of fiscal year 2009, by $399 billion in 2010, and by $134 billion in 2011.[1]

In a February 11, 2009 letter, CBO Director Douglas Elmendorf noted that there was disagreement among economists about the effectiveness of the stimulus, with some skeptical of any significant effects while others expecting very large effects. The Director said the CBO expected short term increases in gross domestic product and employment. In the long term, the CBO expects the legislation to reduce output slightly by increasing the nation's debt and crowding out private investment. The CBO also noted that other factors, such as improvements to roads and highways and increased spending for basic research and education may offset the decrease in output and that crowding out was a not an issue in the short term because private investment was already decreasing in response to decreased demand.

## Table 26-2
## Economic Stimulus Plan Distribution of Expenditures

**Government Spending Description**                  **$ in billions**

| Government Spending Description | $ in billions |
|---|---|
| Higher education modernization | 6 |
| Pell grants | 15 |
| Increased unemployment benefits and job training | 40 |
| Food stamps | 15 |
| Temporary increase in Medicaid matching rate | 88 |
| COBRA | 39 |
| Preventive care | 4 |
| State fiscal relief | 79 |
| Local school districts | 40 |
| Public housing and energy efficiency | 15 |
| Transform energy systems | 30 |
| Clearwater, flood control and environmental restoration | 19 |
| Modernize federal and other public infrastructure | 30 |
| Highway construction | 30 |
| Science facilities, research and instruments | 10 |
| Weatherize modest-income | 6 |
| Law enforcement | 4 |
| Healthcare IT | 20 |
| Broadband internet access | 6 |
| Transit and rail | 10 |
| Tax credits and Incentives | 281 |
| Total Stimulus Plan Spending | 787 |

## THE 2015 FEDERAL BUDGET

Table 26-3 summarizes the President's 2015 budget outlays and receipts. The budget called for large increases in expenditures and budget deficits in every year through 2019.

### Table 26-3
### Proposed Federal Budget for 2015 Outlays and Receipts
### (Dollars in billions)

| Outlays | 2013 | 2014 | 2015 | 2016 | 2017 | 2018 | 2019 |
|---|---|---|---|---|---|---|---|
| Defense Spending | 626 | 612 | 623 | 584 | 570 | 570 | 577 |
| Other Programs | 521 | 562 | 563 | 569 | 576 | 579 | 585 |
| Total Discretionary | 1,147 | 1,174 | 1,186 | 1,153 | 1,146 | 1,149 | 1,162 |
| Social Security | 809 | 852 | 896 | 947 | 1,003 | 1,063 | 1,126 |
| Medicare | 492 | 513 | 526 | 569 | 575 | 589 | 648 |
| Medicaid | 265 | 309 | 336 | 355 | 372 | 392 | 415 |
| Other Programs | 520 | 577 | 700 | 750 | 773 | 767 | 818 |
| Total Mandated | 2,086 | 2,251 | 2,458 | 2,621 | 2,723 | 2,811 | 3,007 |
| Interest and Disaster Costs | 222 | 226 | 257 | 325 | 400 | 483 | 560 |
| Total Outlays | 3,455 | 3,651 | 3,901 | 4,099 | 4,269 | 4,443 | 4,729 |
| **Receipts** | | | | | | | |
| Individual Income Taxes | 1,316 | 1,386 | 1,534 | 1,648 | 1,781 | 1,920 | 2,047 |
| Corporate Income Taxes | 274 | 333 | 449 | 502 | 528 | 540 | 514 |
| Social Security Receipts | 673 | 732 | 758 | 811 | 850 | 898 | 945 |
| Medicare Payroll Taxes | 209 | 219 | 232 | 249 | 263 | 278 | 293 |
| Other Insurance and Retirement | 65 | 69 | 66 | 67 | 81 | 80 | 75 |
| Other Receipts | 238 | 263 | 298 | 291 | 308 | 314 | 352 |
| Total Receipts | 2,775 | 3,002 | 3,337 | 3,568 | 3,811 | 4,030 | 4,226 |
| Deficit | 680 | 649 | 564 | 531 | 458 | 413 | 503 |

**Note:** Other Mandated Programs: Include Federal Employee Retirement and Disability, Unemployment Compensation, Housing Assistance, Veterans Benefits and Other Federal Benefits.

**Source: President Obama's 2015 Proposed Budget – Table S-5**

**The Budget Message Of The President**

The President's message started with some general comments on the on his 2015 Budget. After 5 years of grit and determined effort, the United States is better positioned for the 21st Century than any other nation on Earth. We have created more than 8 million new jobs in the last 4 years and now have the lowest unemployment rate in over 5 years. Our housing market is rebounding. Our manufacturing sector is adding jobs for the first time since the 1990s. We now produce more oil at home than we buy from the rest of the world. We have cut our deficits by more than half since I took office. And for the first time in over a decade, business leaders around the world have declared that China is no longer the world's number one place to invest; America is.

What I offer in this Budget is a set of concrete, practical proposals to speed up growth, strengthen the middle class, and build new ladders of opportunity into the middle class—all while continuing to improve the Nation's long-run fiscal position. Earlier this year, thanks to the work of Democrats and Republicans, the Congress produced an agreement that undid some of last year's severe cuts to priorities like education and research, infrastructure, and national security.

Recognizing the importance of that bipartisan compromise, the Budget adheres to the spending levels agreed to by the Congress for fiscal year 2015. But there is clearly much more we can and should do to invest in areas like infrastructure, innovation, and education that will create jobs, economic growth, and opportunity. So I am including in my Budget a fully paid for Opportunity, Growth, and Security Initiative that provides the Congress a roadmap for how and where additional investments should be made in both domestic priorities and national security this year.

The President's budget message continued on Energy Policy. We also know that one of the biggest factors in bringing more jobs back is our commitment to American energy. The all-of-the-above energy strategy I announced a few years ago is working, and today, America is closer to energy independence than we have been in decades.

The Budget advances this strategy by ensuring the safe and responsible production of natural gas and cleaner electricity generation from fossil fuels. It creates new incentives to cut the amount of energy we waste in our cars, trucks, homes, and factories. It promotes clean energy with investments in technologies like solar and by expanding and making permanent the tax credit for the production of renewable energy. And it continues to strengthen protection of our air, water, land, and communities, and addresses the threat of climate change. Climate change is a fact, and we have to act with more urgency to address it because a changing climate is already harming western communities struggling with drought and coastal cities dealing with floods. That is why I directed my Administration to work with States, utilities, and others to set new standards on the amount of carbon pollution our power

President Obama's message concludes by stating that: Finally, if we are serious about long-term, sustainable economic growth and deficit reduction, it is also time to heed the calls of business leaders, labor leaders, faith leaders, and law enforcement—and fix our broken immigration system. Independent economists say immigration reform will grow our economy and shrink our deficits by almost $1 trillion in the next two decades. And for good reason: when people come here to fulfill their dreams—to study, invent, and contribute to our culture—they make our country a more attractive place for businesses to locate and help create jobs for everyone.[2]

## Analysis of the Proposed Federal Budget 2015 through 2019

**Defense Spending:** From 2013 the current budget fiscal year through 2019 defense spending will decrease by $49 billion. .

**Other Discretionary Spending:** This is mainly the cost of running the agencies of the U.S. Government. From 2014 through 2019 the budget shows an increase of only $35 Billion. This is a start but additional expense cutting is needed to balance the Federal budget in the future.

**Social Security Receipts and Outlays:** total receipts are budgeted to increase by $4,990 billion from 2014 through 2019. However, Social Security Outlays are budgeted to increase by $5,920 billion for the same period. For the six year period, Social Security outlays will exceed receipts by $930 billion. This is an indication that the government will have to use the Social Security Trust Funds from 2014 through 2019 to fund Social Security payments.

**Government Deficit Spending and Debt Held by the Public:** The deficit is projected to increase by $3,798 billion from 2013 actual expenditures through budgeted year 2019. Total Federal Debt Held by the Public will increase by $3,999 billion from 2013 through 2019. Total debt held by the public is projected to be $15,982 by the end of fiscal year 2019. The increase will result in debt held by the public to be 72.0 percent of the Gross Domestic Product versus 72.1 percent in 2013. This is an indication that no progress is planned on reducing the ratio of debt held by the public to the country's gross national product.

**Interest on the Gross Federal Debt:** Will reach $551 billion by 2019. This will make interest owed on the Federal Debt larger than all other government outlays with the exception of Defense, Social Security and Medicare. If net interest on the debt were eliminated from the 2019 budget there would be a budget surplus of $48 billion.

**Individual Income Taxes:** The budget projects and increase in individual taxes of $731 billion from 2014 through 2019. This includes a tax rate increase on those individuals making over $400 thousand per year that was approved by Congress and signed into law in 2013.

**House Budget Committee Chairman Paul Ryan's Statement, Available at his web site, on Barack Obama's 2015 Budget.**

Upon reviewing the President's budget, House Budget Committee Chairman Paul Ryan of Wisconsin issued the following statement. "The President's budget is yet another disappointment—because it reinforces the status quo. It would demand that families pay more so Washington can spend more. It would hollow out our defense capabilities. And it would do nothing to preserve or strengthen our entitlements. The President has just three years left in his administration, and yet he seems determined to do nothing about our fiscal challenges. "This budget isn't a serious document; it's a campaign brochure. In divided government, we need leadership and collaboration. And in this budget, we have neither. Ryan outlined some key facts on the 2015 Budget.

**Spending Surges:** We're not in an "era of austerity." Since 2009, we've added $6.8 trillion to the debt and spent $17.6 trillion. The President's budget increases spending by $791 billion over the budget window and by $56 billion in, 2015 above the Murray–Ryan spending agreement. This is the agreement he signed into law just two months ago. His budget will increase total spending by 63 percent from today's levels over the budget window.

**Debt Explodes:** President Obama's budget never balances—ever. It would add $8.3 trillion to the debt over the budget window. Cumulative deficits would amount to $5 trillion, and gross debt would climb to $25 trillion in 2024. **Interest Skyrockets:** President Obama's plan nearly quadruples interest costs, which remain the fastest growing item in the budget. Interest this year on the debt would be $223 billion, but would rise to $812 billion in 2024 under his plan.

**Taxes Hiked (Again) to pay for New Spending:** President Obama has already increased taxes by $1.7 trillion. Now, he wants another $1.8 trillion on top of that. Roughly half of the new tax hikes would be dedicated to new spending rather than deficit reduction.

**A Booming Washington, D.C.—and a Shrinking American Middle Class:** The share of Americans over 16 who are working is at its lowest level since 1978. Real wages are lower today than in 1999. One in five U.S. households is on food stamps. But what does the President and his party propose? A health law that will remove the equivalent of 2.5 million full-time workers from the workforce; an energy policy that drives up costs and destroys jobs; a regulatory policy that sends U.S. jobs and wealth overseas; a tax policy that closes plants and factories; a welfare policy that discourages work; and a spending policy that that crushes economic growth and threatens the future of America's youth.

## THE ELECTIONS OF 2010

November 2, 2010 was not a good day for many Democrats. Record number of voters including seniors cast their votes against Democrats in the Senate, the House of Representatives and Governors across the country. When the dust settled Republicans had won enough seats to take control of the House, gained six seats in the Senate and nine governorships. The changes are listed below:

| Description | Republican | Democratic | Republican Gain |
|---|---|---|---|
| Senate | 47 | 53 | 6 |
| House | 241 | 193 | 62 |
| Governors | 29 | 20 | 9 |

Note: Two Senators are independents and caucus with the Democrats

Michael Baronet writing in Townhall Magazine offers an historical analysis of what happened in the November elections. According to Barone: The 2010 elections produced results that are unprecedented in the lifetimes of most readers. In nine of the 10 congressional election cycles between 1986 and 2004, no party gained or lost more than 10 seats in the House of Representatives, the one exception being 1994, when Republicans gained 54. Otherwise, the numbers were pretty static. Not so in the three most recent cycles. Democrats gained 31 seats in 2006 and another 23 seats in 2008. Now Republicans have won significantly more than the 39 seats they needed to regain the House majority they lost four years ago.

American politics has had not such sharp shifts to one party and then the other for more than half a century; not since the elections of 1946 and 1948, immediately after World War II. And then, as now, very fundamental issues about the size and scope of government were at stake. After World War II, the issue was whether the United States would move in the same direction that voters in Britain chose when they elected a Labor government that instituted national health insurance and a cradle-to-grave welfare state. Franklin Roosevelt laid out a similar program in his 1944 State of the Union, and labor unions, bulging with new members due to New Deal and wartime laws, for the first time became a mobilizing force in that year's presidential election. They sought legislation to provide public housing, federal aid to education and national health insurance.

The voting public had other ideas. Unions in 1946 called more strikes than in any other year in American history, and that fall voters elected a Republican Congress. That 80th Congress proceeded to abolish wartime rationing and wage and price controls, enact a record tax cut and pass the Taft-Hartley Act limiting the powers of labor unions. In 1948, Democrats won back control of Congress, in large part because of support from farmers (one-quarter of Americans in the 1940s still lived on farms) and in tribute to Harry Truman's vigorous response to communist aggression in Europe. But the Democrats were unable to repeal the 80th Congress' legislation and failed to pass major housing, education or health care legislation.

The Republican Congress thus put postwar America on a very different path from Britain's. Its enduring public policies laid the groundwork for the generation of postwar prosperity. For six decades, from the late 1940s until the election of Barack Obama and Democratic congressional supermajorities in 2008, Americans were not presented with a clear-cut effort to vastly expand the size and scope of government. Even Lyndon Johnson's Great Society, which gave us Medicare, was directed more at expanding welfare programs that were rolled back in the 1990s. On Tuesday, Americans gave their verdict on the Obama Democrats' sharp increases in government spending and Obama care (The newly passed medical insurance law). It was an resounding "no" as their forebears delivered to the postwar Democrats' welfare state vision in 1946.

In particular, voters in the industrial heartland, states which trended Democratic in the postwar recession years of 1958, 1970 and 1982, this time trended Republican. They evidently see government spending programs as the problem, not the solution, to a stagnant economy. In 2008, Barack Obama and congressional Democrats won with a top-and-bottom coalition, carrying voters with incomes over $200,000 and under $50,000, while losing those in between. In 2010, that coalition has contracted. Turnout among low-income voters was down, while Democratic support among the affluent seems confined to those on public sector and university payrolls.

Democrats and their supporters in the main stream press will trot out alibis and rationalizations, blaming the result on ignorance, selfishness or racism. But voters this year were better informed about the intentions of the Obama Democrats than they were in 2008 and no more racist than the electorate that gave Barack Obama 53 percent of the popular vote, more than any other Democratic nominee in history except Andrew Jackson, Franklin Roosevelt and Lyndon Johnson.
The implications for public policy and for the 2012 presidential election remained unclear. Republicans could fail to offer attractive policy alternatives or a viable presidential nominee.[3]

## THE 2012 ELECTION

The election campaign for the President and member of Congress was a grueling one. The contest was between President Obama and businessman and former Governor of Massachusetts W. Mitt Romney. On November 7, 2012 most of the results were in and Barack Obama was elected to serve a second term as President. Also, the Democrats picked up 2 seats in the Senate. The count was 53 Democrats, 45 Republicans and 2 Independents which are expected to caucus with the Democrats. The House of Representatives remained in firm control of the Republicans with 233 seats to the Democrats 193 seats with 9 contests still undecided as of November 8th.

Linda Feldman a staff writer for the Christian Science Monitor offers some suggestions about the Election results in her article: "Does Obama's historic victory give him a mandate?

An outcome that maintains the status quo in Washington guarantees Obama some important advantages. But the 2012 election results also foretell more gridlock, and the president, by not offering a path out of debt and deficit lacks a clear mandate for action.

President Obama burnished his historic legacy by winning a decisive electoral victory – sweeping most of the battleground states – despite high unemployment, sluggish economic growth, and a bitterly partisan atmosphere. The reelection of America's first black president shows that Mr. Obama's triumph four years ago was not a fluke. Not only did Obama emerge the undisputed victor on November 7th over Republican challenger Mitt Romney, albeit with a smaller popular-vote margin than in 2008, he also appears to have pulled along with him a larger majority in the Senate.

Despite predictions of diminished turnout by Obama's core constituencies – blacks, Hispanics, young voters, and women – they delivered again for both the president and the Democratic Party.

Still, 2012 was a markedly different election. Gone is the optimistic tone of 2008. The road ahead is paved with tough choices, amid worsening fiscal conditions. And the scorched-earth quality of the campaign, fueled by unprecedented spending by the campaigns, the parties, and outside groups, has left many Americans gasping for air.

The continuation of the status quo – Democratic president, Democratic Senate, Republican House – foretells more gridlock. And by not offering a detailed prescription for addressing the nation's unsustainable deficits, particularly on entitlement programs, Obama enters a second term without a clear mandate for action.

In his victory speech, Obama sought to provide a moment of lift at the end of a grueling campaign. "The task of perfecting our Union moves forward," the president told his supporters at McCormick Place in Chicago. "It moves forward because of you. It moves forward because you reaffirmed the spirit that has triumphed over war and depression, the spirit that has lifted this country from the depths of despair to the great heights of hope."[4]

## THE FUTURE, THE ECONOMY AND THE PEOPLE

Will the combination of low interest rates, the troubled asset relief plan and the fiscal stimulus plan get the economy growing again? With interest rates lower than any time since the Kennedy administration and fiscal stimulus including tax cuts and increased government spending, the economy did, as predicted by the Federal

Reserve, start to grow by the end of 2010 and throughout 2011 and 2012. In 2013 the economy has continued to grow but only at 1.9 percent for Real GDP. However, there may be a new threat, inflation. Total federal government outlays according to the President's 2015 Budget is planned to increase by $1,078 billion from 2014 through 2019, the Treasury will find it more difficult to sell government bonds. This could weaken the value of the dollar, lead to higher interest rates and the crowding out of some private sector investment.

America is strong; its manufacturing ability is still second to none. All of the fundamentals are still their including the financial markets, which have begun to recover from the recession of 2008. The war on terrorism will probably not end any time soon, but their threat to the average American should be substantially reduced as the terrorists are hunted down and brought to justice. In Iraq there is a real chance of a lasting Democratic form of Government. By the end of December 2011 America had removed all troops from Iraq. Is the American trained Iraq military ready to take over the security of that country? Only time will tell, but they are off to a good start. Also, the U.S. is committed to leaving Afghanistan by 2014 leaving only a small contingency of armed forces behind to train that county's army.

Tables 26-4 A shows that Real Gross Domestic Product for the four quarters of 2013. During this period Real GDP increased by only 1.18 percent. Personal consumption expenditures increased by only 1.23 percent. The largest increase was in gross private investment of 2.11 percent. The increase in investment spending is an indication that the economy might be paused for additional growth in 2013. Table 26-4 B shows GDP as expenditures on an annual basis. Real GDP was $15,761 on for 2013 compared to $15,471 million for 2012 and increase of 1.9 percent. This indicates a slow but steady growth during 2013. With the steady improvement of 2013 over 2012 a most likely forecast for all of 2014 is a slow growth rate of real GDP of between 2.0 and 2.5 percent.

# Table 26-4 A

## Real Gross Domestic Product for 2013 by Quarter
## ($ in Billions)

| Description | 1st Quarter 2013 | 2nd Quarter 2013 | 3rd Quarter 2013 | 4th Quarter 2013 | % Change 4th qtr 2013 vs. 1st qtr 2013 |
|---|---|---|---|---|---|
| Personal Consumption expenditures | 10,644 | 10,692 | 10,744 | 10,832 | 1.7 |
| Gross Private Domestic Investment | 2,470 | 2'525 | 2,627 | 2,643 | 7.0 |
| Net Exports | (422) | (424) | (420) | (383) | 9.2 |
| Government Consumption Expenditures | 2,892 | 2,887 | 2,888 | 2,850 | (1.5) |
| Real Gross Domestic Product | 15,584 | 15,680 | 15,839 | 15,942 | 2.3 |

**Source: BEA National Income and Product Accounts March 2014, Table 1.1.6**

**Note: BEA Table 1.1.6 contains a residual line which is the difference between total real GDP and the sum of the detailed lines. The residual amounts are small and have been added in this table to the Government Consumption Expenditures line.**

## Table 26-4 B

## Real Gross Domestic Product 2013 vs. 2012 ($ in Billions)

| Description: GDP as Expense | Year 2012 | Year 2013 | % Increase 2013 vs. 2012 |
|---|---|---|---|
| Personal Consumption expenditures | 10,518 | 10,728 | 2.0 |
| Gross Private Domestic Investment | 2,436 | 2,566 | 5.3 |
| Net Exports | (431) | (412) | 4.4 |
| Government Consumption Expenditures | 2,948 | 2,879 | -2.3 |
| Real Gross Domestic Product | 15,471 | 15,761 | 1.9 |

**Source: BEA National Income and Product Accounts March 2014, Table 1.1.6**

## SUMMARY AND CONCLUSION

Even with the current slow growth of Real GDP of 1.9 percent, we are still a great nation and we will prevail. America will continue to be the economic leader of the free world in the twenty-first century, not because of its buildings and equipment or government, but because of the will of its people to live and prosper in a free society. Today even with the 6.7 percent unemployment rate reported by the Department of Labor in December 2013, America is an economic colossus, more competitive, more innovative, and more technologically advanced than Japan and Europe. Ronald Reagan knew why America was so prosperous. Aids close to Reagan have said that whenever Reagan was asked whether he was responsible for the American resurgence, he would reply, "Oh no, it wasn't me. The American people did it. They deserve the credit."

**NOTES:**

**Chapter 26**
**The Twenty-First Century – The Barack Obama Administration**

1.  Congressional Budget Office, <u>Official CBO Report to the Senate Budget Committee</u>, February 4, 2014.
2.  Obama, Barack, <u>Proposed 2015 Budget</u>, March 5, 2014
3.  Congressmen Paul Ryan's Web Site, <u>Paul Ryan's Comments on Barack Obama's 2015 Budget,</u> March 10, 2014.
4.  Baronet, Michael, <u>Voters Reject Obama's Big-Government Ambitions</u>, Townhall, November 4, 2010

# INDEX

www.ingramcontent.com/pod-product-compliance
Lightning Source LLC
Chambersburg PA
CBHW080233180526
45167CB00006B/2261

\* 9 7 8 1 4 9 9 1 2 1 8 1 0 \*